Kundalini Awakening

The Sacred Path to Awakening your Dormant Energy and Living a Meaningful Life. 8 Guided Meditations for Chakra Healing, Opening the Third Eye, and Developing Psychic Abilities

- Mindfulness Academy -

Copyright © 2021 by Mindfulness Academy

All rights reserved. No part of this book may be restructured or used in any manner without the written approval of the copyright owner except for the use of quotations in a book review. For more information, please contact the author.

Table of Contents

INTRODUCTION	4
PART 1	6
CHAPTER 1: INTRODUCTION TO KUNDALINI	7
CHAPTER 2: KUNDALINI YOGA AND ITS GOALS	21
CHAPTER 3: KUNDALINI DIET	77
CHAPTER 4: KUNDALINI VS MEDITATION	81
CHAPTER 5: BENEFITS OF YOGA	92
CHAPTER 6: KUNDALINI EXERCISES	104
PART 2	114
CHAPTER 7: INTRODUCTION TO MEDITATIONS	115
PART 3	140
CHAPTER 8: THE MEDITATION PROCESS	141
CHAPTER 9: INTRODUCTION ON CHAKRAS	151
CHAPTER 10: FOOD AND CHAKRAS	174
CHAPTER 11: CRYSTALS TO KNOW	179
CHAPTER 12: CHAKRA'S MEDITATIONS	197
CHAPTER 13: QUESTIONS THAT ARISE ON THE HEALING PATH	278
CHAPTER 14: THE QUEST FOR SELF-DISCOVERY THROUGH THE CHAKRAS	287
PART 4	290
CHAPTER 15: CONCENTRATION AND BREATH MEDITATION FOR CHAKRA HEALING	291
CHAPTER 16: KEEPING BALANCE: BREATHING PRACTICES TO KEEP YOUR CHAKRAS OPEN	295
PART 5	302
CHAPTER 17: ONE BREATH AT A TIME	303

PART 6   311
CHAPTER 18: ORGANIZING SPIRITUAL WORK ON DAILY LIFE   312
CONCLUSION   322

Introduction

Kundalini meditation is an ancient practice that has been rediscovered in recent years. This book will teach you what Kundalini is, how it affects the body, and how to use it to enhance your life.

You may have heard of Kundalini as something mystical and confusing, or even dangerous. True, Kundalini has sometimes been misunderstood or misrepresented. But the science of Kundalini is based on sound principles and techniques.

The goal of yoga is self-realization and enlightenment—the full awakening of human consciousness through meditation.
This book will arm you with the tools that are necessary for self-realization and enlightenment, as well as the tools that you need to be able to help others come to a higher state of being. You will also learn how to transform fear into love with various techniques of chakra balancing and meditation.
These techniques have their roots in Eastern spiritual practices; however, they can be used by anyone who wants greater consciousness or more happiness in their lives.

Kundalini meditation uses specific breathing techniques, physical postures, and sound vibrations to activate this latent energy in your body.
The most important aspect of Kundalini meditation is your willingness to allow this energy to move through you. This impulse can be blocked at any time, and as a result, the force gets trapped in the body.
This process is similar to the process of spiritual growth—you must let go of blocks and negative attitudes in order to progress. The same thing can be said about Kundalini's movement through your body: if you don't let go, it remains stuck in one spot. Through Kundalini meditation, you will learn how to make this vital energy flow freely again.

Kundalini will not kill you; it will ultimately prove beneficial for mental as well as physical health and well-being.

The aim of this book is to help people to release Kundalini Energy and improve their Mindfulness.
Happy reading!

Part 1

Kundalini Yoga Information

Chapter 1: Introduction to Kundalini

This type of yoga is an ancient science and art which deals directly with the expansion and transformation of consciousness. The end result after dedicated practice is the raising of Kundalini energy, which flows through the chakras. Through the combination of pranayama, bandhas, asanas, mudras, and mantras, there is a build-up pressure, which forces the Kundalini energy to be awakened to rise up through the body. In addition to these exercises, focused attention, projection, and visualization are key to acquiring specific effects.

When a person practices Kundalini Yoga, they are able to unite their consciousness with the Ultimate Consciousness when they practice daily. It is not a quick process, and much care needs to be taken to ensure that specific combinations of exercises are performed. Once a student starts to perceive the movement of energy outside, and within the body, they are able to consciously direct the flow of the pranic energy to unblock, clear, and awaken the chakras. In turn, they will be healing themselves and even others as they become one with the universal energies.

Kundalini yoga has been gaining popularity since the 1980s in the West since Yogi Bhajan brought over the teachings from India. He was considered a Kundalini master at the young age of 16. He first emigrated to Canada in 1968 and moved to Los Angeles, California to teach Kundalini shortly thereafter. His utmost goal was to make each individual holy, happy, and healthy. His non-profit organization named 3HO is still functioning today through his students as he passed away in 2004.

The typical traditional Kundalini yoga sessions include a balanced distribution of physical yoga poses, meditation, and breathing exercises. They also incorporate mantras into their meditations, which assist the newcomer in mediation with the silence, which is required for meditation. These mantras differ from other Sanskrit mantras which are commonly used in Sanskrit because they are usually from the Gurmukhi language.

The combination of different aspects of yoga practice is known as *kriya*, which translates to "action" from Sanskrit. A particular kriya will have a focus such as a physical, emotional, or mental health benefit. These can range from letting go of anger, discovering inner intuition, or eliminating health issues such as lower back pain or poor digestion. Some of these kriyas' names are Kriya for Conquering Sleep, Navel Adjustment Kriya and Kriya for Elevation.

Kundalini Awakening

Kundalini is the extremely strong psychic force that resides within each and every one of us. It's known as Shakti, and it's the life force that propels our inner self forward. It is usually represented as a coiled and sleeping snake, and when we are born, it is dormant at the base of the spine. Kundalini Shakti's snake unwinds and ascends through the Sushumna Nadi in the middle of the spinal column as this force is stimulated and awoken. The Sahasrara, or crown chakra, at the top of the head, is its final destination. Kundalini Awakening occurs when Kundalini connects with our 7th chakra, causing the person to transcend into a heightened spiritual state.

The prana, or life force, contained in the food we consume and the air we breathe is consumed at a much faster pace when Kundalini yoga is practiced. The Apana, which is the energy of elimination or return, is a partner in this transformation. Tappa, or heat, is generated inside the navel center when the prana and Apana energies are combined. The Kundalini force is awakened when the heat from the tappa descends into the Muladhara chakra.

What is a Kundalini Awakening, and how does it happen?
When people begin to feel movement in their bodies, they will most likely feel a stirring of Kundalini energy. As the chakras are triggered, they can feel an energy change that makes their perceptions far more conscious. These moments, however, are brief and only last a few days. Kundalini awakening in its entirety is exceedingly unusual. It happens when all of the psyche's problems and knots have been confronted and resolved. As Kundalini energy surges up from the Muladhara chakra, it passes through the back of the spine and over the top of the head, finally landing in the 3rd eye chakra. The entire system has been changed and awakened at this stage.

Kundalini Awakening and Stirring Symptoms
Since the energy blocks that were part of the spiritual, mental, emotional, and physical bodies are largely responsible for the symptoms, each person's symptoms are special. When these blocks are struck, symptoms are usually felt. The signs will go away until they've been dealt with properly. Many common symptoms, however, are felt more commonly, including:

- Periods of increased imagination
- A flash of insight or wisdom into the complex workings of truth
- Strange sounds, such as thunder, musical instruments, or buzzing, are heard internally.
- Your senses are quickly overwhelmed.
- Emotional mood swings that can be very serious
- Orgasm may be caused by waves of bliss or pleasure.
- Immediately recognizing and learning previously unknown pranayamas, asanas, bandhas, mudras, and kriyas
- Cold sensations all over the body, as well as extreme heat or aches in the spine and chakras

- A sensation of snakes or insects crawling over your body, especially along your spine
- Jerking or shaking of the body that the practitioner is unable to manage
- Lightning bolts or electricity inside the body are energetic sensations.
- Itchy feet or hands are a normal occurrence.

How to Deal with the Signs and Symptoms of Kundalini Awakening

Symptoms will appear even if you have done personal spiritual work on yourself before beginning Kundalini yoga. The onion peel has so many layers that you won't know how far you have to go until you've been through them all. There will always be something that needs to be dealt with, let go of, or transformed.

When all of the above symptoms become unbearable, it's a sign that there are circumstances, feelings, or past traumas that need to be confronted so that they can no longer control you. If you get into the habit of letting go of the burdens you've been bearing, letting go of these stuff can become second nature to you, even though you've been holding onto them for decades. You'll find that you were carrying a lot more weight than you knew or were willing to admit. Sitting and meditating, as well as light pranayama, are two ways to get over the negative symptoms. Determine the location of your discomfort, whether physical or emotional, and perform a breathing exercise that focuses on the corresponding chakra. Meditation will often aid in the relaxation of the mind, allowing you to think more clearly. You can also be led to the answer if you will listen to your inner guidance and intuition.

It's important to note that if these symptoms appear, it means you're on the right track to cleansing your body in preparation for the Kundalini awakening. The obstacles will be hit and hopefully eliminated, allowing you to begin a new life filled with boundless ecstasy and bliss.

Reduce your practice time if you're noticing that meditation or pranayamas aren't making the unwelcome symptoms go away. You can be pushing yourself too hard at times.

It will take determination and perseverance.

During this process, however, you must pay attention to your body. Other things you can do in your day to help with the symptoms and your overall health

Kundalini's regular routine is to go for a long stroll. It will not only calm the mind, but it will also allow the body to work through some of the symptoms while relaxing the Kundalini Shakti. Tai chi is also a great exercise to implement because it will help you to stay grounded.

You are not dissolving the Kundalini energy when you ground yourself. In reality, it is bringing in the masculine aspect in order to balance and calm down the feminine Shakti energies that are felt through our nervous system. Grounding yourself will get your nerves back to normal function every time you feel stressed during a Kundalini session.

If the symptoms begin to intensify or vanish, you can investigate three aspects of your life: habits, diet, and lifestyle. Unbalanced or balanced Kundalini Shakti is caused by these two factors.

When it comes to practices, you can take a close look at the structure of the activities you're doing. Perhaps they require practice on a particular chakra, or the exercises require you to balance the feminine and masculine energies. If you discover that this solves your dilemma, keep making the improvements you've made and go with the flow. However, it often includes more than one aspect. When it comes to the lifestyle side, this can be a big deal. Pose the difficult questions to yourself.

- Should you engage in too much or too little spiritual practice?

- Is it possible for you to strike a comfortable balance between your activities and your everyday life?
- Do you work long hours at work and neglect your other commitments as a result?
- Is your job spiritually supportive of who you are as a person?
- Do your mates distract you from your spiritual concerns?
- Does your partner encourage or discourage you in your attempts to awaken Kundalini?

What If There Isn't Any Feeling?
If you don't have any of these Kundalini signs, what do you do? Maintain your Kundalini workout routine. They will most likely arrive in due time, but they might not be felt at all at times. It all comes down to how you handle the Kundalini awakening process. You would have an easier time than someone who lets their emotions run wild or has a narrow view and views about life if you can let go of things quickly and not let too many things bother you. All is relative. Only know that if any symptoms do arise, you will have a clearer understanding of why they are occurring.

History of Kundalini

It is best to learn as much as we can about the concepts of kundalini and the culture that houses the concepts. Jumping headfirst into intensive practices is careless and disrespectful to the culture. For the most efficient practice and experience, we need to learn the etymology of kundalini and explore its rich history as an obscure Hindu concept to one of the western world's most practiced spiritual exercises. This journey is complex, but we will keep it simple and easy to follow.

Etymology
In Sanskrit, the ancient language of Indian culture and other Eurasian cultures, the word kundalini means 'circular.' This adjective is found in the Upanishads in the 4th through 9th centuries BCE. The Upanishads are parts of the ancient Sanskrit texts The Vedas. These texts are the source of the core principles of Hinduism, Buddhism, and Jainism, containing some of the earliest concepts that are still practiced today.
In the 12th century, we found the word 'kundalin' used as a noun to mean 'serpent.' There are also similar words used to mean 'ring' or 'coil.' The 12th century also found a similar word 'kundali' as a nickname for Durga, a goddess and one of the forms of Shakti. This name was used in many traditions, such as shaktism and tantrism. A few centuries later, we find that Hatha Yoga traditions using similar terms to mean 'coiled power,' often found at the base of the spine.

History
Kundalini's actual origin is difficult to pinpoint. Just like most ancient spiritual concepts, kundalini has traveled throughout its respected homeland, influencing different traditions and evolving into what we know it as today. As a core principle of spiritual practice, kundalini is central in Saiva Tantra, a sect of Hinduism that reveres Shiva as the Supreme Being. Tantric traditions considered kundalini as an inherent intelligence that embodies consciousness. We see that there is a wide use of similar words with varying meanings.
The first known use of the actual word kundalini is found during the 8th century, although similar concepts existed before the use of the word. For instance, the idea that there is a pranic force that is moved up a central energetic pathway through the spine was known as Sakti long before kundalini was recognized as this vital force. This concept of a feminine force vital to life is also synonymous with the term boghavati, which is defined as both 'joy' and 'coiled.' This links the

kundalini again with pleasure and liberation, symbolic of Shiva's enjoyment of his union with Shakti.

A notable mystic and philosopher Abhinavagupta claimed there are two kundalini energies. One that starts at the base of the spine and moves upward and one that starts at the top of the spine then moves down. This would be symbolic of the dance between Shiva and Shakti, logic moving down and contracting, and creativity moving upward and expanding. This mystic lived in the 1s century AD and had a prominent influence on Indian culture, namely Kaula and Trika traditions.

The idea that this vital force is the source of manifestation for all of our experiences is key to understanding this energy. Pleasure and pain, breath, and body, all experience is influenced by kundalini. While there are plenty of modern interpretations of this energy, the more open-minded approach is key to getting the most out of our practice. There are kundalini yoga classes and specific kundalini meditation techniques springing up everywhere in the west. These classes are typically not affiliated with any religion and mainly focus on the physical practices we can perform to stimulate the kundalini energy. Here we see that all-inclusive nature of kundalini, it is open to all people, and in fact, it is a gift from the universe that we need to accept and implement it into our daily lives gladly.

Modern

The modern take on yoga and meditation has seen a watering down of sorts, focusing on the scientific understanding of what takes place when we are practicing these arts. This is unfortunate since there is a wealth of spiritual knowledge available through these practices. The concept of kundalini acts to unify these arts in the face of materialist science, and it's doing just that. Let's take a look at how kundalini made its way into the modern sphere.

Like many powerful practices from around the world, globalization has made it easier than ever to share foods, ideas, technology, and spirituality. Many people find this to be very important to the progression of the world, while others think it is a sign of end times. Many people want their culture to be maintained as pure and not become watered down by tourism and the adoption of their traditions by other cultures. But with the Internet and worldwide travel, this is inevitable.

Many have used this new technology to take advantage of spiritual practices, selling them to other cultures through classes and books, while others have selflessly shared these practices for free online and in person. Even more so, especially in the west, we see people adopting these practices and teaching them to others as their own newfound spirituality. Anyone taking credit for their own new spiritual model should be avoided. More often than not, these people have simply stolen ancient ideas and try to sell them as their own.

As for kundalini, she has seen a rise in popularity, much like the use of yoga and meditation. This serpent energy cannot be taken advantage of in the same way that many other Indian and eastern traditions can. If kundalini is not approached with respect and humility, she may very well turn on you, offering a negative experience that can leave one scarred for life. These are not fear tactics but in actuality the very behavior that makes kundalini so powerful. Many negative kundalini experiences can be found online but also plenty of positive ones. As she makes her way to the west, we must take even more precautions not to utilize this ancient knowledge for evil or selfish purposes. Let's take a look at the rise of kundalini in the modern west.

For millennia the concepts of kundalini were held a secret. The practices and philosophies of ancient India were kept hidden by masterful yogis and wise men. These masters would pass down the knowledge to their dedicated students, who they believed were ready for such powerful teachings. It was widely frowned upon to teach these practices in any other way. Sharing them openly was taboo, and there was also an Indian elite that kept close tabs on the spreading of these teachings. This group of elites believed that the Indian public was not ready for these practices.

These secret groups felt that if this knowledge was widespread that it would be used in unholy ways, or even allow the public to empower themselves in ways that would challenge the elite's social and political status. For centuries, these teachings were kept a secret from the Indian public and the rest of the world.

As technology became more advanced, and British colonization was running rampant, these traditions were starting to be shunned and ridiculed in the face of Christianity and Empirical power. Still, the masters of these traditions held their secrets and did not allow them to be adulterated or spread widely. Many foresaw these ancient secrets getting lost in the timeline as Great Britain tore through India, hoping that their precious traditions weren't lost.

As time wore on and global travel became accessible to everyone, there was much debate about sharing these traditions with the wider world. On the one hand, these traditions would be preserved in modern technology and the new students who would adopt the practices. On the other hand, these ancient arts may become adulterated or used for the wrong reasons. While many masters maintained their convictions that these secrets should not be spread worldwide, there were many who felt otherwise, most notably Yogi Bhajan. Bhajan was a Sikh rebel who is widely regarded as the man who brought kundalini to the west.

Yogi Bhajan

In the year 1968 Yogi Bhajan took a flight from Punjab, India to Toronto, Canada to make his way west to explore the cultures and ideas found there. Little did he know that this flight was the beginning of an incredible journey that would alter the course of western spirituality forever. From Toronto Bhajan made his way south into the United States, he found himself in southern California amidst the late sixties counter-cultural revolution. The ideas and philosophies being shared during this era were ones of social upheaval and distrust for the government. These young people were not interested in the paths of their fathers. They protested the wars, denounced the Catholic Church, and began experimenting with psychedelic drugs that offered spiritual insight and expanded consciousness.

Indian philosophy was also becoming popular during this time, yoga practices and mediation were alternatives to drugs that offered the same insights. An entire generation was turning on to other cultures, sharing their homes and food, and boldly attempting to redesign the American dream.

Yogi Bhajan saw these young people and noticed familiar glimpses of his own Sikh philosophies in their ambitions. He found that their hearts were in the right places but that they may have needed some guidance. He pointed out that this generation was longing for truth through a godly experience, but that they were being exposed to half-baked mysticism and drugs. This combination would not allow them to reach the goals that they desired.

Yogi Bhajan was well aware of the fact that to teach kundalini outside of an Indian lineage was forbidden, but he was troubled by the half-baked mysticism being presented to the young people in America who so desperately needed spiritual guidance. Soon Yogi Bhajan had a realization. While he was meditating in Los Angeles in 1968, he had a distinct vision of a spirituality that blended both ancient bits of knowledge with modern implications. He understood that the world was changing dramatically and that modern technology was going to alter spirituality all around the world, whether the Indian elite liked it or not. He soon found that keeping these secrets from other humans simply because they are not from India was unfair, proclaiming that it was every human's birthright to be happy, healthy, and holy. He suggested that kundalini yoga was the way to reclaim this birthright. Yogi Bhajan stayed in Los Angeles sharing his knowledge, and in only two years established the 3HO Foundation and the Kundalini Research Institute. 3HO, also known as the Healthy, Happy, Holy Organization was dedicated to spreading his philosophy, and the Kundalini Research Institute, was dedicated to finding connections between science and kundalini practices. This was the beginning of a new era of western philosophy, aided by Indian mysticism.

Yogi Bhajan acted quickly on his realization, teaching thousands of classes and opening his first teacher training program in 1969. He trained thousands of future yogis and teachers, several of them moving on to open their own studios all around the United States and around the world. Bhajan wrote many books on his teachings and even worked with governments to develop projects that promoted peace and unity in the world. He established International Peace Prayer Day, promoting the idea that it is our responsibility as humans to establish peace among our feuding countries. He taught that it was our responsibility through new technology and knowledge to promote peace and further our society into a unified future. Even after his death, the United States Congress passed a resolution honoring his contributions to world peace.

Yogi Bhajan's contributions to the acceptance of kundalini are immeasurable. It would be easy for these wise yogis to keep their ancient secrets and not share them with the world. But Yogi Bhajan went out on a limb and risked ridicule to bring these practices to the west. There is no other individual as responsible as Bhajan for the advent of kundalini in the modern world. Even as the kundalini resided secretly in India, she was not shared; now, that she has a place in the west, she is shared with the entire world.

The many kundalini classes and websites we see today can be attributed to Yogi Bhajan and his students. It may be tough to navigate the Internet with all the false gurus and greedy sites aiming to capitalize upon spiritual models, but there is still plenty of pure and mindful information available. Many of Bhajan's lineages still exist, and his 3HO network is alive and well. For kundalini resources, his teachings and organizations are the best places to begin.

The cultural changes that took place in the 1960s are not comparable to any other decade. We can safely say that something shifted in the collective consciousness during these times that open new paths for humanity. The technology, spiritual collectivism, and overall furthering of a globalized civilization culminate to create a new path to help us navigate this world. A path that is inclusive and accepting, breaking old traditions and building new ones.

We find that the journey kundalini as taken over the centuries is allusive, partly due to the fact that its existence was held secret by the purist yogis and masters, but also because of the nature of spiritual history. It is always difficult to find the exact origin of these practices and ideas. It is safe to say that although the earliest recorded source of kundalini can be found, the concept itself existed well before written history. The Upanishads are our earliest known sources for these concepts, while also being the source of many core principles of Hinduism and Buddhism. This is the physical origin of these concepts, but kundalini has no beginning or end, it is omnipotent as a fragment of the source.

While the actual term kundalini can be used to highlight important moments in this concept's history, we must remember that the concept of a divine feminine is as old as time. There is no documenting her history; she has no beginning or end and is prominent in almost all cultures. The symbolic serpent and various energetic visualizations used to access this power are products of certain regions and cultural practices. In essence, kundalini is one of the most prominent spiritual forces in the world, but simply the Indian version of it. We need to take care when we contemplate this timeline and really open our minds to the fact that most religious concepts stem from one place. A source, in some sense, where all knowledge and experience comes from and inevitably returns to. Kundalini seems to be the most effective way to work with this divine energy, offering a distinct and powerful narrative that doesn't exclude any student seeking to work with these energies.

As we continue, we need to keep what we know about kundalini's history in mind. It has found its way west for a reason and aims to unite the world with its practice and power. It is important to contemplate this long history, but we must also keep the power of the present moment in mind, holding close our slogan; Wherever you are, you live fully in the here and now.

Chapter 2: Kundalini Yoga and its Goals

Kundalini yoga is a specific yoga practice designed to awaken, balance, and harmonize Kundalini energy. Individuals who embark on a Kundalini yoga journey often report that they begin experiencing the awakening symptoms after just one or two sessions. This awakening furthers as they move deeper into their Kundalini yoga journey. This yoga form also helps support the Kundalini energy, keeping it awakened, complete, and thriving in the individual practicing it.

Kundalini Yoga
Not all yoga practices are done equally. Some are designed to stretch out the physical body, some are designed to facilitate a mind-body-spirit connection, and others are designed for specific purposes, such as Kundalini yoga.
Kundalini yoga does not emphasize the physical as much as other practices, such as Hatha yoga. Instead, it incorporates meditation and mantras as a foundational part of the overall practice. The combined experience of the mind, body, and spirit being brought together through these three practices encourages Kundalini awakening and supports Kundalini flow. The body is supported and awakened by the yoga poses, the mind is supported and awakened by the mantras, and the spirit is supported and awakened through meditation.
Introduced by Yogi Bhajan in the 1970s, Kundalini yoga is still relatively new to the Western regions. It is, however, rising in popularity as more individuals seek to incorporate the mind, body, and spirit connection in their lives.

The Bodies
There are ten bodies associated with Kundalini yoga. All ten bodies are awakened through Kundalini yoga, allowing

individuals to begin to continue feeling full Kundalini flow. These bodies are as follows.

The Soul Body

The soul body is your flow of spirit. This is where you connect to your Soul and to infinity. The soul body is considered to be the foundational body and your true self. It provides you with the ability to live from your heart. This body responds to any form of heart work, as well as the raising of your Kundalini energy.

The Negative Mind

Your second body is your negative mind. This is one of our strongest bodies, as it consistently works toward assessing the environment and circumstances you are in and if there is any danger present as a result. This body is responsible for your ability to stay alive and gifts us with what is often called "a longing for belonging," which is a phrase coined by Yogi Bhajan. Your negative mind can be balanced through integrity and discipline.

The Positive Mind

The third body you have is your positive mind. This works toward assessing what is positive, beneficial, and affirming in your environment and circumstances. This body allows you to see where opportunities lie and where you may be able to access resources. The playful mind is responsible for bringing willpower and playfulness into your life. Everything you do with your navel point, or your core, contributes to your positive mind. You can also balance it by increasing your self-esteem.

The Neutral Mind

Your neutral mind is responsible for guiding you through assessing the information coming in from both your negative and positive minds. The neutral mind is compassionate, recognizes polarities, and works on intuition. The neutral mind can be balanced through meditation, which is a foundational part of Kundalini yoga.

The Physical Body
Your physical body is your temple. This is where all of the other nine bodies come together to exist in harmony. This body allows you to be able to balance yourself and your life. You can also sacrifice for your hopes, dreams, and the greater community through your physical body. The physical body possesses the energy of the teacher. It is balanced through regular exercise. The physical body also loves to share what has been learned with others.

The Arcline
Your arcline body is like a halo that wraps around your head around your earlobes, brow, and hairline. If you are a woman, you have a second arcline that exists across your breast line. Your acrline body allows you to intuit the world around you, as well as project yourself upon it. You can use this body to help you focus and meditate. Any practices associated with the pituitary gland or the third eye (pineal gland) support the arcline body's awakening.

The Aura
Your aura body is your electromagnetic field of energy that extends around the physical body. It is responsible for holding your life force energy and shielding you and providing protection. Through your aura body, you can elevate yourself both energetically and consciously. Natural fibers are worn on the body as well as meditation both contribute to awakening and balancing your aura. You can also incorporate the color white into your life and practice, which is believed to magnify and expand your aura.

The Pranic Body
Your pranic body is supported by your breath, which brings life force energy into your physical body. This allows you to experience accomplishment and energy in your life. You interact with this body every time you breathe in and out. The pranic body is awakened and supported by pranayama practices.

The Subtle Body
Your ninth body is your subtle body, and it is responsible for helping you see beyond the physical matter and into what else exists. This body is deeply connected to your soul body, as it carries your soul body after your physical body dies. Many wonderful teachers and gurus continue to teach us through their subtle bodies despite no longer being in the physical realization. Your ability to master anything exists within this body. If you want to experience mastery, do a Kundalini practice for 1,000 days in a row. Then, your subtle body will be balanced.

The Radiant Body
Your tenth and final body is your radiant body. This body is responsible for giving you radiance, courage, and nobility. When you meet someone who is naturally charismatic and magnetic, they have a balanced, radiant body. To balance and awaken your radiant body, you need to have commitment. Through the art of being committed to your practice, truth, kindness, and excellence, your balance and awaken your radiant body.

Embodiment
Though not technically a body itself, the embodiment is an important element of awakening the 10 bodies. Embodiment suggests that all ten bodies are awakened and balanced. This is the ultimate goal with Kundalini. When you practice

Kundalini yoga, you are awakening, balancing, and strengthening your ten bodies.

Yoga Poses to Awaken the Bodies
The following yoga poses are written in the sequence in which they should be completed. There are 14 poses in total, all of which are designed to help you awaken your Kundalini and your 10 bodies. You must remain mindful of your breathing and use each of these as a pose to meditate in. You can also repeat a mantra to help you further integrate your mind, body, and spirit.

Easy Pose
Easy pose, known as Sukhasana, is the first pose you are going to start with. This pose requires you to sit on the ground with your legs crossed and bringing your hands in front of your heart. Bringing the hands in front of the heart in this way is known as the prayer mudra. Rub your palms together a few times, warming them up. Then, relax your thumb joints into your sternum.

Stretch Pose
Gently move from easy pose down to your back, with your legs stretched straight below you and your arms straight down by your sides. When you are ready, bring your heels together and point your toes away from your body. Gently lift your head about 6 inches off of the ground and look down toward your toes. If this feels like it is too much or like it is bringing discomfort, you can slide your hands under your lower back and use them to support you. As you do this, practice the breath of fire (explained below.) Hold this sequence for about 1-3 minutes. If you are pregnant, do not practice this pose or the breath of fire.

The breath of fire is pranayama. To do it, you want to inhale while pushing your navel away from your spine, then exhale, pulling your navel back toward your spine. This allows you to fill your diaphragm, lungs, and throat with air and then exhale all of the air from your throat, lungs, and diaphragm.

Knees to Chest Tuck
While laying on your back, after you finish the stretch pose, you can move into a knees-to-chest tuck. Simply bring your knees up, wrap your hands around them, and then gently pull them toward your chest. If you are feeling confident, you can lift your head up. Your nose should be pointing between your knees. Use the breath of fire and hold this position for about 1-3 minutes. If you are pregnant or are experiencing a heavy menstrual cycle, you should substitute the breath of fire of long deep breathing. Breathe in for about six seconds and out for about six seconds. Do not hold your breath at any point.

Ego Eradicator
When you are done with your knees to chest tuck, you want to come back up to a seated position with your legs crossed in front of you. Begin creating the easy pose by bringing your hands back into the prayer mudra in front of your chest. Then, curl your fingers in and point your thumb up toward the air, as if you are giving someone two thumbs up. Your fingers should only be lightly curled, with the fingertips gently touching the palms and the majority of the palms remaining exposed. Then, put your hands up above your head and out to the sides. This opens and exposes your chest and core. Close your eyes and practice the breath of fire for about 1-3 minutes before moving into the next pose. Again, if you are pregnant, refrain from using the breath of fire and instead practice deep breathing.

Hold Your Toes
Now, you want to uncurl your legs and stretch them out to the sides in front of you. Your legs should be spread in a wide "V" shape in front of you. Keep your feet flexed with your toes pulled back toward your body. Do not push yourself to stretch

further than is comfortable in this pose. Allow yourself to relax into it and trust that the more you practice, the more flexible you will become and the easier this pose will get. When you are ready, take a deep inhale and stretch your arms over your head. Then exhale and stretch your hands out to your feet, holding onto your toes and relaxing into the pose. Hold this for about 1-3 minutes.

Grasp Your Shins
Cross your legs once more, returning to an easy pose. Hold each of your shins. Then, inhale and flex your spine forward, curling it over as if to expose your back. When you exhale, flex your spine backward as if to expose your chest. You should be getting a good relaxed stretch out of this, so keep it calm and intentional. Do this pose for between 1-3 minutes before moving on to the rock pose.

Rock Pose
To complete the rock pose, you will need to tuck your feet under yourself and sit on your shins with your knees together in front of you. You should be sitting on your heels with your feet relaxed. Let your hands gently come to a resting position on your thighs before flexing the spine as you were in the previous pose. Your eyes should be closed and gently rolled toward your third eye if you feel comfortable doing this. Continue this stretching pose for about 1-3 minutes.

Grasp Your Shoulders
Remain in the same seated pose as you used for rock pose, with your heels underneath you. Keep your torso and head pointed forward, looking directly in front of you. When you are ready, lift your arms up and gently grasp your shoulders with your hands. Your left thumb should be behind your left shoulder with your fingers rested above your left collarbone. Likewise, your right thumb should be behind your right shoulder with your fingers rested above your right collarbone.

Sit in this stretch pose for a few moments. Then, on each inhales, twist toward the left, and on each exhale, twist toward the right. Your arms should remain lifted, keeping your biceps parallel to the floor during this pose. Do this for 1-3 minutes.

To take this pose a step further, stay in this posture, return your torso, and head to center, looking directly in front of you. Your hands should remain in the same position, with your elbows extended out toward the side. Each time you inhale, lift your elbows up, drawing a line toward the sky. When you exhale, draw your elbows down, returning to your original position with your biceps parallel to the floor. Do this stretching pose for about 1-3 minutes.

Shoulder Lifts

Take a few moments to return to a crossed leg position. Then, gently rest your hands on your knees and allow them to relax completely. Refrain from drawing your knees up in this position, as these shoulder lifts can sometimes result in tight hips causing your knees to draw up toward the sky. Allow them to relax toward the floor instead. When you are ready, inhale and lift the left shoulder toward the sky. As you exhale, lower the left shoulder and simultaneously lift the right shoulder. Continue this for 1 minute before reversing the process. As you reverse it, lift your right shoulder on the inhale, and drop it to lift your left shoulder on the exhale. Continue the stretch on this side for another 1 minute.

Double Shoulder Lifts

After completing your alternating shoulder lifts, you can begin lifting both shoulders at the same time. For this, you want to lift them and try to pull them toward each other on the inhale. Then, drop them and push them away from each other, allowing them to relax on the exhale. Continue doing this double shoulder lift practice for 1 minute.

Turn Your Head

As you continue to hold the easy pose with your legs crossed in front of you and your hands rested gently on your knees, you can begin turning your head. This will stretch out your neck, upper spine, and upper back area, allowing you to experience a pleasant, relaxing sensation. Each time you inhale, turn your head to the left. When you exhale, turn your head to the right. Your head should remain level, and your nose should draw a line around your head that is parallel to the floor. After you have done this for one minute, reverse the breath. On each inhalation, turn your head to the right, and on the exhalation, draw your nose across the front of you, turning your head toward the left. When you are done with this reversed breathing part of the pose, bring your head to come back to a resting position in front of you, slowly exhale, and relax your body.

Frog Pose

This will be one of the more advanced poses of the yoga session. The frog pose requires you to come up into a squatting position, resting on your toes. Your heels should be drawn up toward the sky and touching each other beneath you. Your fingertips can be placed on the ground between your knees, with your fingers separated wide and each tip firmly planted into the ground. Evenly displace the weight between each of your fingers and toes to allow for a centered pose. Your head should be lifted with your chin pointing upward, allowing you to gaze toward the sky. Don't lift your head too hard, but rather allow for a nice relaxed upward focus. As you inhale, stretch your legs out slightly allowing your glutes to rise toward the sky. Remain on your toes for this pose. As you exhale, come down to the original position. Continue holding this rhythm with your breath for about 54 repetitions. However, if this is beyond your skill level, you can always aim for 13 to 26 repetitions. Continue adding more to your practice each time until you reach the 54 repetition mark.

Laya Yoga Meditation

With most of your poses now completed, you can enter the meditation part of the process. Here, you want to sit back into the easy pose — Left your wrists to rest on your knees as you point your palms toward the sky. Then, bring the tip of your thumb to the tip of your index finger and create a circular shape. This is called the Gyan mudra. Now, chant the following mantra. As you are chanting, take the time to visualize energy that spirals from your spine's base to the top of your head. This is the realized energy of Kundalini.

The chant is as follows:

- "Ek Ong Karah,
- Saa Taa Naa Maah
- Siree Whaah, Hay Guroo."

You want to continue chanting and meditating for a total of 11 minutes to experience the full effect of this process. Carry the visualization from the base of your spine to the top of your head during the entire process, allowing it to unfold naturally in whatever way it manifests for you. Refrain from forcing the energy, but rather set the intention and allow it to show you how it wants to be realized, rather than the other way around. This is an excellent opportunity to explore the practice of releasing blocks by allowing the process to unfold.

Savasana

Lastly, you want to end your Kundalini yoga sequence with a savasana pose. This pose requires you to gently lie down on your back, with your feet down and gently separated and your arms relaxed out to your sides. Breathe intentionally but with a natural rhythm here and relax as the energies flow through your body. Instead of trying to create or force anything, receive all that comes your way. This will allow you to integrate the entire yoga experience. You can gently guide your awareness between the ten bodies, balance, and wholeness from this pose.

Kundalini Yoga Practice Benefits: Physical, Mental and Sexual

Clearing and Calming of the Mind
As with any practice which includes meditation, these practices will naturally clear your mind. When you allow yourself to meditate at least 15 minutes a day, you will see that even if you had a racing mind, it would start to calm down. This is a benefit that most people will find beneficial, even when starting with the Kundalini awakening process.

Improvement in Memory
With the combination of the pranayama's and yoga poses, you will be introducing more oxygen into your system. This, in turn, helps the blood to flow more easily throughout the body, including the brain. More blood entering the brain improves the cognitive functions and the pituitary and pineal glands.

Physical Ailments Can be Relieved or Cured
During the process of Kundalini awakening, you are working towards cleaning out your nadis and chakras to facilitate Kundalini Shakti's movement. This cleansing brings about an environment in your body that diseases cannot survive, so they will be greatly reduced or eradicated.

Increased Physical and Mental Strength
There is no doubt that the dutiful practice of yoga poses will get you into shape. Coupled with the other exercises in Kundalini, your mind will become sharper and focused, which in turn increases your mental fortitude. You will find that you will be able to control your emotions, as well.

Proven Build Up of Willpower
There is no doubt that some of these Kundalini exercises are difficult. There are some that you will need to practice other exercises before you even think about graduating yourself. With the need to continue to push yourself systematically strengthens your willpower and drives you to succeed.

Feeling One with the Universe
When you can connect with the higher energies within yourself, you will realize that we are all just from the same source. No matter what your background, education, upbringing, belief system, or marital status, we are based in the same energy of the Ultimate Consciousness.

Tap into Inner Intuition and Guides
As you dig deeper within yourself and can silence your thoughts, you will start to hear another voice that will never steer you wrong. This inner guide is your intuition, your gut feeling, which always has your higher interests at heart. Learn to trust this voice, and you will excel more quickly during the Kundalini awakening process.

Emotional Balance
Because you have strengthened your body and cleared your mind, body, and soul of troubling aspects which have occurred to you, this makes you more in control of your emotions, and you will find you simply will not react as much, if at all. You realize what the bigger picture is, and you do not allow petty things to ruin your day.

Feeling Overall Bliss and Peace
When you go through the Kundalini awakening process, there certainly are low points. However, just as quickly, you can be sent up to soaring heights which blow your mind. You cannot even imagine this state at this point in your journey. Feeling

these emotions certainly makes up for any hardships you will go through.

Psychic Abilities Are Enhanced
You will find that you will become more sensitive to the sounds, colors, and vibrations around you. This happens when you come more in tune with your body and then it radiates from there. When your intuition becomes more enhanced, you will start to know everything that you need at the moment that you need it.

Slower Aging Process
When you get to the higher levels of Kundalini yoga practice, you will see a glow that will start to show in your skin. This is partly because of the cleaning process. It is also because you are balancing out the elements within your body to function more efficiently. Your body will no longer need to work so hard in maintaining itself.

Connection with the Divine
This is the ultimate goal of Kundalini yoga and awakening. When you can be in direct connection with the creator, anything is possible. You lose all earthly bounds and are able to achieve the so-called unachievable. Going back to the Source is the perfect prize for all of the hard work and dedication you have put into your practice.

Sacred Chant
Many of the chakras can be healed through a sacred chant. When you use a mantra, rhythm, and breath, it has been found to have beneficial effects on well-being and health. It can also bring joy to the heart and the soul. The sacred sound is known as Naad Yoga. The experience comes from how your voice's vibrations can have a positive effect on the body, the mind, and the spirit. In fact, the sound can change the chemicals in your brain.

Inner Soul Guidance

Through Kundalini Awakening and Kundalini Yoga, you will learn all about the power of your intuitive mind. As we mentioned before, you need to learn how to listen to the voice inside your head. Each person has this voice, but it is up to you to choose to listen to it. As you clear your mind, especially your subconscious mind, you will learn how to listen to your thoughts without needing to rely on others. This way, you can always be present and sense your intuition. The more you practice, the stronger your ability to face choices and decisions will come!

Karma

It is thought that it takes you out of the karma cycle when you practice Kundalini. As you begin to practice, your positive intention will grow, therefore putting you into Kundalini Kriyas. These are exercises that help you burn off karma. As you practice more, you will become more intuitive to your decisions as well as your conscious. As you do this, you will begin to walk on a Dharma path instead of living according to karma.

Spiritual Chain

As you now know, Kundalini has been taught for thousands of years. Originally, it was taught by the Master to the student. In a Kundalini Yoga class, you will chant, "Ong Namo Guru Dev Namo." As you do this, you will be linked to spiritual masters from the times before your existence. The lineage is known as The Golden Chain. Through spiritual awareness, it will guarantee Kundalini's teachings to make sure you will remain unadulterated and pure.

Emotional Balance

What you may not know is that by balancing your Kundalini, you will also be balancing your glands, purifying your blood, strengthening your nervous system, and cleaning out your subconscious. As you awaken your Kundalini, you will gain the strength to choose how you respond to your thoughts and feelings instead of just reacting. You will also have a greater awareness during your daily activities. As you practice more, you will also learn how to let your emotions go. No longer will you just react emotionally? By developing a neutral mind, you may find yourself living a more positive life. The key is to act instead of reacting.

No More Negativity
As you practice awakening your Kundalini, you will begin to expand your aura. This is the energy field that surrounds you. Its main job is to alert you of any positive or negative emotions around you. At this point, you probably have a weak aura. When it is weak, you can easily allow negative influences to affect you. As you strengthen your aura, it will keep you centered, and you will know your true identity.

New Lifestyle
In life, we make a lot of excuses that keep us unhappy. Luckily, Kundalini Yoga is meant for people with busy lives. That means that it can be done quickly and still work effectively. It is a yoga that can fit into many different lifestyles. Whether you attend weekly or bi-weekly, there are many benefits to be found. There are also yoga teachings that can change other parts of your life. Whether you want to change your hygiene, child-rearing, or conscious communication, there is yoga for that!

Relax
As we mentioned earlier, Kundalini yoga will work to strengthen your nervous system. If your nervous system is weak at this point, you are probably susceptible to stress. Through yoga, you will learn how to relax like you have never felt before. You may find that you will reach a rejuvenating state through yoga to bring you to total relaxation. Through

regular practice, it can help you build resilience to stress and give you some extra stamina.

Community
On your journey, you do not need to do this alone. Often, yoga brings people together who are like-minded. This can be a very powerful tool as you travel along your consciousness journey. If you weren't already aware, many Kundalini yoga centers and studios could help welcome you into a community. With other people, you will develop a community that can meditate and chant together. It also helps to have people to help you make positive changes in your life.

Befriending Your Soul
As you practice Kundalini, you may begin to get a grip on your ego. You will slowly be learned about your soul's depth so you can learn the truth of your connection to your soul and the Universe. Through more practice, you will learn how to unite yourself with the Infinite. Gaining the experience can help you forget your insecurities of knowing who you are. This way, you will let go of the past and healthily manifest your destiny.

Difference Between Kundalini Yoga Other Types Of Yoga

The Basics of Kundalini Yoga
This type of yoga is an ancient science and art which deals directly with the expansion and transformation of consciousness. The end result after dedicated practice is the raising of Kundalini energy, which flows through the chakras. Through the combination of pranayama, bandhas, asanas, mudras, and mantras, there is a build-up pressure, which forces the Kundalini energy to be awakened to rise up through the body. In addition to these exercises, focused attention, projection, and visualization are key to acquiring specific effects.

When a person practices Kundalini Yoga, they are able to unite their consciousness with the Ultimate Consciousness when they practice on a daily basis. It is not a quick process, and much care needs to be taken to ensure that specific combinations of exercises are performed. Once a student starts to perceive the movement of energy outside, and within the body, they are able to consciously direct the flow of the pranic energy to unblock, clear, and awaken the chakras. In turn, they will be healing themselves and even others as they become one with the universal energies.

Kundalini yoga has been gaining popularity since the 1980s in the West since Yogi Bhajan brought over the teachings from India. He was considered a Kundalini master at the young age of 16. He first emigrated to Canada in 1968 and shortly thereafter moved to Los Angeles, California to teach Kundalini. His utmost goal was to make each individual holy, happy, and healthy. His non-profit organization named 3HO is still functioning today through his students as he passed away in 2004.

The typical traditional Kundalini yoga sessions include a balanced distribution of physical yoga poses, meditation, and breathing exercises. They also incorporate mantras into their meditations, which assist the newcomer in mediation with the silence, which is required for meditation. These mantras differ from other Sanskrit mantras which are commonly used in Sanskrit because they are usually from the Gurmukhi language.

The combination of different aspects of yoga practice is known as kriya, which translates to "action" from Sanskrit. A particular kriya will have a focus such as a physical, emotional, or mental health benefit. These can range from letting go of anger, discovering inner intuition, or eliminating health issues such as lower back pain or poor digestion. Some of the names of these kriyas are Kriya for Conquering Sleep, Navel Adjustment Kriya and Kriya for Elevation.

Hatha Yoga

Known as the most popular form of yoga in the West, Hatha yoga is focused more on the physical practice of yoga compared to Kundalini. However, the physical practices were taken from Hatha yoga to be practiced in Kundalini yoga. People who practice Hatha yoga do not perform the mantras and pranayamas into their exercises.

Hatha yoga was born out of Tantric yoga practices and is believed to be approximately 5,000 years old. The first text which was written about Hatha yoga was written by Swami Swatamarama in the 15th century. The core belief of Hatha is that enlightenment could be attained when you strengthened the connection with your physical Self.

The traditional practice of Hatha consists of some breath work or a short meditation in which they proceed with many different yoga poses. Some of the poses which are common to Hatha yoga are Warrior, Mountain, Child's, and Downward Dog pose. As the individual is practicing the yoga poses, it is a slow process that is marked by precision and striving to make the pose correct and perfect. It is not necessarily a fast-paced or physically demanding type of yoga; however, there are always exceptions.

In respect to Kundalini yoga, Hatha yoga share several of the same physical positions and breathing exercises. Sometimes a Hatha practitioner may even use some of the mantras which are used in Kundalini yoga. The largest difference between the two is how the yoga sessions are structured with Hatha yoga focusing on bettering the physical Self and Kundalini yoga's focus is on the spiritual experience, which can be felt inwardly. However, both types of yoga strive to increase awareness and flexibility, remove stress, and have a goal of becoming balanced in body, mind, and spirit.

Bhakti Yoga

This style of yoga is understood to be the path to a devotion, which is based on emotion and reality based on our emotions.

Emotions are the root of the most intense experiences we have in our reality. Feelings are able to make us experience the highest highs and the lowest hells. They can unite people together for their lifetime or burn bridges without the thought of looking back. Certainly, everyone can agree that emotions are the number one intense experience that we can have as human beings.

The purpose of bhakti yoga is to teach a way to control these intensely emotional experiences so that they can live their life for the better. The devotional path of bhakti teaches their students how to transform their negative emotions into more pleasing ones. The way they view life is through eyes of love. When you focus your mind on love and how it makes you feel, it can make everything in your life look that much brighter. It also plays on the Law of Attraction.

Being in a state of love also has a chemical effect on the brain. There is more dopamine released into the brain when you are feeling love or remembering memories that are close to your heart. When you feel this way, you tend to ignore or forget about all the negative things in your life and around you.

Some people may think this is too much of an unrealistic way of viewing life. However, it is very detrimental to be bogged down with negative emotions of anxiety, anger, sadness, or stress. There needs to be a happy medium. However, bhakti yoga only focuses on this one aspect, whereas Kundalini yoga is much more profound on an internal and external level.

Gnana Yoga

For those who want to strengthen their intellect and mind, jnana yoga is right up their alley. However, this is not necessarily for the Harvard graduate. How we define intelligence in today's society, it is very ego-based and materialistic. True intelligence cannot be measured by test scores, complex thoughts, or big words. No, the real type of intelligence is not attached to a value or a particular outcome.

This type of intelligence is gathered in a particular way because of your awareness level of activities occurring around you. It brings about complete focus without getting wholly involved. You could say that the motto of jnana yoga is "it is what it is" as they embrace this fact. It is a form of detachments as intellect disbelieves nothing and simultaneously believes in nothing.

Karma Yoga
There is a misunderstanding that there is good and bad karma. However, the truth of the matter is there is simply karma. The definition of karma is the use of the physical energy within your body. The belief in karma yoga is that there is a coiled spring located inside of each of us which much be released during physical activity. If this spring is not released, there will be a buildup of energy with us which will need to be released. When this becomes the case, it causes people to become nervous and agitated.
During karma yoga, the eternal actions which are performed are expending the karma which is centered around this coiled spring. When energy is dispersed each day, it can be a liberating experience rather than entangling. The activities that are performed are not necessarily things that you want to do, but because they need to be done.
The end result of this activity is that it causes a stillness within you that becomes your reality. It is not just an idea because it becomes your life.

Kriya Yoga
This type of yoga focuses on the emotions, mind, and body being external to you as they are not what defines you. Instead, they are your realities based on your experiences in life. Kriya in this sense if your energy which is a reality experienced internally.
The motto which could be used for this type of yoga is that "everything happens for a reason," and it is not part of the

practice to come to the bottom of the reasoning. However, the purpose of kriya yoga is to put trust in the process and open yourself up to the possibility that nothing can have an explanation in the physical world. The reasoning for this thought is that the ego tries to explain everything as it assigns, meaning the insignificance and chaos of our individual lives.

They believe they are just energy which the use of a body and mind which helps to facilitate their experiences in this life. They are able to separate their physical experience of living from their energy. They want to understand the inner workings of the energy and soul within them.

Of course, when it comes to Kundalini yoga, all these types of yoga are just smaller pieces to a larger puzzle. Kundalini digs deeper than any of the other types of yoga. It also much more physical and requires a great deal of dedication if you want to realize the true end goal of Kundalini - to have the coiled serpent rise through all of your chakras. The end result is the liberation and freedom from the confines of this bodily existence. It is surreal and unimaginable and quiet difficult to attain without guidance. However, there are steps that anyone can take to start on the path to enlightenment.

In short, all other types of yoga focus on one central point within ourselves. Kundalini yoga makes you take apart each part of yourself to examine and polish or toss away parts of ourselves that do not mesh truly with who you are inside. There is simply no comparison. As long as you come to this path of yoga with sincerity and respect without expecting to experience actual awakening after doing it for a few months, then you are prepared to start.

Kundalini Yoga Asanas & Mudras

All of the poses listed are recommended to use during Kundalini Awakening as well as clearing out the chakras to prepare for the Kundalini energy to rise.

Adho Mukha Svanasana - Downward-Facing Dog Pose (Variation)

- Position your hands and knees on your mat. Place your knees straight below your hips.
- Set your hands together with your only thumbs touching and angle your fingers slightly angled outwards.
- Exhale as you lift your knees while keeping them slightly bent and the heels just above your mat.
- Stretch your spine and press lightly towards the pubic bone. This will take the stress off your shoulders.
- Contract the outer arms and press against the base of your index fingers.
- Your head should be kept steady between your arms and not drooped down.
- Take long and deep breaths for 3 minutes as the prana is allowed to flow towards your brain.

Benefits of Adho Mukha Svanasana

- Strengthens the feet, shoulders, legs, and arms
- Relieves fatigue, insomnia, headache and calms the mind
- Aids in healthy weight loss
- Lengthens the spine and increases lung capacity
- Energies and rejuvenates the body
- Treats the symptoms of sciatica as well as lung disorders such as asthma
- Eliminates menstrual discomfort pain
- Improves digestion and eliminates constipation
- Treats sinusitis and other allergy symptoms
- Strengthens the bones and prevents osteoporosis
- Relieves the symptoms of menopause

Bakasana Crow Pose

- Stand on top of your mat with your arms loosely at your sides. Keep your feet at the edges of the mat.
- Bend your knees and lower your hips as you come down to the position of a squat. Keep an equal amount of weight on both of your feet.
- Keep the thighs set slightly wider than the shoulders.
- Lower your chest slightly and place the upper arms at the inside of the knees.
- Keep your spine straight as possible while slightly pressing inwards at the pelvic bone.
- Hold this pose for half a minute up to 3 minutes before proceeding.
- Place your palms flat on the mat about shoulder-width apart and spread your fingers.
- Hold your shins against the back of your upper arms. Make sure to keep the knees as near to the underarms as you are able.
- Round out your back and contract the muscles in the abdomen. The tailbone should be tucked in towards your heels.
- Focus on the area of the mat between your hands.
- As you continue to lean forward, lift your feet off of the floor, and push your heels towards your buttocks.
- If lifting both of your feet is too difficult at first, try lifting one foot at a time.
- Balance your legs and chest on the back of your upper arms.
- Be sure to have even pressure throughout your fingers and palms as you straighten the elbows.
- Keep the shins and knees touching the armpits and keep your forearms touching your core.

- Press your navel towards your spine as you touch your big toes together while keeping your breath steady and smooth.
- Exhale and slowly lower your feet to the mat. Stay in the squatted position with your feet slightly wider than shoulder length apart.
- Form the Anjali mudra again and press your elbows once again to the insides of the knees.
- When complete, lay down on your mat either in a lotus position or in savasana to notice the effect of the exercise.
- Return your breath to a normal rate.
- Pay special attention to the physical area of the perineum, tailbone, and hips.

Benefits of Bakasana

- Increases physical and mental strength
- Allows the body to be more flexible
- Strengthens the shoulders, wrists, abdominal and forearm muscles
- Cleans and energizes the sacral chakra

Bhekasana - Frog Pose

- On your mat, place your heels together as you place your fingers on the mat in front of you.
- Inhale through your nose as you straighten your knees.
- As you exhale again through your nose, bend down to a squat position.

Benefits of Siddhasana

- Stabilizes the nervous system and reduces symptoms of anxiety and mental frustration

- Aids the practitioner to control sexual functions and sexual urges
- Helps the Kundalini energy to move upwards as the heel is pressed into the perineum.
- Prepares the body for meditation

Sukasana - Easy Pose

- Sit on your mat with your legs crossed at the ankles.
- Press the lower spine slightly forward so that the back is erect.
- You can also perform this pose sitting in a chair with your feet both planted firmly on the floor.

Benefits of Sukhasana

- Stretches the back, neck and spinal cord
- Reduces fatigue and lack of energy
- Helps the joints of the hips, knees, and ankles to be more flexible
- Balances out the mind and body so you feel calmer
- Strengthens the back muscles while improving your posture
- Expands the collarbone and chest

Supta Utthita Tadasana - Stretch Pose

- Lay down flat on your mat with your arms lying next to your sides.
- Simultaneously lift the feet and the head up to 6 inches off of the mat.
- Lift the arms still outstretched with the palms facing the mat.

- Fix your gaze upon your toes.

Benefits of Supta Utthita Tadasana

- Improves circulation, respiration, and posture
- Heightens concentration and focus
- Opens the practitioner to feelings of happiness and love
- Enhances emotional balance
- Aligns the chakras
- Particularly balances and charges the heart chakra

Swastikasana - Auspicious Pose

- Sit on your mat with your legs lengthen out in front of you.
- Set your hands on the mat next to your hips with your palms touching the mat and your fingers facing forward.
- Shake the legs a few times to relax the muscles.
- Bend your left knee and set the sole against the inside of your right thigh and your heel against your perineum.
- Hold on to your right foot by using your right hand to hold the front of your ankle and use your left hand to grip your big toe.
- Place your right foot in between your calf and thigh so that only your big toe is showing.
- Place your hands on your knees with your palms facing down and your arms relaxed.
- Stretch your spine and neck so that they are erect.

Benefits of Swastikasana

- It is a good position for those who are not able to perform the asanas of Padmasana and Siddhasana.

- It is a good position for those who have leg pains or varicose veins
- Promotes calmness of mind
- A good position for concentration during meditation

Ustrasana - Camel Pose

- Kneel on your mat and place your thighs and hips at a 90-degree angle to the floor.
- Keep the muscles of the shins loose as your press the top of your feet firmly into your mat.
- Move your thighs inwards and bend backward.
- Touch the soles of your feet with the palms of your hands.
- Be sure that your face is upward towards the ceiling as you arch your back.
- Press your shoulder blade inwards to allow your chest and heart chakra to be more open.
- Relax the muscles of your throat while you audibly hum on your exhales.
- Hold this pose for up to three minutes while deeply breathing.
- When the pose is complete, breathe deeply and fill the lungs. Hold your breath for a few seconds.
- During your exhale, slowly lift your head as you lower your hips gradually so that you are sitting in rock pose on top of your heels.
- Allow your breathing to come back to normal and contemplate the effects of the asana.
- If this stretch is too much when you start to practice, place your hands on the small of your back rather than your feet as you arch your head.

Benefits of Ustrasana

- Clears and balances the chakras
- Activates the thyroid glands
- Improves and stimulates the nervous and respiratory systems
- Stimulates the digestive system, kidneys, and endocrine glands
- Reduces fatigue and anxiety as it energies the body
- Strengths the back, thighs, arm and shoulder muscles
- Loosens the spinal cord, improves posture and opens up the hips
- Stretches the hip flexors, quadriceps, abdomen, and chest.

Vajrasana - Rock Pose

- On your mat, sit on top of the heels of your feet like the top of your feet are lying flat on the mat.
- Stretch your spine and neck so that they are erect.

Benefits of Vajrasana

- Aids in proper digestion and liver function
- Relieves symptoms of indigestion, constipation, nerve issues, and sciatica
- Balances out the acidity in the stomach and prevents ulcers
- Strengthens the pelvic and back muscles
- Reduces menstrual cramps and eases labor pain
- Prepares the body for meditation

Benefits of Vajrasana

- Aids in proper digestion and liver function
- Relieves symptoms of indigestion, constipation, nerve issues, and sciatica
- Balances out the acidity in the stomach and prevents ulcers
- Strengthens the pelvic and back muscles
- Reduces menstrual cramps and eases labor pain
- Prepares the body for meditation

Savasana - Corpse Pose

- Lay on your back on your mat and bend your knees slightly.
- Keep your arms straight at your sides.
- Center your head while facing straight at the ceiling.
- Extend both of your hands to the sides parallel to the body.
- Breathe normally, and let the air flow smoothly.
- Close your eyes and relax the facial muscles starting with the eyelids and forehead.
- Secondly, relax your tongue, lips, and cheeks.
- Continue to relax all the muscles in your body methodically going in section towards your feet.

Kundalini Energy and Chakras

In this part we are going to explore the means of which this energy moves through our bodies. The coiled serpent energy does not just awake and explodes out in all directions. It travels certain energetic pathways that are found in our subtle energetic bodies. These pathways are known as nadis, and they culminate at energy centers well-known as chakras. When kundalini is awakened, it travels these pathways through the chakras, opening these energy centers and sparking a union of our physical bodies and subtle energetic bodies. But what is the nature of these energetic pathways when the kundalini is still dormant? Let's explore the chakras and nadis more thoroughly to get a better understanding of these energetic highways.

The Seven Chakras

The most popular system to work with the chakras is the seven chakra system. Over the centuries, there have been many differing chakra techniques and systems, but the one that has found the most success in the western world is the seven chakra system. This system is comprised of a working method of visualization, mantra, and other attributes that relate to a set of seven main chakras that run along the spine, respectively.

It is thought that there are thousands of chakras throughout our subtle energetic bodies, but many of these chakras are minuscule or so subtle that we cannot even feel them working. The seven main chakras, on the other hand, are very prominent in our lives. We can actively feel them moving and intentionally work with them to improve our health and our lives.

The chakras are energy centers that act to bridge the gap between the physical and energetic bodies we thrive within. Any physical ailment or experience can be attributed to a chakra. The attributed chakra allows access to our energetic bodies so that we may work to heal ourselves. These energy centers are key to performing any energy work, and this includes kundalini. Let's look at the seven main chakras and their attributes.

Sahasrara – Crown Chakra
This chakra is known as the crown chakra. It is thought to be the highest chakra in regards to spiritual development. It is said that the masculine, Shiva energy is seated at the crown chakra, and when the kundalini rises up to pierce this chakra, then the union of Shakti and Shiva begins. This is no small feat, raising your energy this high takes practice and patience. This unification achieves self-realization for the student, the ultimate goal of the kundalini practices.

It needs to be said that achieving this unification may come easier to some students than others. Everyone's path is different and unique. There is a major problem in many spiritual communities with false gurus claiming to be enlightened. This comes along with them trying to take advantage of new students or to get money from tourists or other seekers. This is unfortunate, it makes navigating these communities very difficult and often deters seekers form this holy path. In any community, there will be people there trying to cash in on the popularity of spiritual practices, tread lightly and don't trust anyone claiming got be enlightened. For what it's worth, no one who is truly enlightened will ever boast or brag about it.

The crown chakra's yantra or symbolic representation is a thousand-petaled lotus flower. This image is often associated with infinity or the formless unseen forces that we find during spiritual endeavors. This image also represents the oneness that is attained through the union of Shakti and Shiva, the thousand petals seemingly infinite in number. This wholeness is the overall objective of our practices in this book.

- The color associated with the third eye chakra is indigo/purple or colorless. Wearing indigo will help to balance this chakra.

- The stone associated with the third eye chakra is diamond. Wearing this stone in jewelry will help to balance this chakra.
- The metal associated with this chakra is gold. Wearing this metal in jewelry will help to open and balance the crown chakra.
- The mineral associated with this chakra is fluorine. If your diet is lacking fluorine or too high in fluorine, the crown chakra may become unbalanced.
- The musical key associated with the crown chakra is B. Listening to songs in this key or meditating on the B note will help balance this chakra.
- The seed sound for this chakra is Om. Chant this sound or listen to recordings of these chants to balance the crown chakra.
- The pineal gland is associated with the crown chakra. If your pineal gland does not function properly, then you may have a blocked crown chakra.
- There is no flavor associated with the crown chakra.

Ajna – Third Eye Chakra
The Ajna chakra is well-known as the third eye chakra. The third eye is associated with the pineal gland, often being associated with spiritual insight, second sight, and intuitive visions. The third eye is located between the eyebrows, just as the pineal gland sits just behind this area inside of your head. Kundalini is thought to break through the barrier between the physical and the spiritual at this chakra, opening a new perspective to the student and offering them intuitive abilities beyond their sensory capacity.

The concept of the third eye is not only found in Indian culture, but even science also validates this area as distinct with studies of the mysterious pineal gland. Other cultures have this idea as well, consider the Egyptian priests with a cobra spring forth out of their headdress right where the third eye is located. We see here how these concepts are not limited to one religious sect or cultural system, these energetic power centers are inherent in all humans, whether our culture acknowledges it or not.

The yantra of the third eye chakra is a two-petaled lotus flower with a triangle pointing downward in the middle. It is also taught that the nadis cross at this chakra, switching roles and preparing the student for the union of the divine feminine and divine masculine. This crisscrossing acts to rid the student of duality, to give them the capability to see the non-dual perspective of the world. With this insight, we can see the balance of the light and dark, male and female and positive and negative.

- The color associated with the third eye chakra is violet. Wear this color or decorate your home is violet to help balance this chakra.
- The stone of the third eye chakra is opal. Carry this stone or wear it in jewelry to help balance this chakra.
- The metal of this chakra is silver. Wear jewelry that is made of silver to help stimulate and balance the third eye chakra.
- The mineral associated with the third eye chakra is chlorine. If you have too little to too much chlorine in your diet, your third eye chakra may become blocked or unbalanced.
- The musical key of this chakra is A. Listening to songs in this key or meditating on the note A will help to balance this chakra.
- The seed sound of this chakra is Om. Chant this sound or listen to recordings of these chants to balance the third eye chakra.

- The pituitary gland is associated with the third eye chakra. If this gland is not functioning properly, then this chakra may be unbalanced.
- The flavor that is associated with this gland is sweetness. If your diet is too sweet or lacks freshness your third eye chakra can become unbalanced.

Vishuddha – Throat Chakra
The Vishuddha chakra is known as the throat chakra in English. It is located under the chin or near the top of the spine. This chakra is associated with the akasha, the element of ether. It is thought in some systems that the akasha holds records of human history, as well as spiritual insight. This chakra influences our ability to communicate effectively. If it is blocked or unbalanced, we may have trouble expressing ourselves or getting the attention of others with our words. People have also experienced a sense of being invisible or overlooked due to these blockages.
The balancing of this chakra is crucial if we wish to express any emotions. Socializing and joyous occasions are also greatly affected by this chakra. When unbalanced this chakras may make it difficult to thrive within a community, or to join in on communal get-togethers like family dinners or charitable events. Essentially any task that requires clear communication can be troublesome, and as you know, almost anything you wish to achieve will require some, if not a lot, of clear and concise communication.
The throat chakra's yantra or symbolic image is a sixteen-petaled lotus with a triangle pointing downward and a circle at its center. The communication issues with this chakra are not only limited to communicating with others. We must communicate truthfully to ourselves as well. If we are not able to be honest with ourselves, then we will not be able to be honest with anyone else around us. This is the lesson of the throat chakra.

- The color of the throat chakra is blue. Wearing this color or decorating your home with this color can help balance the chakra.
- The stone associated with the throat chakra is quartz. Carrying this stone or wearing it in jewelry helps to open and balance this chakra. A necklace would be fitting since this chakra is located at the neck.
- The metal of this chakra is mercury. Mercury can be used for chakra workings, but it's not recommended for beginners since it is highly toxic.
- The mineral associated with this chakra is silicon. If your diet is too high or too low in silicon, then your throat chakra may become unbalanced.
- The musical key associated with the throat chakra is G. Listening to songs in this key or meditating on the G note will help balance this chakra.
- The seed sound associated with this chakra is Ham. Chant this sound or meditate on recordings of this chant to open and balance the throat chakra.
- The thyroid gland is associated with this chakra. If your thyroid is not functioning properly, you may have a blocked throat chakra.
- The flavor associated with the throat chakra is sour. If you ingest too many sour foods or too small of an amount, this chakra may be unbalanced.

Anahata – Heart Chakra

Anahata is also known as the heart chakra. It is located in the middle of the chest or the paralleled area on the spinal column. This chakra governs self-love and the ability to accept and share all kinds of love. In Buddhist traditions, the acceptance of love and developing compassion for others is key to reaching enlightenment. Compassion and empathy can be seen as types of unconditional love; therefore, these emotions are greatly affected by the health of your heart chakra.

Love is the defining factor that separates the higher chakras from the lower chakras. Developing a sense of unconditional love is crucial to our development as humans. If we only give love for something in return, we have missed this point altogether. We must learn to give and accept love as it is, not with ulterior motive or great expectations. Love is a defining factor as to whether or not our lives are fulfilling and enjoyable. If we cannot properly accept love or be grateful for love, then we cannot find contented wholeness in this lifetime. Without a compassionate sense of love, we cannot move further up with our chakra workings. We need love to determine our path as humans, to communicate openly and to work through intuitive processes. It truly is amazing how life changes all aspects of our lives, not only through sharing it but by loving ourselves as well.

A twelve-petaled lotus symbolizes the heart chakra's yantra with two interlocking triangles in the middle. These interlocking triangles are popular as the Star of David, but these symbols hold many meanings and have been used for centuries. These triangles may be symbolic of the relationship between fire and water, as well as various protective powers found in esoteric traditions. Overall this symbol will represent the union, and the transformative results that love can offer.

- The color of the heart chakra is green. You can wear green or decorate your home in green to help balance this chakra.
- The stone attributed to the heart chakra is sapphire. Carry one of these stones or wear them in jewelry. A necklace is best since it will hang near your heart chakra.
- The metal of the heart chakra is copper. Wear this metal in jewelry or carry a piece to help balance the chakra.

- The mineral of this chakra is potassium. If your heart chakra is unbalanced, you may be ingesting too much or too little of this mineral.
- The musical key for this chakra is F. Listen to songs in this key or meditate on the F note to balance the heart chakra.
- The seed sound for this chakra is Yam. Chant this sound or listen to recordings of it while meditating to balance the heart chakra.
- The thymus gland is associated with the heart chakra. This gland may not function properly if our heart chakra is unbalanced.
- The flavors associated with this chakra are astringent in nature. Having too much or too little of these flavors may cause your heart chakra to become unbalanced.

Manipura - Solar Plexus Chakra
Manipura is also known as the navel or solar plexus chakra. It is housed at the navel or stomach area, as well as the paralleled location on the spinal column. This chakra is often seen as the energetic center of our personal self-discovery. We develop our personality and move past primal instincts to develop a sense of individuality at this chakra. The solar plexus chakra is also seen as a battery for our physical energy. Not unlike the sun, this chakra works to light the way on our path, giving rise to new growth as an individual.
This chakra acts as a threshold from the primal lower chakras to the heart chakra, where we find compassionate love. Working with the solar plexus chakra will allow us to define who we are and what we want to contribute to the world. Discovering our place in life will allow us to find love within these goals of social contribution.
The solar plexus is symbolized in a yantra by the ten-petaled lotus flower with a triangle pointing upward in the middle. This triangle symbolizes fire and the burning desire to find our

calling. This burning desire gives rise to conscious evolution and burns away, primal fears or negative urges.

- The color of the solar plexus chakra is yellow. You can wear yellow clothing or decorate your room with yellow to help balance this chakra.
- The stone of the solar plexus chakra is ruby. This stone can be carried in your pocket or worn in jewelry.
- The metal of this chakra is iron. This metal can be worn as jewelry or carried with you in a pocket.
- The mineral of the solar plexus chakra is sulfur. If your solar plexus chakra is unbalanced, you may be ingesting too much or too little of this mineral. Alter your diet accordingly.
- The musical key of the solar plexus chakra is E. If your chakra is unbalanced, you can listen to songs in this key or meditate on the E note to balance it.
- The seed sound of this chakra is Ram. Chant this sound or listen to recordings of it to balance your solar plexus chakra.
- The pancreas is associated with the solar plexus chakra. If your pancreas is not functioning properly you may have blockages in this chakra.

The flavors associated with this chakra are pungent flavors. Balance your diet with these flavors to ensure your solar plexus chakra stays balanced.

Svadhishthana – Sacral Chakra

This chakra is also known as the sacral chakra and is near the sexual organs or the paralleled area of the spinal column. This lower chakra influences creativity in the broadest sense, as well as sexual drive and desire. Balancing and opening this chakra is key to developing our self-expression and desire to procreate. If we cannot learn to express ourselves or express desire in a balanced way, we will remain controlled by our selfish and primal desires.

The creative abilities dictated by this chakra are creative in the sense that we are artistic and creative by nature, but also our desire to create life. The creation of life can be referring to having children, but also the creation of life within us. Instead of living a primal and instinctual existence, we find life inside of us as creative expression. Understanding this concept is key to developing a sense of individuality and personality. We must create the person we wish to be, expressing our contributions to our society and the greater world.

A six-petaled lotus flower symbolizes this chakra's yantra with a crescent moon in the middle. The moon relates to the water element and also fertility. This chakra is fluid and always changing, which can make it tough for some to balance and open. Through a healthy sex life, control of desire, and creative endeavors, this chakra can be opened and worked with directly. We must find what we have to offer with this chakra. We are not just automatons seeking food and shelter. We have a creative expression to share in the form of art, music, technology, philosophy, and nurturing.

The color attributed to the sacral chakra is orange, we can wear orange or decorate our room in orange to help balance this chakra.

- The stone attributed to this chakra is beryl; we can carry this stone in our pocket or have jewelry made using this stone.
- The metal of the sacral chakra is tin. We can use this metal to make jewelry or carry it with us to help balance the chakra.
- The mineral of the sacral chakra is sodium. If your sacral chakra is unbalanced, you may be ingesting too much or too little of this mineral.

- The musical key of the sacral chakra is D. Listening to songs in this key or meditating on the note D will help balance this chakra.
- The seed sound of the sacral chakra is Vam. Chanting or meditating on recordings of this sound will help to balance the chakra.
- The sexual organs are associated with this chakra. If your chakra is blocked, you may experience a lack of sexual drive or inefficient organ function.
- The flavor attributed to the sacral chakra is salty flavors. If you consume too much salty food, or too little, your sacral chakra could become unbalanced.

Muladhara – Root Chakra
Muladhara is also known as the root chakra. It is located at the base of the spine. This chakra influences our most primal needs governing our ability to survive. The basic necessities needed to thrive, such as shelter, food, and procreation are all essential aspects of this chakra. These are the basic instincts of every human; these impulses are found at the root of all of our choices in life. When this chakra is unbalanced or blocked, we are susceptible to our most basic impulses, regardless of the repercussions. Gluttony, promiscuous sex, anger, and selfishness are all negative qualities that can arise if we are not working to improve the health of our root chakra. Keeping a home and providing for your family will also be interrupted if this chakra is not balanced.

This is also the general area where the kundalini energy resides. She is coiled here, dormant until we approach our survivalist needs and balance them. It is thought that these primal urges must be contemplated and utilized in an evolved way for kundalini to awaken. This adheres to the idea that we must start at the lower chakras and work our way upward to get the full benefits and properly open these energetic centers for our advantage. If we attempt to approach kundalini with no prior experience with this energy, we can potentially awaken the serpent prematurely, resulting in negative experiences that can cause permanent damage to our psyche. This is why it is recommended that we work casually with the seven chakras before intentionally addressing the kundalini energy. Experimenting with basic techniques is suggested before attempting more advanced practices. We find that the more open and clear your chakras are, the less likely you will have an adverse kundalini experience.

The root chakra's yantra is symbolized by a four-petaled lotus flower with a triangle pointed downward within a square in its middle. The primal nature of this chakra is the base for which all our chakra work will be built upon. Although primal urges must be managed properly, we still need these urges to motivate us to survive and perpetuate our bloodlines. Ancestral lineages may need repairing as well through work with this chakra. Our most basic needs cannot go unnoticed, but we also may need to balance them out, so our most basic instincts don't consume our ability to be selfless or empathetic.

- The color of the root chakra is red. We can wear red or decorate our home to stimulate the chakra.
- The stone associated with this chakra is onyx. We can carry this stone in our pocket or wear it in jewelry to balance the root chakra.
- The metal associated with the root chakra is lead. Lead is toxic, so it is not recommended to be used by beginners.
- The mineral associated with this chakra is calcium. We can balance out the root chakra by including more or less calcium-rich foods in our diet.
- The musical key for the root chakra is C. Listening to songs in this key or mediating on the C note will help to balance this chakra.

- The seed sound for the root chakra is LAM. Chanting or listening to recordings of this sound can balance this chakra.
- The glands associated with this chakra are the gonads.
- The flavor attributed to this chakra is bitterness. Balance your diet with not too much or too little of its flavor to balance the root chakra.

Minor Chakras

Aside from the main seven chakras of the chakras system, there are also minor chakras that are much more subtle and more difficult to work with. These chakras are minuscule compared to the main centers of energy. Not only are they difficult to work with, but they are also hard to feel. Working with these chakras requires very advanced techniques, and they also are attributed to very specific aspects of our lives. When we work with our main chakras, many of these minor chakras are affected as well; in a sense, these minor chakras are all interrelated to the major chakras we have learned about.

It is thought that there may be upwards of about 88,000 minor chakras. It is impossible to tell for sure, but these energy centers seem to be infinite, all interconnecting to each other, forming a web that connects everything in the universe. These are the connections that we feel to everyone and everything.

Some of the more prominent minor chakras include the Bindu, talu, and manas chakras. The Bindu is quite popular, even being implemented by some new age communities. The Bindu is often visually expressed by certain Indian cultures wearing a jewel or gem on their foreheads, also known as a bindi. The actual word Bindu is dated back to the Rigveda. We also see some more prominent minor chakras on the hands. These chakras are great for working with other people's energy and manipulating our own with physical movement. The feet are also known to have important chakras for massage work or reflexology practices.

You may never work with these minor chakras on your journeys on the path to kundalini awakening, but it is good to know how these systems work. The complexities of life could not all be filtered through only seven chakras. It makes sense that there are thousands of chakras working to bridge the gap between the physical and energetic bodies. There are more advanced studies on the minor chakras, but for our intents and purposes, we will focus on the seven chakra system.

Chakra Etymology

The actual word chakra can be translated loosely to disc or wheel. This is because the chakras are actually circular in shape, and when healthy, will spin in certain directions. This spinning can be felt on subtle levels, and sometimes can be more intensive while the chakra is being worked with. In some traditions, they teach that chakras should be spinning in a certain direction. This is difficult to verify in person, but generally, if your chakra is spinning, it is open and healthy.

In many cultures, chakras are at the core of philosophical and physical life. These energy centers can be attributed to basically every human experience or ailment. Physiological issues, as well as spiritual ones, can be healed or attended through these energy centers. The idea that energy flows all around and through us is no secret. Even science has proven that humans are electromagnetic in nature. It makes sense why these cultures adhere to these philosophies and practices, not only does history validate the techniques as useful, but science is gradually getting on board with the concepts.

Chakras are also aligned with other aspects of our lives. There are attributes to each chakra that entail almost all aspects of life, if not all of them. Stones, herbs, colors, musical keys, metals, and so many more attributes are associated with certain chakras. These attributes can be seen as energetically similar to the chakra they are assigned to. Many modern traditions believe these attributes to be symbolic representations, but the ancient practices saw these attributes as literal aspects of the chakras themselves, viewing the physical attributes as manifestations of certain conscious energy. By extension, even manmade products can be seen as attributed to certain chakras. So our physical health and psychic health play a role in the balance of our chakras, but so does our environment. Just as the energy flowing through us connects us to our subtle bodies, this energy is also connecting us to our surroundings. This brings up the question of pollution and the destroying of the natural world. Since we are connected to this world energetically, its destruction affects us, but we may also heal it with our energetic practices if we so choose. The awareness of this universal energetic connection is overwhelming at times but also helps to promote mindfulness about our environment. If we can live in a more balanced world, then our chakras will be more balanced as well.

The idea that we are all connected energetically is not only found in the chakra systems of India. This idea is found under many guises throughout all spiritual cultures. One of the most prominent is the traditional Chinese medicine. These practices are built on the idea that we are energetic beings. Acupuncture and acupressure techniques are based on energetic meridian lines that flow throughout our bodies. Modern technology has shown that these ancient meridian lines are closely paralleled to the nervous system. We can also view the Chinese lay lines as being similar to nadis in the Hindu traditions. Energy travels through these lines, so we must keep them clear and healthy to avoid blockages.

Acupuncture and acupressure can be seen as ways to open and stimulate the energetic lines through our bodies, but what about working with our energy on an individual level? Not everyone will have the means to see a licensed professional or spiritually adept practitioner to help with our chakra blockages. When we think about how to work with our energy, we need to consider the aspects of life we wish to change. More often than not, we know intuitively which chakras need the most attention. Since these energies manifest in our physical lives as ailments or adversity, we can assume that the troubles or challenges that we face are related to our chakra health.

As beginners, we should focus heavily on the chakras that need the most attention. Working individually with each chakra individually before beginning a more advanced routine will allow us to prepare the energy centers for the more intensive practices. This will ensure that we will not face adverse effects from our practices. These energetic centers are very potent and can be intense to work with, especially if you haven't had any previous work done on with them in the past. Many people discover that their chakras are not healthy and functioning at all; this can make releasing them much more intense since there is so much build-up.

When we become more adept, we can centralize our routine to focus heavily on the relationships between the chakras and how they interact with each other. Eventually, we can see the clear connection between all seven of the chakras. Being able to move energy through two or three different chakras for a specific reason is an advanced skill that allows us to target very specific aspects of our lives.

When approaching chakra work, we must personalize our practice and focus on the most basic principles of energetic work. We need to open our chakras and then continue to move energy through them, removing any blockages, and ensuring that we have a consistent flow. The spiral motion of the disc-like shape of the chakra is the easiest movement to feel at first, but eventually, you will be able to feel the full seven chakra system as it pulses through your being.

Opening and Healing

As a basic first step to working with your chakras, you need to test the waters a little bit. A large part of working with these energy centers is able to feel the energy. All of us have felt an energetic jolt of excitement or surprise. Many of us have likely felt a 'bad' energy in a room or a certain building. This is feeling the energy around you. It is a distinct feeling that almost feels electric as it moves through you. When working with kundalini energy, it feels very much the same, but more intensive. A good first step to learning to feel the energy is to sit down in a quiet place and simply feel. Take note of the smell of the room around you, the temperature, the sounds, and any other notable experiences. Then turn the observational sight inward, seeking the energy flowing through you. Try and notice any movement through your body, listening closely to your heart pumping, try and move energy on your breath. You can also practice feeling the energy with your fingers or palms. Many like to visualize a ball of energy between their hands, trying to manipulate it. There are many different versions of these energy practices, find methods that suit your needs as you begin these basic exercises.

As you begin to learn the basics of how to feel and move energy, you can begin to work directly with the individual chakras. By placing our hands directly over the area that the chakras reside, we can try and feel our chakras. For the most part, the chakra's energies all feel similar. The main difference between the way these chakras feel is going to be the more movement when they are open. If you are trying to feel your chakras and you find tightness or no movement, your chakras may need opening and clearing. It is best to start with the lower chakras as you begin. See if you can feel their energy at all, it may take a few sessions of listening to your body to really adapt to what the energy feels like.

To open blocked chakras, we need to focus predominantly on the chakra's blockages. We can sit quietly in a room, and visualize this chakra. Immerse yourself in its attributed color or hold its attributed stone in your palms as you focus. Clear your mind a focus all of your attention on this chakra. Now visualize the chakra being filled with white light, breathe deeply and see the chakra move with your breath. Maintain this visual for as long as possible, then relax.

Keep note of any experiences you have. If a certain technique works really well, then keep that one in your routine. As you progress, you will notice tightness and warmth in the chakra areas. This is very common and is often a sign of the chakra opening. Once you feel that the chakra is open, you can again try to feel its energy with your hands, if you notice more movement or a swirling movement then this chakra is open.

When these chakras open, you will notice non-physical results as well. The emotions related to this chakra will be balanced; you may even notice certain aspects of your environment changing. Keep track of any significant experience and see how it relates to what we know about the attributes of the chakras. For instance, if you are having problems maintaining a steady home and providing for yourself or family, you may have root chakra blockages. Work with the chakra to see if it is, in fact, blocked. Then work to unblock it, see if you can feel a difference in the energy. Once you have successfully opened or cleared this chakra see if there are any drastic changes in these aspects of your life.

Notes on Energy Work
The use of energy work to improve our lives is no new discovery. These kinds of practices have existed for millennia, under many different names. Using our gifts as humans to manipulate energy and improve our lives is a key component of living that is all too lost in western society. We can feel the energy all around us. There are distinct differences in the energy of certain places and buildings. Energy can be disorienting, or even frightening at certain locations. All of us have felt the loving energy of a friendly embrace or smile. These forces in our lives cannot be ignored. And if left unattended will cause blockages that only get worse over time.

We have the capabilities to move this energy, not only with our own physical bodies but also with our minds through visualization and other energetic practices. We can liken the moving of energy to that of a river or stream. They are always moving, but we can change their direction or swiftness with a little effort. One of the most prominent times that energy is very obvious is when we are emotionally aroused. Anger and sadness are such intensive emotions that the energy literally pours out of us. It is often impossible to hide the fact that we are upset due to those energetic releases. These releases may also be beneficial in the end, offering to clear on their own accord. This is why crying and really embracing strong emotions is key to dealing with them.

Many people, intentional or not, use their energetic skills to manipulate others. These cruel practices come in many forms, often as emotional drainage or a sort of energetic vampirism when people drain others of energy simply by being near or causing disruption. Some people who do this may not even realize they are doing it, but there are those who intentionally use their energy for selfish and evil reasons. This type of energy work is not recommended for any reason, and in fact, will cause even more damage to your own chakra system in the long run. These attacks may also trigger premature kundalini awakening when used intentionally. Combined with a vindictive mindset, this could potentially be very detrimental.

Developing your energetic skills for the greater good is the most balanced path to walk with these practices. Not only can we heal ourselves with these skills, but we may even wish to heal others. These practices are common in many cultures, taking forms like massage or reiki. These practices are very common in the west and are found in many new age circles. The role of the healer is very important in our current society. With the advent of synthetic drugs and unhealthy diets, we need healers of all kinds to lead the way through this messy era. If you feel that you have a knack for healing, then most certainly follow this path and seek assistance to hone your skills. The communal healer is one of the most important roles in society. Consider the ancient shamans who would travel to the underworld to heal the land or protect his community.

These are incredibly complex and dangerous feats, but the shaman takes these risks for the good of the community.

Many find energy work to be very challenging when they are starting out, while others may be more skilled at the practices. There is no reason to be discouraged, as we have mentioned, everyone is energetic and has the potential to hone these skills. Clearing and opening the chakras will be the first steps you need to take when developing your energy work skills. With plenty of practice, we can find which skills we are best at and focus on them as we work towards our kundalini awakening.

Clearing Exercise

A simple and effective clearing exercise is a must-have for your arsenal of energy work techniques. Using a clearing exercise one a week will ensure that your chakras to not become blocked again and again. These exercises work well to clear chakras and keep them clear. As you manage to open your chakras, you will want to keep them clear so you can further your work and progress on your holy path.

This exercise is really simple and uses visualization and breathing to clear the chakras. We will need a comfortable, quiet place to sit and relax. Breathe deep and clear your mind of any chaotic thoughts. Once you are calm and relaxed, visualize a pure white light above you. Let this light fill the skies and immerse yourself within it. Continue breathing and on an inhale to draw the light down from the heavens and let it enter your body through the crown chakra. Maintain this connection and try to move the light down through all the chakras until you reach the root. Keep this light connected and let it mingle with your chakras for as long as you see fit. Once you are finished you let the light leave your body, potentially taking any blockages out with it.

After this white light exercise, continue to breathe deeply. Visualize the blockages leaving on your breath with each exhale. Breathe deeply for a few minutes, really letting your breath fill your body, carrying out any remnants of blockage away with it on every exhale. When you are finished, take a few minutes to relax.

This simple practice is easy to do and will help keep your chakras clear. You can even modify this practice and use it in a more spontaneous way. This is helpful when you are on the go or at work. Do the same white light exercise listed above, but don't worry about sitting or deep breathing, just take a minute or two to visualize the light entering your body, then leaving your body.

Keep this easy practice handy throughout your path on the way to kundalini awakening. It is one of the easiest and most effective means to maintain clear chakras. Use this exercise at least once a week at first, but as your practice develops, you can do it less often, perhaps once or twice a month.

Chakras in Motion

As we work with the chakras, we must take into consideration how they move. This will help us learn to feel the energy and know where and how it moves. We know that the chakras are disc-shaped, but why are they disc shaped? The chakras actually move in a circular motion rather than being disc-shaped. The circular motion makes the chakra seem to be a disc, but it is actually the motion of the energy that creates this shape. May traditions find that this spinning is often a good way to tell if the chakra is healthy. It is thought that if you cannot feel the spinning energy that the chakra may be blocked or unbalanced. If your chakras are completely closed, you may not be able to feel them at all.

Many traditions believe that chakra should be spinning in a certain direction. It is thought that the chakra should be spinning in a clockwise motion. If the chakra is not moving or is moving counter-clockwise, then it may be unbalanced. Some traditions believe that if your chakras are spinning the opposite direction that they are overstimulated. This concept is debatable, and for our purposes in this book, we will stick with the idea that if they are open and moving, then they are healthy and can be worked with directly.

When we visualize the chakras, we can see the circular motion that they make, this will help us understand how to work with any particular chakra depending on how it is moving. If there is an intensive movement, then the chakra is certainly open. If it is overstimulated, you may feel an overabundance of heat or energy in that area. Typically, the root and sacral chakras are the ones that are easiest to overstimulate. Sexual desire is the most common culprit for overstimulation.

When we are working with our chakras, we need to be very aware of the movements they make. Developing this mindfulness and awareness is key to keeping track of your chakra health. An adept practitioner can sit down to meditate and instantly know whether or not their chakras need work. These skills take time and effort to develop, but eventually being aware of your chakras becomes second nature. This also brings up the power of the present. If we are not in the present moment, we will not be able to be mindful of our chakras. In fact, not being here in the present moment makes us oblivious of all our surroundings, leading to delusion and false experiences of what is actually going on.

Blockages

With years of wear and tear and not efforts to heal, chakras can become unbalanced and blocked. These blockages can cause serious problems in the physical world. If our energy is not flowing correctly, we will not be living a healthy life. Just as there is an energetic counterpart to our physical bodies, there are energetic counterparts to physical ailments. These blockages cause the chakras to close, not moving at all. When this happens, we are left to lead half-lived lives full of trouble and sickness.

Most of us have probably experienced a chakra blockage, although we may not have attributed the problem to our chakras. When a chakra is blocked, it feels like a knotted up ball where the chakra is, then it inevitable manifests in a physical ailment or even a problem in relationships or careers.

These blockages can be handled with a little bit of energetic work. Depending on how unhealthy your chakras are, you may even be able to unblock them in only a few days. Now when we say unblock, we aren't necessarily saying they are open and functioning optimally. Removing blockages is the first step to getting the chakras moving and opening. You will want your chakras to be open and healthy before you awaken kundalini. If she is awakened and your chakras are blocked, you will have major problems as she tries to pierce each chakra. It will be like all your stored problems and emotions flooding through you all at once. This is enough to drive anyone crazy or dramatically interrupt life in negative ways.

To unblock chakras, we must use meditation, yoga, and visualization to move the energy through them, removing blocked energy out of our bodies.

Nadis

The nadis are important factors when it comes to any energetic workings. Energy is moved through the nadis, they may culminate at chakras where they access the physical world, but to move freely form chakra to chakra they rely on nadis. Nadis act as a highway system to channel the energy from chakra to chakra. These energetic highways need to be worked with as well. They can become blocked and unbalanced just as the chakras do. Working with the nadis is similar to chakra work, we can use the same practices and techniques. In fact, when we work with the chakras, we affect the nadis as well. Chakras will not become unblocked if the nadis are blocked; this is an integrated system that relies on its parts to work effectively as a whole.

Nadis are at the heart of the energetic model that Hinduism relies upon for existential understanding and knowledge. The concept of the nadis is well over 3,000 years old. And just as there are thousands of subtle chakras, there are thousands of nadis that interconnect these chakras. This energetic road system is often compared to meridian lines in traditional Chinese medicine or our physical nervous system.

Ida, Pingala, Sushumna

Just as there are seven main chakras that we aim to work within this book, there central and major nadis as well. It is taught that there are three main nadis, the ida, pingala, and sushumna. These are the most vital nadis to our energetic bodies. They are the highways that most of the potent energy that reaches the major chakras travel upon, eventually reaching a heightened intensity as it culminates at the chakras and influences our physical world.

The nadis are related to the arteries, veins, and nerves throughout our bodies. The nadis plays the role of the subtle energetic counterpart to our physical system that carries actual nutrients and oxygen to all parts of our bodies. This makes more and more sense as science discovers the mysterious nature of the human body and its complex systems. It is safe to say that all physical presence has an equal twin in the energetic or spiritual world.

We work with the nadi channels at the same time as we work with chakras. These channels are also engaged in the same way we would approach the chakras; only the nadis are not culminations of energy like chakras. The nadis act more as channels for energy. Working with the nadis allows us to move energy throughout the body, clearing blockages as it travels. If we were to only focus on the chakras, we would have no means of moving the blockages without the energetic channels that connect these chakras.

The ida and pingala nadis are considered to be parts working together to create a whole. This whole is likened to the feminine and masculine energies that flow through us. Many traditions teach that ida and pingala cross paths over each other at the chakras. While other traditions say that ida and pingala run along their attributed side of the body, the ida is on the left and the pingala is on the right. In all traditions these channels run from the sides of the genital up to the third eye chakra where they do cross and lead out the nostrils. This is where we see the distinct role of breath in energy work. If the nadis exit at the nostrils, then our breath most certainly plays a role in this operation.

Our breath and our nadi channels work together to move energy. Breathing is one of the most important aspects of any energetic system, including the kundalini workings. We often take breathing for granted, but being in control of our breathing is one of the most basic steps to improving our lives for and developing a preliminary practice for kundalini workings.

Ida and pingala are often recognized to be attributed to the two hemispheres of the brain. This concept adheres to the idea that the right and left sides of our brain govern different human experiences and behaviors. This is a popular view in the west. This idea claims that the right brain is responsible for creativity and spontaneity, and the left side of the brain is responsible for reasoning and problem-solving. Let's explore ida and pingala more thoroughly.

Ida

The energetic channel ida is related to lunar energy and feminine energy. It offers a cooling feeling and is nurturing. The fluidity of this nadi results in erratic changes if left on its own unattended. This channel is also known to stimulate deep thought and contemplation.

Pingala

The energetic channel pingala is associated with the energy of the sun and masculine energy. Its warming effect is very noticeable when we are enjoying ourselves. This channel is often associated with reasoning and logic. The pingala energy is extroverted and responsible for survival tactics and stamina.

Sushumna

The energetic channel called sushumna runs directly through the middle of the spine from the root chakra to the crown chakra, connecting the other chakras along the way. This is the core channel that Ida and pingala are guided by as they move energy around the body. All the thousands of nadis are said to connect to sushumna, revealing its importance to energy workings and kundalini practices. Many people who have experienced a kundalini awakening report that they absolutely feel sushumna being energized as they are experiencing the event.

The nadis are a popular concept found in many ancient philosophies; the balancing of feminine and masculine energies, lunar and solar energies, or watery and fiery energies are all found throughout the world's ancient cultures. This validates these balanced philosophies as very important to the progression of humanity.

Balancing the feminine and solar energies is as easy as maintaining a healthy lifestyle and a positive mindset. We can take action in the physical world to balance these energies, but we must also act in the energetic world to balance these energies fully. In fact, the workings you perform for your energetic body versus your physical body is a balancing act in itself.

We see that the relationship between the chakras and kundalini awakening is key to our purposes in this book. We must act to engage the energetic chakra system and get it into healthy shape before we attempt any kundalini centered exercises. Having our chakras cleared in preparation for kundalini not only shows our dedication to the practice but will also lessen the chance of any negative effects from the intense kundalini awakening.

We are seeing the complete energetic body system taking shape. This complex system is the active body that we engage in anytime we are performing energy work. It is actually unavoidable to not interact with this body. Our physical selves and this energetic system work together to create a life experience. Perspective, consciousness, and all of our emotions stem from the health of these systems. If we cannot keep one side healthy, then the other side will suffer as well. As we begin to approach working directly with kundalini, we must take time to get these systems into shape, familiarizing ourselves with their behavior and cycles.

We also need to see the relationship between these two bodies. We should develop awareness and mindfulness when it comes to these relationships, taking notice of how they interact and influence each other. As we will learn, these two bodies are acting together as one system, creating all that we know and love about life.

Chapter 3: Kundalini Diet

Believe it or not, your diet has a major impact on Kundalini energy. What you fuel your body with is a form of energy in and of itself. Not only does it provide you with physical energy, but it also works together with your aura and other non-physical energy. It truly does impact you on many different levels. If you want to have a powerful impact on your Kundalini and support it in the best way possible, be sure to pay attention to your diet and what you are eating.

Avoid eating two to three hours before you plan on doing your kriyas and asanas. Since this yoga uses many different body locks, breathing exercises, vigorous movements, and asanas, you may feel extremely uncomfortable if you are doing so on a full stomach. If you feel you lack energy, have an energy bar beforehand.

Most yoga practices recommend consuming a Sattvic diet, which promotes clarity and calmness, instead of rajasic or tamasic diets; because of the energetic and physical nature of this yoga, consuming some rajasic food isn't that big of a deal. Rajasic foods promote activity. It's still recommended that most of your diet be sattvic. These include fresh and sweet foods like nuts, vegetables, fruit, etc. Rajasic foods are spicier and stimulate, like tea, fish, eggs, garlic, onions, etc. Tamasic foods are meats, stale foods, fatty foods, and so on.

It's important to drink plenty of water after practicing a kriya because it is designed to get your vessels, nerves, tissues, and organs to release toxins. Water will help you cleanse out the toxins.

Adjusting Your Diet for Kundalini Awakening
Many people believe that to promote a healthy spiritual flow, you need to eat a vegetarian or vegan diet. With Kundalini, this is not believed to be necessary. However, it is important that you learn to adjust your diet to suit your body's changing needs. As your spiritual energy changes, your physical body

will typically desire to change what it consumes as well. Those who are awakening or who have awakened already tend to avoid eating any foods that introduce unhealthy energies into the body.

Common things that you will likely feel naturally drawn to avoid when you are awakening include things like: alcohol, recreational drugs, red meat, sugar, and excessive chemicals such as the preservatives they put in convenience meals. You may begin to find yourself wanting or even craving more water, whole organic foods like vegetables and fruits, fish and poultry, or otherwise. Some people may even find themselves naturally drawn to releasing meats of all varieties and instead pursue a vegetarian or vegan diet. That is perfectly fine, too. The idea here is to listen to your body and what your body wants instead of trying to eat a diet that has been manufactured for you by someone else. Only you know what you need. Following these natural requests from your body will greatly impact your ability to feel your best and allow your Kundalini energy to flow fluidly.

Listening to Your Body
Your body is already well aware of what it needs to survive and thrive. As you are right now, your body has likely been consuming foods that would keep it comfortable amidst a high-stress lifestyle that may have involved many difficult or painful emotions. This is natural, especially in the Western world, where emotional self-care is less popular than in other cultures worldwide.

Learning to listen to your body takes some time. Additionally, you may find yourself realizing that as you awaken more, your body needs to change. They may even change beyond diet, encouraging you to exercise differently, use different body care products, or even rest at different times. Being able to really tune into what your body needs is a powerful practice that can truly help you so much in your awakening.

As you grow used to communicating with your body, recognizing what it needs and what it no longer wants becomes significantly easier. You can begin to intuitively recognize anytime something is causing your body to feel sluggish, slow, or otherwise "off." You can also begin to recognize anytime your body feels empowered, high energy, and positive. Naturally, you will want to begin practicing more of what makes you feel good and less of what does not. This is how you can intuitively support your body and begin using diet, exercise, and overall physical wellbeing to promote and support your Kundalini awakening and balancing.

Ayurveda Diet and Kundalini
One form of diet that regularly finds itself incorporated in Kundalini awakening and energy is Ayurveda. Ayurveda is a traditional Hindu system of medicine that uses diet, herbs, and yogic breathing to promote physical, mental, and spiritual wellbeing.

Seeing a professional Ayurvedic practitioner who can assess your unique body type and provide you with advice on how to balance your energies through diet can be powerful. This practice can help you use your diet as a tool to awaken your energies further and thrive, allowing you to feel your best as often as possible. It is a highly recommended tool to use when performing your Kundalini awakening, even when you are balancing your energies.

Dietary Restrictions and Purification Exercises
Part of bringing your physical body into balance is being conscientious about what you put into it. There's no one correct diet for following Kundalini yoga—the point of dietary restrictions is to eat moderate amounts of simple, healthy, nourishing food that will support your body without overstimulating or punishing it. Different teachers have different opinions but agree that aspirants ought to adjust and perfect their diets depending on their own bodies' needs.

Typically, simple foods like milk, fruit, lentils, nuts, and vegetables are recommended, while meat, salt, alcohol, and strongly flavored foods are forbidden. Eat only as much as you need to, and make your meals simple and regular. Attachment to food only creates more attachments to the particulars of the earthly world, making the transcendence of it impossible—you can't negate your individuality if you're craving something particular. Overeating also makes the body sluggish and less responsive to hatha yoga training.

Also, as a preliminary to the strict exercises involved in Kundalini awakening, traditionally aspirants practice various bodily purification exercises involving the digestive tract, sinuses, lungs, and other body parts. These practices are an important part of preparing the body for the strenuous process of kundalini awakening.

Chapter 4: Kundalini vs Meditation

The relationship between meditation and kundalini energy is very important. Meditation aims to clear the mind, letting thoughts roll by and not distract us from our one-pointedness. This clear-headed state is imperative to a successful kundalini working. We need a clear mind to focus our energy and attention on the task at hand. If we are distracted, we will not be able to engage our inherent energy. Without some sense of attentiveness, we will not be successful in our efforts to manipulate this energy.

Meditation's ultimate goal is to clear the mind and offer a sense of oneness. While we don't particularly need to be in this blissful state for a kundalini working, it helps us understand this state. The most important factor that meditation can offer for our kundalini workings is a focused mind. If we can put aside all of our mundane thoughts and memories for enough time to focus our attention on our energy, we will be more aware of the kundalini progress and workings. This one-pointedness that meditation offers is incomparable to any other practice.

Meditation is unique in its ability to offer a sense of clarity for the mind. Simply sitting and breathing is safe and easy; it truly is remarkable how powerful such a simple exercise can be. When we sit down to meditate, we are, in essence, sitting to enter a different state of consciousness, blissful and comforting. These practices are crucial to any balanced lifestyle, and for kundalini, they are invaluable.

There are thousands of different meditation techniques, each of them with its specific use or traditions. As we explored above, it is difficult to find a solid definition for meditation, but overall its goal of achieving a truly clear mind is at the heart of any meditation exercise.

For our kundalini meditation, we must treat it similarly to kundalini yoga. You will not want to have a full stomach for these workings, and you will want to warm up a bit before beginning. We suggest doing some casual yoga and short breathing exercises before performing the following practice. You will not want to go from a normal state of consciousness and then try to jump right into a heightened one. We need to ease ourselves into these more advanced practices to ensure we do not have unwanted outcomes.

There is a common misconception that when you sit down to meditate that your mind will quiet itself. This is misleading; the mind is so chaotic that it will not quiet itself easily. When we meditate, we look inward to discover that we are the listener to our thoughts. How can this be if we are just one person? This is duality, and to eliminate this duality, we must be in the present moment. If we can fully be here now, we can eliminate the distracting thoughts from our past or future. This is a very powerful state to be in, and meditation is the tool to get us here.

When we meditate, we will get distracted. It's inevitable. But we cannot give up on our practice. We must shed the distracting thoughts and not let them trip us up. When we do get distracted, we must realize this distraction and brush it off, continuing our practice from the start. This is not a failure, but a simple challenge, a bum in the path on our way to kundalini awakening. Do not be discouraged. Even the most experienced yogis get distracted by the chaotic nature of the mind.

Meditation is a blissful and comfortable place that we can enter at any time and in any environment. This cozy and welcoming place is found through rigorous effort and dedication to the power of the present. This comfort stems from the oneness that accompanies expanded consciousness. Even when distracting thoughts arise, we must see them off. They will not hook their ugly thoughts onto you if you are attentive and one-pointed. Let them wash away on your breath.

Kundalini philosophy: The Yoga of Awareness

I believe yoga philosophy has the potential to affect every aspect of your life. With a regular practice, yoga can help transform your mind, heart, body and soul. Yoga Philosophy is a demanding discipline that requires great dedication and commitment to achieve spiritual fulfillment.

In ancient yogic terminology, Kundalini refers to an inner energy that is located at the base of your spine. It is often depicted as a coiled serpent or worm-like creature who is asleep at the base of your spine.

Kundalini yoga masters have stumbled upon this powerful energy through years of diligent and concentrated practice. By learning to control this energy, they were able to achieve greater peace of mind, better health and heightened states of awareness. And while it's not easy to learn how to awaken this force, it's certainly worth the effort because Kundalini can transform each aspect of your life.

Kundalini is similar to Qi (the Chinese word for life force) and mana (a Hawaiian word for spiritual energy). These words indicate the vital force or energy that we are all born with.

Many highly intelligent people are able to tap into this energy through meditation, concentration and prayer. And while it is true that some channel this energy into positive ways, there are also those who use it for destructive purposes.

The wakefulness of Kundalini can be compared to a sleeping person, and the suppressed form of this energy can be compared to a person in deep sleep. Yogananda described Kundalini as "a woman deeply dreaming". Unlike most people who are in deep sleep, Kundalini doesn't dream - she is fully aware of her surroundings. And while she is dreaming her own dream, she has access to information and insights that are unavailable to most people.

Kundalini dreams can be compared to a 'consciousness' experience. The person who is directing her dreams can wake her from the sleep state and return her to waking consciousness. But if she falls asleep again, there's little chance of ever waking up because the delusion of deep sleep will become the reality of her life.

The yogic analogy for Kundalini is a sleeping woman who never sleeps. In ancient Sanskrit texts, this person was called Yoga-Sakti - Kundalini in the guise of goddesses and sages.

Is it Kundalini Yoga a safe practice?

Is Kundalini Dangerous? NO! In simpler words it is not dangerous if you know what you are doing. All the incidents we listen to ultimately lead to the conclusion that the guru was not well trained, or we do not have a clear idea about the process of kundalini. When you do not know what you are doing can have an immense impact on your life then you might get confused and start having symptoms of a mentally retarded person. If you are not spiritually attached to the kundalini, then you will have side effects that will freak you out. The awakening of the kundalini is the moving of the prana stimulation throughout the body. Not all the energies developing inside you are kundalini, kundalini is indeed the primary base for all the energies be it mental, physical, spiritual or emotional. The shift of energies within a person can ultimately awake for a while the chakra, behavior modes can be strange. In kundalini awakening, the whole system has come to life as there is a surge of energies that purifies you too if you are not prepared you will be considered as paranoid.

Kundalini Yoga is a ground-breaking practice; however, should its strength give you delay? Here, I will demystify the normal worries about this old practice.

Ever Googled Kundalini Yoga? You may have experienced list items cautioning of a "risky" practice that could incite trepidation in even the most prepared yogis. While the facts confirm that enlivening kundalini vitality releases colossal force—which can degenerate if it isn't utilized appropriately—Kundalini Yoga as instructed and brought toward the West by Yogi Bhajan has been sharpened and tried. As an accomplished, confirmed Kundalini Yoga teacher myself, I instruct and practice this style of yoga in an efficient, synergistic way that ensures a protected, transformative encounter. Here, I disperse 6 greatest fantasies about Kundalini Yoga.

1. It's Hazardous
No one on record has ever gone insane from Kundalini Yoga as instructed by Yogi Bhajan. Kundalini is a normally adoring, mending, and edifying vitality. Through adjusting in and warming, the organized practices educated in my course, Kundalini will get ready for you and your body for a safe and transformational experience. You will confide in your instinct more profoundly and interface with your higher self. Individuals from everywhere throughout the world and varying backgrounds have rehearsed Kundalini Yoga and encountered its extraordinary force.

2. It's a religion
Kundalini Yoga associates you with the vitality of your being. Regardless of what religion you do (or don't) practice, Kundalini Yoga will improve your feeling of the soul. The mantras are widespread. Truth be told, most originate before every cutting edge religion. While the word God is utilized a considerable amount in Kundalini Yoga, you don't have to have confidence in a particular divinity. The God in Kundalini Yoga is deciphered as the "Sustainer of All." Feel allowed utilizing an alternate word that feels progressively normal to you, for example, holy, universe, divine, source, soul, or nature.

3. Arousing This Vitality Is Alarming

To the vast majority, the enlivening of normal kundalini vitality resembles a wonderful flood of heavenly nature that mends and opens new sensations. It can feel like an inward ecstasy that begins in the spine and spreads all through the body. Some have said that it feels exotic. Freshness is possibly terrifying if you clutch previously established inclinations and examples. When kundalini rises, yogis might be guided to surrender meat, liquor, and medications to clear vitality channels. On the off chance that somebody proceeds with those practices when guided not to, she may confront difficulties. At the point when you are obstructed inside, it might set aside some effort to free the trash from a lifetime—including the past karma of your predecessors engraved in your vitality field.

4. You Need to Wear a Headpiece.

The covering of the crown chakra is an antiquated strategy to help contain individual vitality and the sacrosanct affectability of the tenth entryway, which opens to the heavenly vitality of the universe. Consequently, numerous Kundalini Yoga specialists decide to cover the highest point of their heads with normal fiber while rehearsing. It is discretionary; there is no compelling reason to wear a turban.

How to practice in totally safe Kundalini Yoga

Kundalini Yoga uses asanas, which are movement-based poses, combined with breathing and meditation techniques. It's designed to stimulate the awakening process in the body and mind while activating both chakras—the spiritual energy centers within the body.

There are several ways in which you can practice Kundalini Yoga safely. The first and most important thing to do is to perform the yoga asanas properly. A lot of people just jump up and start moving without any attention to detail. They simply want the process of awakening in the body, which is an amazing experience, to begin, with as little pain or injury as possible. They are impatient and want to get there fast, so they will often skip some of the preparatory exercises in order not to have a potentially painful introduction. Other people avoid certain postures because they are unfamiliar or feel that they are risky - all these reasons should be addressed and discarded before you start practicing Kundalini Yoga effectively.

The second factor you should take into consideration is breath control (pranayama). Without proper breathing exercises, the energy will not flow as it should and you may find you cannot feel anything in your body.

Before you begin practicing with others, which is highly advisable in Kundalini Yoga group classes, make sure you can perform all the poses correctly and focus on your breathing. This will improve your understanding of the energy flow within the body and enhance your individual experience.

The third safety measure to take is putting safety first if you decide to practice by yourself rather than attending a class or getting instruction from an experienced teacher of yoga. Here, the most important thing is to learn the correct sequence of postures and understand the technique and mechanics behind a pose so that you can be certain to never go beyond your limits at any stage.

Once you have practiced the postures in this book you should be able to perform them perfectly individually. You will then begin practicing with others and be safe while doing so. The last and the most important step to take is to focus on your breathing technique and meditation. You should always pay attention to how you feel while performing the postures. If something hurts - stop immediately.

If you can't be sure that you will never go beyond your limits, practice with others so that you can learn from their experience as well as put them under pressure to hold the poses correctly and not go beyond their limits. As you progress in your practice, remember that going too far does not mean you are progressing at all; it's better to gradually increase the intensity of a pose than risk an injury or major pain right from the start.

Remember: physical injuries are often symptoms of a deeper problem. They should not be seen as an obstacle to practice. They're just a symptom that should be addressed and treated by your guru. If you can't sit in a pose, but you can stand up, you can begin first with standing postures: standing headstands, balancing postures, and chaturanga dandasanas.

Finally, one of the most important things to take into consideration is not to force any posture. If you find it difficult to go deeper in any posture it is likely that the pose is not suitable for you and your body type - either because of your physical condition or size or simply because it's too advanced for you at this point in time.

How to find a nice Kundalini Yoga teacher

Oftentimes, yoga instructors are a dime a dozen. But finding the right one can be difficult. Here are three steps to find your ideal Kundalini Yoga instructor:

1. Research online reviews and testimonials for instructors near you. Kundalini Yoga is largely an internal practice, so it's important that you feel comfortable with your instructor on an emotional and spiritual level before committing to classes.

2. Visit their studio if possible and see the vibe for yourself; some studios have a more relaxed aura while others are bustling with energy, which can really affect how well you learn in the space.

   Check out the teachers' bios. You'll notice that some teachers have specific training in yoga therapy, and others do not. If you or your friend has physical ailments, make sure the teacher you choose is a practicing yoga therapist.

3. Find out how long the instructor has been practicing Kundalini Yoga. It's important that they have been practicing for at least three years to ensure they are well versed in all aspects of the practice, even though there is no official certification process for Kundalini Yoga instructors.

It is always a good idea to check out the instructor's website first before signing up for a class. If the website is not professional or doesn't have any information about the teacher at all, then that is a red flag. There are three things you want to know about your teacher before signing up for private sessions or beginning classes with them:

1. What type of training do they have? It's important to know what kind of training they have for teaching Kundalini Yoga; many instructors do not have any formal education and claim to be Kundalini instructors simply because they practice it on their own, and this is not necessarily the best option.

2. What makes them attracted to this type of yoga? The energy that surrounds Kundalini Yoga is unique and can be very intense. To be able to teach it, you must have the ability to feel and connect with this energy, which is not something you can learn by reading a book on it or watching videos of it online.

3. What program will they be teaching? There are many different programs out there; some teach different variations while others focus on different aspects such as meditation or chanting for example. You'll want to make sure your teacher will be covering the exact basics of the practice and nothing more than that.

You'll have to be comfortable with your instructor before continuing on to more advanced techniques. There are many different levels of Kundalini Yoga practice, and the teacher's training will determine which level they will teach. Some instructors may only teach three or four different techniques whereas others may cover a variety of practices. The ability to expand your practice is important and you'll want to make sure that if you do advance with your instructor that you are on the same page with them.

A Kundalini Yoga teacher is someone who has a lot of wisdom and knowledge about Kundalini Yoga, so it's imperative that you feel comfortable around them before taking any instruction seriously.

How to use Kundalini Yoga to giving up bad habits forever

It is time. You have tried to stop smoking, eating fast food, spending too much time on social media, drinking too many nights in a row — and you gave up. You are ready to give it one more shot. To make this go the distance this time, you need a better plan than last time.

Kundalini yoga has been found to be very effective in helping people to give up bad habits.
Stay focused on your goal with the help of meditation techniques for making positive change. These include tips for understanding and refining your motivation, finding the hidden obstacles that are keeping you from achieving your goals, and using visualization to form empowering visions for your future.

This is extremely important when you are trying to quit smoking. Kundalini yoga can help in many ways. It boosts lung capacity, making it easier to resist the temptation of lighting up a cigarette or swigging from a bottle. The postures also strengthen abdominal muscles, which can be pulled back, tightening the diaphragm around your lungs, so that you inhale less smoke and expel more of it with each exhalation.

Yoga will help you to become more disciplined and goal-oriented. It is hard to stay focused on what you want, however, if your mind is filled with other distracting thoughts. Once you have reached a certain level of proficiency in a yoga pose, however, the consequences of failure are so immediate and visible that it helps to keep your mind on task.
Doing yoga regularly also helps you to develop flexibility and endurance — both of which are essential skills if you are going to quit a bad habit. You need stamina if you are going to withstand the cravings. And you need the flexibility of mind that lets you redirect your focus from what doesn't work in your life to what does.

When your mind becomes more flexible, it can accept new ways of looking at things, which opens up new possibilities for change. When your mind is less cluttered with repeating thoughts about the past or future, you can focus on the now - on the present moment — which is where true change happens.

Chapter 5: Benefits of Yoga

There is a plethora of ways in which yoga benefits the body—too many to count, in fact. So, let's explore 15 different benefits of yoga in daily life.

1. Improves flexibility - This is one of the most fundamental benefits of yoga. You may not be able to touch your toes or bend all the way forward in your first class, but you will notice over time that your body begins to loosen up, and with that will come a decrease in muscle pain as well.

2. Builds strength - Yoga is the best way to build a healthy amount of strength while balancing it with flexibility. The strength of your muscles contributes greatly to your posture, how you walk, and how you power the daily physical tasks that you may have. Lifting weights builds muscle too, but that (more often than not) takes away from your flexibility.

3. Improves posture - People underestimate the weight of their heads! When you slouch, the amount of tension of your heavy had leaning beyond your spines center of gravity can have lasting effects. Yoga encourages and promotes healthy standing and sitting positions, so you will learn over time how to sit and stand properly which will increase the longevity of your back and neck especially.

4. Stops joint/cartilage breakdown - The body is more like a machine than anything else. Like most machines, it has to be well oiled and taken care of with great compassion. Your cartilage is a spongey substance that cushions the area between your bones within joints. Yoga takes you through full ranges of motion that will loosen those joints and promote proper maintenance of your cartilage. Without going through the motions, your cartilage will likely wear

with age, and eventually will be scraped down until you're experiencing the trouble and pain of two bones rubbing together without any cartilage between them. Many elderly experience this, hence why they most so slowly. Yoga can solve this problem!

5. Spinal Protection – Spinal disks are the shock absorbers of your back, and require a healthy amount of movement to stay limber and effective. In yoga, there are many motions that involve light twisting and turning to ensure that your spine stays strong and supple through the years. Back problems affect millions of people, so it only makes sense to find a solution that can remove you from that statistic!

6. Promotes bone health – This is important for women especially! You've seen the commercials about the prescription pills that are supposed to combat osteoporosis. Well, this is a natural, much less rigorous way to prevent it. The stances and poses that you take in yoga help to strength the bones of your arms and legs especially, which is where osteoporosis likes to start. In addition to that, yoga as a whole helps to lower the amount of stress hormones produced in your body, which lowers the rate at which calcium is lost in your bones.

7. Blood flow goes up – Although yoga isn't the same as running or lifting weights, it actually is much more effective at evenly distributing oxygenated blood throughout your body. In fact, going through the motions in a session promote a higher blood flow to the areas of your body that may not always receive it as they should (hands and feet). A consistent practice will also lead to more oxygenated blood circulating healthily through your organs and tissues, and even can help with people who have had heart or kidney problems and don't get the appropriate amount of blood to certain areas of their bodies. In addition to that, this

increased flow reduces your chances of unhealthy blood clots.

8. Assists immune/lymphatic system – Everything in yoga from the contraction and stretching of a muscle, to transitioning between poses allows a fluid within immune cells to break free and "drain", if you will. As it drains, your body will be able to fight off infection more readily. It also makes it so that cancerous cells are broken down faster, and also so that the toxic waste within these cells is disposed of more quickly.

9. Improves heart health – Regularly increasing your heart rate during exercise can lower your risk of heart disease as well as the chances of depression because of the endorphins released during exercise. Yoga isn't an aerobic exercise by default, but there are variations that can be done in order to simulate a situation where your cardiovascular fitness is challenged. And even for yoga that isn't ass vigorous, it still lowers your resting heart rate and improves your overall endurance.

10. Lowers blood pressure – If you have HBP (high blood pressure), you too can benefit from yoga. The constant movement combined with the cardiovascular challenge will regulate your blood pressure, and eventually will lead to an overall drop due to the consistent practice of raising and lowering it with different forms of exercise.

11. Regulates adrenal glands – Cortisol is a stress induced hormone that appears when in a time of crisis, embarrassment, etc. Yoga reduces the amount of that this hormone sticks around. Which it first becomes present, it's helpful and makes you more alert, and even boosts your immune system. The real trouble comes when the situation that caused the increase passes and the cortisol sticks

around. An overabundance of cortisol has been related to depression, osteoporosis, HBP, and insulin resistance (which can lead to diabetes). It also has been said that a constantly uninhibited influx of cortisol can lead your body to a state of crisis, and in this state the body stores most things that you may eat or drink as fat for safety purposes. Nobody wants that!

12. Improves moods – It is no secret that any form of exercise improves your overall moods, and promotes a happier existence. The consist practice of yoga will promote an increase in those "happy" hormones like serotonin and the endorphins that fill you with joy, which can be a great combatant of depression.

13. Encourages a healthy lifestyle – There is a spiritual, mental, and physical aspect of yoga. When combined, these things will trickle into other areas of your life from how to eat to how to you think act around others. Yoga encourages a heightened self-awareness, and in gaining a great appreciation for yourself, you will be more likely to begin taking better care of your wellbeing.

14. Fights diabetes – Yoga lowers your bad while increasing your good cholesterol. It makes your body more sensitive to insulin, while managing your cortisol and adrenaline levels which usually contribute to weight gain and the urge to take in more sugary foods. With a lowered blood sugar comes a lessened chance of attaining a heart disease, kidney issues, blindness, and other sugar-related diseases.

15. Improves focus – In yoga, there is no moment but the present one. The only way to master a pose is truly to focus within yourself, and to maintain that focus throughout your sessions. As your mind becomes accustomed to going to that present moment space, it will begin to show in

other areas of your life as well, which can greatly improve things as small as driving to things as large as your professional career!

As you can clearly see, implementing yoga into your life would bring nothing but goodness into it. Now, imagine these health benefits coupled with what Kundalini Yoga can do for you.
Skepticism is a healthy practice, although I would not suggest it here. When it comes to the spirit, there are no gimmicks; no tricks. There is only what works, and what doesn't. This works. So, just to further prove how amazing of a practice yoga can be, I've added another 15 benefits to utilizing yoga as your physical activity for the day.

1. Relaxes your system – The relaxation aspect of yoga shifts the balance from engaging the sympathetic nervous system (fight or flight responses) to the parasympathetic nervous system (relaxation, lowered heart rates, calmness).

2. Improves balance - Proprioception refers to the ability of a person to stay aware of where their body is in space as well as how to counterbalance certain actions to keep from falling. Yoga greatly improves your proprioception, which leads to the ability to balance your body for great stents of time.

3. Maintains the nervous system – With the mastery of yoga comes a level of bodily control that many can't fathom. There are yogis in the world that can harness the usually involuntary power of their nervous system and make voluntary changes, like lowering one's heart rate at will, or forcing blood to accumulate at a specific location in order to heal or even to incubate something (for women who want to create a healthier environment for pregnancy).

4. Releases tension – Our daily cause a lot of tension, and we don't even notice it! Everything from how you drive, to how you sit, to how you hold your face, and other subconscious actions require your muscles to operate in a certain way. Yoga will essentially help you to see where you hold tension, and in practicing you will also see it relieved over time.

5. Improves sleep experience – Along with the stimulation that comes from improved focus is the byproduct of the meditation that occurs during yoga. This byproduct of increased relaxation and decreased stress can also lead to easier, deeper sleep.

6. Improves immune cell functionality – The meditative nature of yoga increases your body's ability to respond appropriately to foreign pathogens. As needed, your body will begin to produce more antibodies and other defensive structures within the body to properly maintain homeostasis.

7. Improves lung health – Those deep breaths aren't for nothing! A constant practice of total lung expansion during yoga decreases the average amount of breaths per minute, while also increasing the level of oxygen within your blood—resulting in improved respiratory health.

8. Combats digestive trouble – Many issues of the abdominal area can be stress induced, and if they are, they can be handled by regulating your cortisol levels. As we know by now, yoga has a phenomenal effect on stress hormones. Movement promotes faster processing of foods and other materials in the body, allowing for a more regulated digestive system which can prevent constipation, colon related issues, and trouble with your digestive tract.

9. Grants peace of mind – Because of the level of inner peace attained after consistently practicing yoga, your general levels of sadness, anger, and frustration will go down. You will learn to live more in the moment, without taking things as personally or as seriously because you will learn that most of what stands before you cannot be controlled, and that your original frustration comes from attempting to control it all.

10. Increases self-confidence – Many of us deal with the burden of thinking we aren't good enough. Yoga not only promotes the idea that you are good enough, but also that you don't need to be anything but who you are in this very moment. We live in a society of constant movement, and of chasing everything without being grateful for what you have. Yoga gives you a sense of gratitude for self, which will show in your future social interactions as confidence.

11. Assists in pain management – This can occur on a physical, mental, and spiritual level. On the physical level, yoga is great for those who experience joint pains, arthritis, and other muscle or bone related aches.

12. Grants mental fortitude – You will find that in staying dedicated to yoga, you will have gained a new level of discipline. Within this discipline lies a greater strength of mind, which most have said is the best benefit of yoga. This will translate to all other aspects of your life, and you will find that you can do more now on a social, professional, and sexual level than you ever thought you could.

13. Provides grounding – The trick to having a successful start with yoga is to find a good teacher. This teacher will essentially facilitate the beginning of your growth as a student of yoga, and will serve as a mental, physical, and

spiritual guide for those who feel lost.

14. Replaces drugs with healthy habits – As you have read, you've seen now that yoga serves as a great, natural combatant to several diseases and ailments that can plague your life. Usually, each sickness comes with a list of pills that have to be taken in order to suppress or maintain them. But one thing that you must remember is that yoga is thousands of years older than modern medicine, and yet the people who lived thousands of years ago, still will able to overcome overwhelmingly more powerful illnesses! So, rather than jumping on the prescription pill train, try implementing some yoga into your daily life and see how differently you feel. The only side effect of yoga is a happier, longer life!

15. Creates greater sense of self – In gaining a greater understanding of yourself and the world that surrounds you, you will begin to be able to dissect and pinpoint where your own troubles and challenges exist within your life. It is said that rage and hostility can be just as contributory to heart problems as poor eating and physical stagnancy. So, even if you are currently experiencing something that you don't want to experience, your new level of understanding about yourself will help you to figure out what the cause of your problem is, and to do everything within your power to remedy that situation within you.

If these benefits aren't enough to prove how awesome yoga is for you and your wellbeing, I don't what to tell you! All that can truly be said is that if you really desire a greater quality of life as well as an even more powerful sense of self, this is the path for you.

Mental benefits of kundalini yoga practice

Yoga is a form of yoga that was originally practiced in early 20th century India. The central concept of Kundalini Yoga is to achieve the ultimate spiritual consciousness by raising vitality through various postures, breathing techniques and meditation.

Practicing Kundalini Yoga can have many mental benefits according to practitioners. Some of the mental benefits of kundalini yoga practice are as follows:

1. Kundalini Yoga helps improve concentration. Concentration is one of the most important aspects of spiritual attunement as it helps in increasing the power of self-control within the individual.

2. Kundalini yoga balances all the meridians and organ systems in the body which also means that it balances our emotions and feelings. This helps us to live a happy life and lead a good life in all situations of life.

3. Kundalini yoga helps to decrease stress and tension in the body. It helps us to calm our mind and to improve our tolerance level towards pain which makes a good living condition possible.

4. Kundalini yoga helps us to improve our knowledge and learning capacity. By practicing kundalini yoga, we force our body into the right positions and cycles of breathing which enhance the brainpower of the individual. This in turn will help him/her to learn things in an easier way and thereby increase the knowledge about life.

5. Kundalini yoga helps to increase awareness in the mind of the individual. This awareness helps us to be aware of our

own body and mind and also about the outside world. Therefore, we are able to judge what is right from what is wrong and thereby make right decisions that will help us lead a good life.

6. Kundalini yoga helps us to have better memory power within ourselves. It helps us to memorize things easily and thereby improve our ability to learn new things easily.

7. Kundalini Yoga also enhances the feeling of happiness within oneself which makes it easier for an individual to live a happy life in all situations of his/her life.

Psychic benefits of kundalini yoga practice

Kundalini yoga is designed to awaken dormant spiritual energies and improve one's intuition.
Some of the psychic benefits of kundalini yoga practice are as follows:

1. Improves Relationship with Subconscious.
Practicing kundalini yoga not only helps to cultivate a strong mind and soul but also encourages one to listen to the voices of the subconscious. Through deep listening, we often come into contact with new ideas or insights that are not apparent at first. A practice of kundalini yoga can bring about greater access to one's subconscious mind which yields a heightened awareness and greater understanding of oneself as well as others.

2. Intuitive Insight.
Through individual personal practices and group sessions, students may develop increased understanding of how their own thoughts work in conjunction with other people's thoughts in order to make judgments that are based on intuition rather than intellect alone. One may begin to develop a greater sense

of connection and understanding with other people, while also developing more awareness of one's own thoughts.

3. Influences the Ego
Often, in our culture, we are taught that an individual's ego is something to fear. Through kundalini yoga practice it may be possible for us to approach ego as something that can be used for the benefit of others and ourselves. Through observing the attitudes and actions of others as well as through deeper personal practice, we can change our own way of thinking and seeing about our ego in order to experience a new level of humility, empathy, simplicity, and compassion towards others.

4. Subconscious Focus
A regular kundalini yoga practice may help to re-focus our minds. Through the power of concentration, students can train the mind to move minutely, releasing other thoughts in order to focus on what is occurring in the moment. This is a great form of therapy for people who have trouble focusing on one task at a time or for those who take their attention away from their current experience too often.

5. Mindfulness and Concentration
Through practicing awareness exercises like pranayama breathing, students often begin to develop greater concentration and mindfulness as they become more present and aware of everything they are learning in class and outside of class. Being aware of one's own sense of "I-ness" is essential when trying to understand other people's wants and needs.

6. Improves Ability to See the Bigger Picture
Kundalini yoga exercises can help students improve their ability to see the "bigger picture." Through regular practice they may come to understand how their actions affect others around them (and vice versa) and how every decision has a consequence whether positive or negative. This is an important

lesson for everyone, but especially for hyper-sensitive people who can get quite bogged down by what they imagine as negative outcomes from doing something that makes them feel uncomfortable.

Chapter 6: Kundalini Exercises

Just as with the yoga and meditation kundalini exercises, we must be confident that we are prepared for these practices. Approach these advanced exercises just as you have been with your routine, find your practice space, clear your mind, have an empty stomach, and overall be respectful of kundalini.

Kundalini should be approached with the utmost respect. You may even wish to leave an offering or prayer before your practice advances. As we begin these practices, let's keep in mind the power of the present moment. Just as a meditation practice aims to achieve, our mind is clearest in the present moment. We are the most attentive and efficient when we are at this moment. We need to maintain this focus when working with kundalini. She requires our attention and respect as we wake her. We do not want to startle her or anger her as we approach these techniques. We must be in the most attentive and focused state that we have ever experienced to achieve the results we seek,

One final note before the exercises begin: Listen to your body. If you do not feel that you are ready to approach kundalini, then absolutely do not do it! There is no shame in being honest with yourself about your practice. As we have mentioned throughout this book, not everyone will progress in the same way. We need to be honest with ourselves about our progress and be truthful when we ask ourselves if we are ready. For what it's worth, the more practice you have before approaching the serpent, the more likely you will be successful in your endeavors. Take your time and be patient. Hone your skills and have an enjoyable experience as you do. This is not a career or a job. There is no deadline or strict structure. Create your path by listening to your body and mind. You will intuitively know that you are ready when you are ready, do not approach kundalini until you are sure that you will be able to adhere to your promises to her.

Starting Out

As we mentioned, the present moment is key to these practices. Stay in this moment and do not worry about the past or future. If you can to stay in the present moment, you will begin to dissolve the deepest illusions your mind has constantly been creating about nature's true reality. You can start by seeing the reality of the endless energy of divine bliss in everyone and everything. This bliss is always there. We just need to see it. If we buy into the delusions of the chaotic mind at any moment, our kundalini working will have failed, and we will need to start over. This is very common, so do not be discouraged.

By staying consciously here in this eternal moment, the phenomena of psychic abilities, unseen powers, and magical manifestation will naturally begin to happen in your life. Combined with the practices in this book, we can optimize these powers. Kundalini will give you the capacity to attract anything in the world you desire. Since these practices act to merge the kundalini's infinite power with your subtle energetic and physical bodies, we effectively upgrade our existence. This upgrade may even protect us from emotional attacks or various otherworldly disasters.

As we are willing to live in this present moment, we will empower ourselves as individuals. With these kundalini workings, we can essentially tap into the source of the universe and keep it near throughout our lives. Sure, we can work with our chakras with kundalini still dormant, but to get the absolute most out of these practices, we will need kundalini to be awake, piercing our chakras and opening them fully to the universal power. When each of the seven chakra centers in your body is ignited, you will transverse the world as you know it. No longer bound to time or worry. The God and Goddess, Shiva and Shakti, within you will become very apparent, and you will know without a doubt that powers are inherent in your body and mind. From this point, there is no turning back, your life is altered completely, and you now are familiar with some secrets of the universe.

Practices
The following practices will combine what we have learned throughout this book. Meditation, yoga, mantra, and visualization is the key component of the following exercises. These practices are the most complex and challenging and are specifically designed for kundalini awakening.

Keep the serpent energy in mind as you practice these exercises. Visualize the dormant snake at the base of your spine. Imagine the infinite potential in the awakening of this energy that is a fiery spark of consciousness just waiting to rise inside you. As you take on these final practices, you will awake this energy. If you have put in the time and effort, you will build this relationship with kundalini. This energy may rise slowly or gradually make itself known, but there are many times that this energy bursts out of its slumber, rise aggressively through your spine. Many have described this feeling online and in spiritual communities. This flood of life is incredible and changes the lives of the experiencers forever. Raising this energy will essentially begin your new life; you will be living fully for the first time. There is an infinite potential of where to go from that point, eventually unifying Shakti and Shiva, allowing them to dance the creative expression of oneness through you.

Kundalini Exercise 1
This is a sequence of exercises that ignites the fire within in hopes of waking kundalini. The mantras used is related to the name of truth and acts to stimulate our entire being with its vibration. The yoga poses and visualization act to engage your energetic body as well as your physical body to really get the energy moving.

Practice these exercises after your body is sufficiently warmed up after some light yoga or breathing exercises.

1. Kneel onto your knees, sitting on the heels of your feet.

2. Inhale and bend forward, touching your brow to the ground
3. Breathe deeply for ten breaths, relaxing into the position.
4. Chant the following mantra, internally or out loud:

Sat, Sat, Sat, Sat, Sat, Sat, Naam.

As you chant, each Sat should be vibrated into a chakra, starting with the root and rising through the other chakras until we reach the crown chakra and chant Naam. Continue this exercise for ten minutes, then move onto the next step for Kundalini exercise 1.

After you have completed the Sat Naam exercise, you can begin the next sequence. This practice is simple and helps to relax after the Sat Naam practice.

5. Raise your brow from the floor.
6. Slowly stretch your legs outward, extending them in front of you.
7. Straighten your back and raise your hands above your head.
8. Bend at the hips and try to grab your toes; hold this position.
9. Breathe deeply for seven breaths.

Each of the seven breaths should engage a chakra. Visualize the breath penetrating the root chakra, then upward through the other chakras until your seventh breath. After the seventh breath, immediately move onto the next sequence.

This part of the exercise is a winding down of sorts. You will feel the energy in your body shift dramatically. Take note of the changes you experience as you relax.

10. Raise up from touching your toes then lay down on your back.

11. Relax your body with your hands at your sides. Breathe deeply.
12. Lay here motionless for seven minutes.

As you lay quietly, visualize kundalini lying dormant. Not unlike your motionless body, she lays asleep. Visualize her as a literal snake, just let the details come as they will.

Once you have reached seven minutes, rise up slowly, visualizing kundalini awakening. Sit quietly with your visualization and see what happens. Sit quietly and breathe normally.

This is the end of the first kundalini exercise, but after you relaxed, you can perform it again and again. It is best not to perform this exercise more than three times per day.

Kundalini Exercise 2

This sequence of exercises is designed for purification of the body and chakras. It acts as an overall clearing and opening, making way for the kundalini energy to rise. This purification is much needed in a world of synthetic drugs and foods. This exercise pairs well after long work weeks or before healing baths.

1. Stand up straight, balancing your weight on our feet.
2. Stretch your leg behind you with the top of your foot staying on the ground.
3. Bend the other leg until you have a ninety-degree angle at your knee, your weight will be on the bent leg.
4. Place your palms together, and hold at your chest, focus your vision on your brow.
5. Deep breathe in this position.
6. Stand up and switch legs performing the same exercise.

This practice is a physical work out that helps to get the body moving and engage the chakras in preparation for the next sequence.

7. Sit down and cross your legs comfortably.
8. Put your hands on your hips and raise your diaphragm.
9. Breathe deeply in this position for three minutes.

The next sequence is more intensive, you can view the first sequences as a warm-up for the next ones.

10. Stay seated and breathing consistently.
11. Interlock your hands at your chest, forearms parallel to the floor.
12. Inhale as deep as you can.
13. Forcibly exhale all the breath as fast as you can.
14. Inhale fully and hold breath.
15. Exhale completely and forcibly.
16. Continue this practice for three minutes.

We should be raising the energy up through the chakras as we practice this, the forced breaths engaging the solar plexus chakra and heart chakra. The next sequence contacts the throat and third eye chakras.

17. Stay seated with your legs crossed.
18. Extend the arms out at the sides like wings.
19. Roll your eyes up gazing at your brow.
20. Breathe deeply and hold this position for 3 minutes.
21. Press your hands together and straighten your spine.
22. Push firm on your hands and hold this position for three minutes.

This exercise is excellent for purification purposes but also works directly with kundalini energy. Visualizing kundalini being purified with this practice can add to the potency as well.

Exercise for Blockages
This exercise is great for clearing blockages in your chakras and nadis. It acts as a great precursor to kundalini works while also engaging the kundalini. Practice this exercise on a weekly basis. It ensures your chakras do not become clogged.
1. Sit with your legs crossed and raise your hands over your head. Practice a range of motion, stretching your arms in circles.
2. Clinch your fists at your heart and roll your shoulders forward and backward.

This exercise becomes quite fun as you move through the steps quickly. It can almost become a dance of sorts. This exercise can be performed before an intensive yoga or meditation session to get the energy flowing smoothly.

A Note on Ancestral Lineage
This exercise is great for breaking ancestral blockages as well. Consider all the people in your ancestral line, only a small fraction of them that you have met. These lines can get blocked just as energetic channels get blocked by day-to-day life. There may be criminals or other troublemakers in this lineage.
The advanced techniques of working to clear our energetic ancestral lineage are powerful and complex. Use the blockage exercises above to heal your ancestral lines visually. You can imagine the line of ancestors going all the way back to the source of consciousness, healing it along the way. You may even want to leave offerings or call upon your ancestors to assist you in this work.
Ancestral practices are very complex and would need a whole book to explore properly. For now, use the blockage techniques to clear your family line.

Chakra Balancing Exercise
Stimulating the chakra system at least once per day is good practice to ensure that your chakras will not become blocked or

unbalanced in the future. Deep breathing exercises and a consistent yoga routine go a long way to achieve this balanced system, but we also must practice more intensive exercises, especially if we have yet to awaken the kundalini energy.

1. In a standing position, place your feet shoulder-width apart.
2. Squat down so the thighs are parallel to the floor.
3. Reach towards your toes; placing the palms on top of the feet, be sure to keep your back straight.
4. Lift your head and look forward.
5. Move to a kneeling position, sit on the heels, and stretch the arms straight over your head.
6. Interlock your fingers except for the index fingers, which should be pointing straight up.
7. Begin to chantSat Naam' emphatically in a constant rhythm.
8. On Naam, relax the stomach.
9. Continue for three minutes.

This exercise is great for stimulating the entire chakra system. The second section continues this practice. If you wish to practice the above before moving on to the second sequence, then do so until you are fully prepared to perform the entire exercise. This is your practice, so make it what you want and go at your own pace.

10. Kneel sitting on your heels, rest the hands on the thighs.
11. Begin inhaling in short sips through your pursed lips until the lungs are full of air.
12. With your breath held, raise up and rotate the hips around in a circle.
13. Exhale and sit back down on your heels.
14. Move to a lying position and bring the hands to the Navel Point. The left hand is closest to the body, and the right hand is over the left.

This is a great exercise for learning to feel the chakras as well. Step 16 is essentially asking you to use your hands in circular motions to feel and manipulate the chakras. Move on with the next steps after you have sufficiently felt and moved the chakras.

15. Remain on your back and extend your arms straight above you.
16. Make fists of your hands and pull your fists into your chest.
17. Release your clenched fists and repeat three more times.
18. Resting on your back, place the left hand on the heart and the right hand over the left.
19. Breathe deeply and engage your heart chakra.
20. Release your fists and place your hands at your sides.
21. Lay comfortably for five to ten minutes.

This exercise acts to clear away chakra blockages while also acting as a great warm-up exercise to start your day or begin your kundalini practices. These complex exercises have so many steps because this is the effort needed to stimulate the kundalini energy.

The kundalini exercises above are the methods that will skyrocket your practice from a humble beginner's practice to a full-fledged advanced routine. When these exercises are practiced consistently and approached with respect and seriousness, you will surely open your chakras and awaken the kundalini energy. These practices should all be performed on an empty stomach to avoid cramps or indigestion. This is why we recommend performing them in the morning when you first awake. Your belly will be empty, and you will have a fresh canvas to work with as you start your day. Not to mention these exercises get the blood moving; you may even be able to skip your coffee!

Conclusion

Kundalini is a way of cleansing one's mind and body. In a way, it's like you're detoxifying yourself without actually having to make green juices or changing your diet in a 180-degree manner. Kundalini works in such a way that once it is awakened, you can expect it to clean and refresh your body 24 hours a day, seven days a week.

It is also a way of cleansing your chakras, or the parts of your unconscious mind and body that is also known as energy points where vital energy and life forces meet. You will not be able to make the most out of your chakras if you don't awaken your Kundalini.

When your Kundalini is activated, you will begin to sense what it really means to be alive. You will know how to use up the energy that is stored deep within your own mind and body. You will also learn how to work with it so that you can improve the quality of your existence.

Kundalini meditation is also an important aspect of any spiritual journey. As a matter of fact, without Kundalini, you might not even reach a certain level on the path towards enlightenment and self-discovery.

Many people are hindered by their own flesh. So before they can really work with Kundalini, they need to cleanse and purify their own soul. Once you do this, only then will you be able to meditate on the spiritual level.

You will learn how to control and direct your energy. Through this, you can have a greater sense of inner peace and better physical health. You will also be able to perform spiritual healing without first going to a specialist.

As you have seen in the book already, there are many different techniques that you can practice on your own or with friends and family members in order to awaken your Kundalini.

Part 2

Kundalini Meditations

Chapter 7: Introduction to Meditations

Meditation is a practice that has been around for thousands of years and is the subject of many books and articles.

The goal of meditation, in essence, is to cultivate awareness. With the help of various techniques that regulate attention, we can alter our way of experiencing thoughts and emotions.
If you would like to be more reflective, present or attentive in your daily life, then meditation may be for you.

There are many ways to practice meditation, and the choice of what form of meditation is most accessible to you depends on a number of factors.

Earth meditation

Kundalini is a form of yoga that many people worldwide practice. Kundalini doesn't mean that you have to be a guru, witch, or mystic in order to practice it. It's actually a very personal and natural way for the individual to explore and discover their own inner-self and their potential for spiritual growth. The goal is to awaken the kundalini as part of your daily self-care routine.
Here is how to go about with earth meditation;
Kundalini can be completed with or without vibrations. A vibration is a form of shakti that helps activate the kundalini. Shakti is a Sanskrit word that means energy, god, or goddess. Basically, it's the flow of life force energy/power/cosmic force that moves through us. When you are in a state of kundalini, you will be awakened and rejuvenated by this shakti.
This type of meditation is done while seated and is usually done facing the rising sun. You may also do this in a standing position, however, it's usually easier to focus when doing it from a sitting position. Sit down in your lotus or half-seated

position with your palms resting on your knees. Before beginning, use candlelight or incense to create an aura around your body. This helps to heighten your sense of smell and touch as well as to relax the sense of sight.

Meditate for at least 6 to 8 minutes. Then open your eyes and begin focusing on the sun rising in the east. This will guide you into your awakening process, which means that you will soon feel a tingling sensation throughout your body. This is always accompanied by a feeling of bliss inside as well as outside of your body.

You may also be able to recognize a sense of heat or burning within your body (especially on the tip of your tongue). Pay attention to this burning sensation and try to identify it's meaning for yourself.

If the sensation is too strong or uncomfortable, close your eyes and try to calm yourself.

Once you're able to handle the sensation, it's time to focus all of your attention on the point between your eyebrows. This is known as the "third eye" or "ajna," and it's located in the center of your forehead. It serves as a direct connection between you and the sun. This helps in enhancing sensory perception as well as to help replenish energy.

Keep focusing on this point until you feel a tingling in this area and a sense of heat (in addition to the heat that you may be already experiencing).

Water meditation

Here is how to go about with kundalini water meditation:
-Sit in lotus or half-lotus position
-Close your eyes and take deep breaths
-Take a sip of boiled water
-Exhale the water through your mouth, making a hissing sound like a faucet. This is referred to as "water sounds"
-Repeat the process 3 more times, always beginning with deep breaths

-Inhale deeply and hold it for 10 seconds before exhaling out any air

Step 1: Sit in a lotus or half position on a yoga mat. Make sure you are comfortable. Close your eyes and make sure to take deep breaths to clear your head before starting meditation.

Step 2: Take a sip of boiled water. Take it in your mouth and slowly bring it up to the back of your palate. Hold it for 10 seconds before slowly exhaling out any air through the nostrils. This is the first "water sounds"

Step 3: Repeat step 2 again, this time making hissing sounds when you exhale out any air

Step 4: Repeat step 3 again, this time making more hissing sounds when you exhale out any air after inhaling deeply

Step 5: Repeat step 4 and 5 three times quickly, taking deep breaths between each

The breathing is done only to cleanse your head and do not count on it to get your mind active or alert. The real meditation begins when you do water sounds and not while inhaling or exhaling through the nostrils. With the kundalini meditation, you begin to feel the water moving upwards from your stomach to your chest and then your throat just like water sounds.

After you have made about a hundred water sounds, take a sip of boiled water. Don't count this as one of the three sips that you will do. Exhale it out and then start on step 1 all over again. Continue doing this until you feel that your stomach has been cleansed and everything is moving up properly, i.e., upwardly in place of downwardly as it is usually in normal breathing. Then you will be able to feel the energy moving in downward direction through the pituitary gland.

Step 6: Repeat step 4 and 5 two more times

Step 7: After you have done step 5 twice, switch to water sounds again

Step 8: Continue with steps 6 and 7 two more times before going back to water sounds. However, each time you will have to take a sip of boiled water and do water sounds before getting back to steps 6 and 7.

Step 9: After you have done step 6 three times, switch to water sounds again. This time you will have to do two sets of steps 6 and 7 before going back to water sounds.

Air Meditation

Step 1: Sit with your spine erect, close your eyes, and take a few deep breaths.

Step 2: Place the left hand on the stomach, with palm facing upwards and the right hand on top of it.

Step 3: Inhale deeply through the ribcage while simultaneously pulling in both hands towards the navel. At this moment, you will feel a rising sensation in the stomach area which is called "kundalini".

Step 4: After that, exhale and release both hands to sit as before during meditation. Repeat this cycle for 10 minutes or until you start feeling tired.

Step 5: When you are finished, sit as you did in step 1, with the spine erect and eyes closed. Draw the energy up to the third eye by pointing both index fingers at it and inhaling deeply. Exhale through both nostrils.

Note: Do not practice this kundalini meditation if you have high blood pressure!

Fire meditation

Here is how to go about with kundalini fire Meditation:
"You are sitting cross-legged on the ground. You're going to start with a 'Sun Salutation'

1. Feet are pointing down toward the ground
2. Bring your palms together forming an oval shape (left over right) and placing them against the top of your head and fingers touching your forehead

3. Begin bending from the waist, coming onto both knees at an angle, maintaining a straight back (don't look up! Keep your gaze focused on the floor)
4. Take three steps forward with one foot, keeping it flat on the ground and bring that same foot out behind you
5. Bend again at the waist, bring that same knee forward and back
6. Repeat steps 3 through 5 on the other foot
7. Bend your knees until you are sitting on the ground, facing your palm out to the right and your feet pointing out toward the left (leave a little space between them)
8. Meditate, find peace within yourself first, then extend it to all beings around you."

5-Minute Meditation Sessions

The following meditation can be applied for about 5 minutes, but you are also free to use them for as long as you would like. These are excellent meditation techniques for beginners, and they can have profound effects. The more you practice these meditation techniques, the better you will get.

Affirmation meditation
You are probably aware of the use of affirmations. For example, when people are feeling afraid, you might hear them say, "I can do this." It is like affirming what they want to happen. Although this is something that is very common, the truth is that only a few know how to use it properly. What you need to know is that affirmations are more effective when they are recited in a meditative state. But, before we discuss them meditation technique itself, you should know how to create your own affirmation. Here are the steps:

Keep it short and clear
You should keep your affirmation short and to the point. As a rule, try to make it just a short and single sentence only. Take

note that you will be reciting, almost like chanting, your affirmation, so do not make it too long. Just around less than 10 words would be nice. Also, avoid using hard to understand words. Instead, use simple words that are easy to understand. Examples: I am strong, I am courageous, I am feeling better every day, I am happy, I am healthy, I am getting stronger, and the likes.

Use the present tense
When you make an affirmation, you should use the present tense. Do not say, "I will become a clairvoyant." Instead, you should say, "I am a clairvoyant." Consider this as some kind of trick of the mind, if you would. The reason here is that if you use the future tense, then it might happen only after so many years; and if you use the past tense, then it means that it no longer needs to happen. Therefore, you should use the present tense, to make it manifest right now or at least as soon as possible.

Believe
It is also important that you believe in what you affirm. Without faith, then it would not be of any good. But, as the saying goes, "With faith, nothing is impossible." Therefore, believe in what you affirm. Believe that it has been realized already, and it shall come true. Again, consider this some form of a trick of the mind, but this is how the universal law works and is the secret to make your desires turn into reality. If you do not believe in what you say, then the affirmation loses its power.

Repeat
While you are in a meditative state, you should repetition your affirmation as many times as you may need to make it sink into your subconscious. Use it as a kind of mantra or focus of your meditation. Let your mind absorb it and sink into its

meaning. Let your affirmation be the sound of the universe at that moment.

Only use one affirmation
It is not good to use different kinds of affirmations at once. Just focus on one affirmation, and do not change it until you have achieved its objective or if you are ready to just give it up. Using more than one affirmation at the same time can be confusing, and your mind might now know which affirmation to absorb fully. Hence, do it one at a time.

Now that you know the important points about making an affirmation, it is time to move on to the actual meditation process:

Assume a meditative posture and relax. Be sure that you already have an affirmation that you want to use. Do any basic meditation, such as the breathing meditation. The objective is simply to reach a meditative state. Once you reach a trance or meditative state, start saying your affirmation. Use your affirmation as the point of focus of your meditation. Focus on it and be one with it.

When you are ready to end this meditation, simply stop saying your affirmation and just bring your attention back to your physical body. Slowly move your fingers and toes and gently open your eyes.

Mantra meditation
The mantra meditation is another very popular and powerful meditation technique. What is a mantra? A mantra is a sound, word, or syllable that acts as the point of focus in meditation. It helps to silence the mind as well as to evoke certain toes of energy. For this meditation, we are going to use the mantra, OM.

The mantra OM is very famous and powerful. It has been used by many spiritual masters and monks. It is also very common in Buddhism and Hinduism. It is believed that OM was also the very first sound in the universe. When you use the mantra OM, you do not just identify yourself with others who meditate, but you also tap the energy of many other spiritual masters and gurus in the world. Let us now move to the actual meditation proper:

Assume a meditative posture and relax. Now, start to say your mantra. In the beginning, you will have to say it out loud. However, after some time, the mantra will be a natural part of you that all you will need to do is close your eyes, and you will be able to hear it with your inner ear (clairaudience or clear hearing). This will happen once you get used to your mantra and have established a good connection to it. Keep your focus on your mantra. Relax and follow your mantra.

As you can see, this is a very simple technique, but it is also very powerful. This is why it has been a long time favorite among meditators, beginners as well as well-experienced ones.

If you are not comfortable with using the mantra OM, you are free to use other mantras. You can even come up with your own mantra. However, when it comes to making your own mantra, you need to take note of some important points:

It has to be neutral

The mantra must not evoke an image or anything. For example, it is not good to use the word elephant as a mantra since it will make you imagine an elephant, which can cause your focus to be divided. Instead, choose a mantra that will not make you visualize anything so you can focus on it without a problem.

Easy to recite

You will have to say your mantra countless times, so be sure to use one that is easy to pronounce. It is also recommended to use a short mantra for convenience.

Use it many times

To establish a good connection with your mantra, you should use it many times. A good advice is to say your mantra even when you are not engaged in an actual meditation. For example, while driving or cooking. The point here is simply to get used to it and make it more a part of you. The more that you become closer to your mantra the more effective it will be. Just like with the use of affirmations, it is advised that you stick to using the same mantra. Hence, early in your spiritual journey, you are not encouraged to make time to try and choose the right mantra for you.

It is worth noting that a mantra does not need to mean anything. Its primary purpose is to help you still the mind by making the mind think of only a single thought (the mantra) instead of having too many thoughts (the monkey mind). Remember that your mantra should help you focus and still your mind.

White light meditation
This is a good meditation technique especially if you want to trigger a lucid dream, also known as conscious dreaming. It is also a good way to just give you a relaxation as it will tend to make you fall asleep. The way to do this is as follows:
Close your eyes and relax. Consider everything that you see that is not black as light. Now, focus on the light. Be as relaxed as possible, even fall asleep, but keep your focus on the light. Let go.

What will happen here is that you will most likely start to see images after some time. These images will soon turn into a vision almost like a dream, but you will be conscious of it. Hence, you can take control of your dream. This exercise can even lead to an actual astral travel once you get good at it. Needless to say, it is not good to expect to see visions for reasons that we have already discussed. Instead, just focus on the light and let go.

Energy charge

This is an excellent technique to get a boost of energy when you need it. This meditation technique fills your whole body with prana. Here are the instructions:

Assume a meditative posture and relax. Now, visualize a ray of white light descending from the sky and allow it to enter your crown chakra, and then into your body. Let it fill you with divine energy. See and feel your whole system filled with the strong current of energy from above. When you are satisfied and ready to end this exercise, simply see the ray of white light slowly fade away, and enjoy the boost of strong energy.

Another way to charge yourself with energy quickly, especially when you are feeling tired is by hugging a tree. As you hug it, feel its energy charging your system. Do not forget to thank the tree afterward.

Bubble shield

This is a meditation technique that will allow you to create a protective shield around you to protect you from negative energies. If you deal with energies, then this is something that you should learn as you will be more sensitive to subtle energy, including negative energies. The steps are as follows:

Assume a meditative posture and relax. Visualize yourself surrounded by energy. For beginners, you can just see this energy as white light. Now, as you inhale, sea and feel that you draw energy from around you and have it form a bubble shield of protection around your body. With every inhalation, continue to charge your bubble shield. See and feel as it gets stronger and harder with every breath. Affirm, "This bubble shield protects me from all negative energies."

Take note that the strength of this bubble shield will dissipate over time. To keep your bubble shield strong, be sure to absorb more energy to replenish it. On average, a typical bubble shield can last for about five hours. The more that you are exposed to negative energy, the quicker that your bubble shield is going to weaken, so be sure to be sensitive enough about it.

If you sense that it is getting weak, then replenish it with more energy. It is good to use this technique before you mingle with people or when you know that you are going to a place where you will be exposed to different kinds of energies, especially if it involves negative energy. It is also noteworthy that this shield gets stronger the more that you get used to it.

Alternate nostril breathing
This is a breathing technique that is used in yoga. When you use this technique, you will feel a sense of balance and tranquility. The way to do it is as follows:
Assume a meditative posture and relax. Try to keep a sense of balance by making your inhalation and exhalation of the same length duration. Relax and continue to focus on your breathing.
Although this may seem a very simple exercise, you might get surprised how effective and powerful it is. It will give you a sense of peace and mental balance, as well as clarity. It is not an excellent meditation technique both for beginners, as well as for experienced meditators. Be sure to give this a try.

Meditation for Kundalini Energy

Kundalini Meditation
You can use this meditation to awaken your Kundalini energy and empower yourself to drop into your center for a balancing experience.

How to Use This Meditation
This awakening meditation should be used at least once per day. Using it first thing in the morning is a great way to awaken your Kundalini energy for the day. It also allows you to balance your energies as you go on, allowing you to continue operating from a gentle and intentional life force flow.

This meditation requires a specific breathing pattern which will be outlined in the script below. As you use this breathing alongside the reflection in your daily practice, you will likely find that the new breathing rhythm becomes your natural breathing rhythm. As this happens, you can be sure that you are effectively infusing your daily life with Kundalini energy. As the energy is at work, this renewed breathing pattern will infuse naturally.

This meditation, as previously mentioned, should take approximately 15 minutes. It is easy to incorporate into your daily routine and can have a powerful effect on all that you do. It will help you destress, awaken, and powerfully approach your day.

You must realize that Kundalini awakening and meditation are both journeys. As such, you need to commit to using these practices daily. This does not mean that you should feel shame or guilt if you miss a day. However, you want to do your best to refrain from missing any days. A truly awakened Kundalini energy will support you in remaining true to your practice day in and day out, which will allow you to continue to awaken your energy further. The more you commit, the more power you will gain from this practice.

The Meditation

Begin by finding your center. You can do this by bringing your awareness to the tip of your nose and then drop it straight down into the center of your body, where your solar plexus chakra resides. Once you have, begin using your breath as your center of focus. You want to block out the chatter in your mind by focusing entirely on rhythmic breathing. Right now is a great time to breathe deeply into your diaphragm, fill your lungs, and then fill your throat with air. As you exhale, empty your throat, then your lungs, and then your diaphragm. Continue doing this without pausing in between. Simply breathe. While you cannot ask your heart to beat at a different rate, breathing steadily in rhythmic breathing can help calm your heart center and bring your body into complete alignment and harmony.

As you continue breathing, begin breathing at a comfortable rate of four counts in... one, two, three, and four, and four counts out. one, two, three, and four. Keep this comfortable rhythm gently flowing through your lungs as you continue to keep your awareness on your center and your breath.

While you breathe, you may begin to recognize the movement in your lower belly area. This signifies that it is time to awaken your energy. This movement is often noticed as a sensation or a fluttering of energy. You can recognize it by the way it feels and keep your awareness of yourself and your inner world.

When you do, continue breathing with your count of four. Let the energy begin to arise, coming up your spine. This rising energy comes from your sacral chakra and continues to flow up your spine, purifying it with life force energy. Rather than visualizing it, simply become aware of the process as it happens. Stay focused on the energy rising, and set the intention to draw it up to your spine. Continue letting it rise until it reaches the crown of your head.

Breathe here for a few moments. In, two, three, four... out, two, three, four.

And as the process completes itself, take a few moments to relax and settle into the sensations that come with it. Then, when you are ready, draw your awareness back to the room and awaken yourself to the life around you. Take a few moments to feel how the sensation continues to reside within you, despite the fact that you are now awakened to the energy of the room. Carry this energy with you throughout your day, allowing it to be infused with all that you do. Let it inspire you, guide you, and continue to awaken you as you move throughout your daily routines."

Tantra Meditation
Tantra is another great practice to use to awaken Kundalini energy. If you have never heard of or used tantra before, you may be fascinated to learn more about it. Tantra is largely based on sexual life-giving energy and its ability to infuse the body with awakened energies. To truly understand the magic of tantra and how it can help you with your Kundalini awakening, we will further explore it. In case you do not yet know what tantra truly is or feel unfamiliar with the entirety of how it serves, we will begin by exploring a bit about tantra itself first. Tantra is an ancient, powerful, and secret spiritual technique from India. The word tantra has emerged from an Indian language, "Sanskrit" which consists of two root words: "Tan" which means Body, "Tra" which means a Process to Expand.
In Tantra, the body is used as a means for spiritual enlightenment. Unlike other spiritual techniques that consider the body filthy, tantra considers the body as a divine temple. Tantra uses sex as a tool for enhancing awareness and consciousness. Tantra merges yoga and sex to reach a new dimension. This new dimension is very deep and subtle that a human mind could ever imagine. In tantra, the practitioner performs several experiments within the human body. Experience, observations, and outcome of these systematic experiments reveal the truth about existence. This truth, when

known to the ignorant mind, results in the attainment of liberation. Tanta is a way to merge body, mind, and energy to reach a higher consciousness level. Sex is an important instrument that is used in Tantra. This instrument, when used with full awareness, leads to awakening. Tantra is a profound meditation that eliminates all the boundaries of body and mind. It removes all the inner blockages. It relaxes the body, opens the heart, and brings the mind into focus. Tantra is not an ordinary casual technique that you want to do for sexual needs and bodily fulfillment. It is a spiritual practice where you awaken your core and merge your entire being in it. Tantra is a journey of human energy from base to infinite.

About Tantra
Tantra is a ritualistic spiritual practice that is rooted in Hinduism and Buddhism. This mystical text dates back as far as the 6th to 13th centuries. Many people hear the word tantra and immediately believe it is about sex. While it does incorporate sexual energies, it is done in a very intentional and ritualistic way to have a specific set of benefits for those using the practice. Tantra, however, has been highly sexualized by the Western culture since its introduction in the 19th century.
Though tantra does incorporate sexual energy, it uses the body as a tool to awaken spiritual energies. This happens through a complex series of rituals, chanting, and transcending.

How Tantra Affects Kundalini
Despite being harmless, Western society has often regarded Kundalini as highly sexual energy. Some people even believe it is rooted in sexual practices and that it may be taboo or bad. This is, however, a cultural bias granted by North Americans who approached the subject with a non-liberal perspective of sexual pleasure.
Kundalini yoga is considered to be a tantric practice itself. Through the chanting of specific sacred words, hand mudras,

and intentional yoga poses, it awakens tantric energy to encourage Kundalini energy's awakening.

Kundalini incorporates tantra as a way of using the body as a tool to achieve liberation. The idea is that, when they are not awakened, our bodies can be tense and tight, often restricting the flow of Kundalini energy. However, our bodies are liberated when we awaken and tend to experience a greater sense of relaxation, pure energy flow, and peace.

The Practice of Tantra for Kundalini Awakening
When done properly, tantra in Kundalini awakening should only be practiced with a guru who is extremely powerful and who has mastered the teacher's inner state. These tantric gurus practice specific yoga practices with you in sequences that require two people to fulfill the yoga pose. This is highly responsible for awakening the Kundalini energies.

Tantric yoga practices for Kundalini awakening are not that different from traditional Kundalini yoga. The primary difference is that they incorporate another being. Because both beings become so energetically charged and awakened during the process, it is extremely powerful. Traditionally and ideally, this practice is accomplished between a man and a woman. This allowed for a balanced introduction of masculine and feminine energies, which ultimately creates the entire outcome.

That being said, tantric Kundalini yoga cannot be practiced on your own and should not be practiced without a guru. The energetic awakening power can be extremely intense and can result in nearly crippling experiences for many. This does not mean Kundalini energy is negative or bad, but it does mean that the experiences you can have due to the powerful energy can be difficult.

Pranayama Meditation
The Kundalini rises, and the chakras are located along the Sushumna Nadi. The Sushumna Nadi, physically located in

the spinal cord, is a major prana channel, or breath energy, through the body. But in addition to the Sushumna Nadi there are many other major nadi, and in addition to those, more minor nadi than could be counted. Many of these nadi gather or originate in the Kama, a location very near the Muldahara chakra, where the Kundalini rests. The chakras can only be awakened if prana is flowing well and purposefully along with this entire system of nadis.

Our physical awareness of prana is in the form of breath. To balance the nadi and promote the flow of prana through them, allowing the chakras to awaken and Kundalini to rise, pranayama, or disciplined breathing exercises, are key. Pranayama helps to regulate the nadis and prana. It should be done diligently, but not to the point of exhaustion or discomfort. Typically, it's done first thing in the morning and holding an asana (described below).

There are many different practices in Pranayama, and to do it fully and gain benefits from it requires the help of a guru. To even begin requires extensive reading, at the very least. Many pranayama exercises involve balancing the flow of prana across the different sides of the body, through practices as simple as inhaling slowly through one nostril and exhaling out the other, more challenging exercises like holding the breath as long as possible and then exhaling silently through one nostril, and very advanced practices that involve taking air into the stomach.

Inner Vision Meditation

This meditation will require you to use your inner vision. Your words carry a vibration, and this imagery that you will picture will carry vibrations as well. You can use any type of image that brings up your energy. Test out a few images to see which will bring you sensations of hope, joy, and peace. To help you out, you can try imagining warm and golden sunlight. As you go through this mediation, your inner vision will likely start to show you things other than what we will discuss. This is perfectly fine as long as it is uplifting.

Find a comfortable and quiet place where you can be undisturbed for a while. Close your eyes and take a moment to scan through your body to see if anything is uncomfortable. Take some time to get adjusted into a comfortable and supported position.

Turn your attention to your breath, but don't try to change it. You may still notice that it changes on its own. It could become slower and deeper. It could also become faster. Don't worry about what it's doing. Allow it to be. All you need to do is watch your breath and be fully aware of how it feels to breathe in and breathe out.

If your mind starts to wander during your meditation, bring it back to your breath. Don't get upset, just return to your breath and how good it feels. Allow your breathing to relax you.

Now that you're relaxed and focused on your breathing picture yourself standing under the rays of a healing and warm golden light. This is a light of complete awareness. This is the essence of you and the essence of all living beings. It's all-encompassing love. It is the purest form of love. It is brighter than anything you have ever witnessed. It shines more than a million diamonds.

Allow this light to flow into your head and spread through your body at its will. Open yourself to the love that the light brings into you. It has your best interests in mind and is clearing out whatever is keeping you from your truth and love. As this light spreads through you, it fills your tissues, organs, cells, and every part of your body. It spreads into your memories and thoughts and fills them with healing. It will allow you to learn from what you have experienced.

This golden light pours through your crown chakra. It spreads into your third eye and opens up your connection to truth.

This warm and healing light flows down into your neck and through your throat chakra, balancing its energy and awakening your freedom. It spills over your shoulder and flows down into your arms and into your wrists, hands, and fingers. It shoots through the ends of your fingers and flows back into the earth.

From your fifth chakra, the light slides down into your heart and fills you with love. It pools in your heart and flows out in every direction. It continues to travel down your chest, front, and back.

The light fills up your solar plexus and fills up your rib cage. This area touches on your memories from your childhood and adolescents and your experiences with parental figures. They are all made new and are provided love, softness, and space. You now know that a Divine Companion accompanied you in everything that you did. This could be a Guardian Angel, Jesus, Buddha, and Love, whatever you choose. This Presence has always been with you and still is with you through all of your challenges.

This light continues to fill every fiber of your being and all of your thoughts as it spills down into your sacral chakra. It embraces the child that is still living in you. The light tells your inner child that he or she is loved for who he or she is. Your inner child is told that he or she hasn't done anything wrong. They only dreamed the things they did. Your inner child is beautiful, whole, and complete. They are loved and safe.

The golden light continues to travel down into your root chakra and spills in all directions. The light opens up your awareness of your connections with the love of family and other people on Earth. This light is awakening your wisdom.

The light heals everything it touches. Everything in your body is being filled with the love of this light. The light flows down your legs and exits your feet, flowing into the Earth.

You are now filled with the flow of this pure light from the top of your head through the tips of your toes. Everything is being rinsed in this golden light on every level. Anything that doesn't serve you is being removed, leaving behind a warm and loving feeling. Relax and allow everything to be released.

Stay in this moment for five minutes or more.

As you are with this light, sense that you are the light. Notice as your body dissolves into the light. Notice the freedom you feel of the light. You are unlimited and unbounded. Your creativity is unlimited because you are the light. You can do everything. You travel in every direction and are one with all beings.

Asana

Asana is what we typically think of when we think of yoga. As such, there are hundreds of them, and the proper way to practice them is widely documented and easy to learn. While the details of asana are unnecessary to document here, it is important to understand their specific relationship to Kundalini awakening.

Pranayama is only helpful when it's practiced in the position of an asana. Asana helps to focus the mind by controlling the body and promotes the physical health and circulation necessary for the prana to move freely and the Kundalini to awaken. This bodily focus helps control physical attachments and discomfort that create worldly troubles and make Kundalini awakening impossible. However, for Kundalini awakening, certain poses are more helpful than others. Simple poses like the lotus position and similar sitting poses are beneficial, and the topsy-turvy and all-members pose, which involve balancing on the head and shoulders, respectively.

Asana is one of the best places to start in the journey toward Kundalini awakening. They lay the groundwork that prepares the body and mind. However, to get the proper benefit from them, they shouldn't be performed as a simple exercise. Practice regularly every day, and strive to keep the mind clear and focused on the body's actions. You'll be able to hold the poses for longer and longer, not merely because your body is becoming more flexible, but also because the mind gains the habit of becoming quiet, still, and patient—free from the passing thoughts and material wants that prevent spiritual awakening.

Transcendental Meditation
Think of yourself as a channel for energy to flow into and fill your body. As a receiver of energy, you must put aside your worries, ego, and thoughts. Think of yourself as a mere hollow capsule. You are an open doorway, a place for the energy in the universe to flow through. You will have an easier time achieving a relaxing, peaceful state if you start each meditation with these beliefs.

Leave thoughts of earthly concerns behind when you enter your holy place. You are no longer on Earth. You are traveling to a higher plane of consciousness. You should do this whether you are practicing by yourself or doing a reading for someone else. You will learn to practice advanced psychic techniques that will allow you to accomplish any goal you may have in mind. Whether it is reading one's emotions, viewing another place on Earth or this universe, receiving messages from another world or time, or locating a lost object, you must always begin with a centering meditation.

The Sacred OM Mantra Meditation
It is hard to nail down a single definition for the mantra because mantras have different meanings in different cultures around the world. Some mantras are used to create deeper relaxation during meditation, while others (like those used for tantra meditation) are considered sacred. Some mantras are based on musical measurements, while others are basic sounds that must be chanted or hummed.

It seems that the best general definition for a mantra is words or sounds that create certain qualities in the mind, with the intent of gaining certain benefits. For the purpose of mantras associated with the third eye, the mantras used should deepen the meditation and heighten the activation of the third eye.

You can also use the mantras to close the third eye or invoke a certain nature, as discussed in the previous section.

Something so rooted in history that is still practiced day must produce some benefits. Otherwise, people would not still be using mantras after all this time. The research shows that there are several ways that mantras work to evoke certain qualities in the mind. On a spiritual level, many meditation masters say that the reason mantras work is because of the vibration. Mantras used during meditation involve grunts and hums; essentially, sounds that vibrate from deep within. These vibrations move through your being, affecting the frequency and vibrations of the molecules in your body. It makes molecular changes that, when paired with meditation and clear intentions, create the results that you experience in your body.

The auditory sense has evolved over time, and science shows that this evolution has created certain constants that affect our perception of the world. It is a combination of syllables, grunts, and pitches that come together to form language. This can be seen in humans as well as animals. Think about the way that dolphins or birds communicate with each other. Echoes are another example of this—think about the way a ball sounds bouncing off an empty basketball auditorium. The reverberation and the echoes create a sound that is unique to the ball and the court.

The reason that mantras are so effective at creating these changes in the body is that they are onomatopoetic. This simply means that you can hear the sound that the words make when they are being said, like a giggle, honk or crash. Sanskrit is a language that is created of onomatopoetic words. As most mantras, at least the classics, are derived from Sanskrit, you can hear the echoes of nature and the world around you. This creates the vibrational energy that brings about the desired effects.

As you mutter mantras, it creates physical events in the body and mind because of the primordial sounds. This is often said to be the echoes of nature traveling through the body and mind. Your intention also has a lot to do with the effects that are created. When you say a mantra, you are expecting a specific result. This is your intention. The utterance of your intention places the idea in your mind and creates the effects. Your consciousness then becomes intertwined with the mantra and its effects, and in this way, you are creating an echo that will produce your effects. Your entire being is now affected by your utterance of the mantra.

The Four Koshas (levels) of the Mantra

Mantras have four levels, each of them with a different intensity. When you first practice mantras, you may not experience the same effects that someone who knows how to increase the intensity would. You will still get some benefit from the mantra, but you will not experience its full benefit unless you deepen the intensity.

The four levels are of mantras are referred to as koshas. They include literal meaning, feeling, inner awareness, and soundless sound. The surface level is literal meaning. During this stage, the meaning of the mantra is understood, but not on a conscious level. Rather, it is experienced as a basic word. Next is the feeling, which is also subtle. However, it resembles feeling the meaning of the mantra. At the inner awareness kosha, you experience the inward feeling of the mantra. This is where it starts to make those molecular changes, and it deepens the experience of the word. The final stage is the soundless sound. This is where you will experience the most profound effects from the mantra. It reverberates inward and changes our consciousness completely, letting us become the mantra that we are uttering.

The goal when you meditate should be to move through all four levels. As you deepen the intention and continue to meditate, the mantra should deepen in meaning, and you should start to feel it internally.

Opening the third eye is all about potential and possibilities. It is about awakening the mind to a higher level of perception and letting our mind analyze the minute details that we overlook. It is about having a certain openness toward the third eye, making your mind receptive to the information that it is sending you.

The most common sound that has been associated with meditation mantras, particularly meditation to induce a state of awareness and enlightenment is the sound 'OM'. The Om sound is pronounced with a long 'o', as 'Aum'. If you have ever seen Buddhist meditation, you probably have heard the sound, as it is traditionally used for opening the third eye.

Take a moment and create the sound with your mouth as you breathe. Your lips should be parted, and the sound should emanate from deep within you, seeming as though the vibration fills your whole being.

If there is one feeling that you could associate with this sound, it would be openness. Your mouth is open, and the sound is formless and empty. This gives it the ability to make your body open and formless, creating infinite possibilities in its molecular structure. A good way to think of the sound is as a gateway to becoming the sound that is created with the mantra. By making the 'Om' sound, you are opening the doorway to becoming this formless being with unlimited potential.

OM Chanting

The Om chant is often called the seed mantra, or the beej mantra. Ideally, you should sit straight up how you are comfortable, with your knees crossed 'Indian style'. Move away from any support, like walls or chairs. When you are ready, settle into the meditation by taking deep breaths and turning your attention to the pineal gland. Chant 'om' loudly, feeling the energy flow through you and the chakra opening. The energy will move through the third eye in a horizontal direction, branching out as far as you can see and merging with the infinite expanse of the universe and beyond.

Increase your volume and chant 'om' louder, Feel the energy of the sound you are making as it vibrates vertically, from the top of your head to the bottom of your toes and into the crust of the earth. Do the verbal chant twice more, then say Om mentally three times.

Continue to chant 'om' verbally and the mentally, as long as you would like. This should increase your focus as stress, anxiety, and fear all melt away. The 'om' chant is what is considered a charged mantra, meaning that it has its own energy. It resonates deeply and reaches into the third eye chakra, causing instant activation. Following the moment of activation, the circumference of the chakra grows, and the chant balances it. It is in this moment when you have the most potential to look inward or to look to a higher sense of realization. By combining this with traditional third eye meditation, the gateway to consciousness is open.

Part 3

Chakra's Meditations

Chapter 8: The meditation process

Meditation and visualization are the basic steps of chakra balancing. It is imperative to understand that chakras are not physical areas. They are the centers where the concentration of some kind of energy is higher than the rest of your body. Abnormal concentration of energy in one place can cause problems. However, there is no way to move this energy physically as these chakras are not present inside your spine. They are outside your spine or alongside your spine. Physical manipulation of this energy isn't possible. However, this energy can be moved through focus. This is where meditation and visualization come into play.

Meditation helps you in bringing your focus to a point and move the energy from one part to another. This energy is directly connected to our subconscious. Our awareness can help in moving the energies into the required areas. You can carry out complete exchange and transition through meditation and visualization.

We are talking of two terms here: meditation and visualization. It is important that you understand the significance and role of both the processes.

Meditation
Meditation is a broader process. It is a technique that helps in gathering your life energies and putting them to optimal use. Meditation can enable you to hold an iron-fist focus that can divert and streamline energies.

For most people, meditation is another way to de-stress. They believe that it is a fancy technique to reduce mind chatter. These are mostly western concepts. In eastern traditions, meditation is the ultimate way to establish a connection with the higher consciousness. Meditation helps you in looking inward, beyond the boundaries of physical perception. The ancient knowledge of the east that is getting so much appreciation today is a result of meditative practices.

Meditation can play a very important role in healing the chakras. It empowers your mind to actually locate the point of the problem and channel the energies to that point for healing. From opening the closed chakra to healing to activate the blocked chakra, everything is possible through meditation. There are several ways to deal with chakras, but meditation is one of the best ways to do so.

Visualization
Visualization is a sub-process of meditation. It is an additional part that can help you in reaching the meditative state faster. It helps the people who don't have the practice of sitting quietly for long hours and thinking in an organized and focused way by guiding them.

Too much involvement of gadgets and technology in life, excessive influence of TV, and other audio-visual stimuli and other such things have made life harder for our mind. To add salt to the injury, we are living life at a breakneck speed. This compels most of us to have to multi-task many things in order to catch up with the speed of our peers. All this eventually leads to clouding up of the mind. We are constantly thinking all the time. Our mind is never at peace. This isn't the end of our worries.

Another big curse of this modern lifestyle is decision-fatigue. We have so many options in everything that we are constantly making a choice. This may look like a boon, but it isn't so for our brain. You stand in front of the mirror in the morning and find yourself confused about which shirt to wear. It is not the shortage of commodity but its abundance that has led to this problem of choice. We have made a boon a big bane for our mind. The choice would leave us dissatisfied. We would keep pondering about not picking up the other one. This would begin the chain of miseries for us. This question isn't important, and it wouldn't have any significance in our lives, but it would keep our mind engaged. It would keep weighing it down. From choosing between tea and coffee to choosing a life partner and from minuscule to magnificent, we are making such decisions every day for all our lives. This makes our brain foggy and tired. It gets into a habit of remaining engaged. It is never silent or straight. It is always making strategies and counterstrategies, even when they are not required.

This can make the simple process of closing the eyes and not thinking of anything near impossible. If you have ever tried to do this, you'll know that it is a lot more difficult task than it sounds. As soon as there is silence, our mind starts racing in all directions, and the continuous chatter makes focusing near impossible.

As soon as we close our eyes, another thing that happens is that our mind starts magnifying or accentuating our fears. It is the right time to generate the fight or flight response for perceived threats on which you might have to make decisions in fear. The mind starts bringing them in front of you. This can scare many people. It also starts running a painful past in the quick flashback as a refresher course to keep you trained and tamed. These are some of the steps the brain takes to keep itself engaged and maintain the habit of constant work.

Majority of people encounter this problem and are never able to really focus. They are never able to achieve the meditative state where they can harness the energy of the chakras.

Visualization is a medium with which you can keep the mind engaged and guide it to the desired point. It is an additional tool in meditation to help you reach the meditative state.

As you close your eyes, a sound in the background will guide you throughout the process to think about some specific things. Your mind would remain engaged and follow the orders. This trains it to think in a positive direction. Slowly and gradually, you can learn to meditate even without the help of visualization and would be able to get better results.

Meditation and visualization together can help you in making the mind chatter inconsequential. They will help you in raising your consciousness levels above your body and guide the energy points. It is a great way to open, activate, balance, and heal the chakras.

Meditation is a complete process. It doesn't require anything or anyone else once you have become trained in it. It is the only path that can be followed for awakening the crown chakra, too. Spirituality and meditation are the only two things combined that can help you in blossoming 'Sahasrara.'

With the help of meditation, you will be able to keep your mind at peace. The mental chatter is not a real problem. Our mind is equipped to several things at a time. It keeps thinking even when you are fast asleep. However, when this chatter starts interfering with your conscious decisions, then it becomes a real problem. If there would be too much mental chatter, your mind would get cluttered. It would lose its sharpness. It would get dull and unresponsive. That will prove to be a problem in your personal, professional, and spiritual upliftment.

With the help of meditation, you can train your mind to ignore this chatter. You will also be able to develop better power of discernment. You will be able to distinguish facts from fiction. You will not get confused between real and imaginary. You will know the difference between truth and myth. All these things will help in clearing the clutter. You will be able to think more clearly. Your mind would feel more energized and focused.

Meditation is the means, and the practice of visualization is a helping tool.

When you use both of these things for chakra balancing, you will be able to get faster results. The risk of failures and disappointments decrease.

Chakra balancing becomes a very simple task once your focus is streamlined. You simply need to sit still and put your focus on the problem areas. Slowly and gradually, you will have to try to pull or push that energy upward or downward as needed.

The Ways to Do It
There are several ways to meditate. Every tradition has established several ways of meditation. Each way only aims a single thing, and that is building focus. There are several meditation techniques that have become very popular all around the globe.
Some of the popular meditation techniques are as follows.

Breathing and Relaxation Meditation
This is a simple yet very effective meditation technique that allows you to develop deep focus by paying attention to your breath. The air that you breath travels to most vital organs on your spinal cord. This is the path on which the chakras are based, and the energies are working. You can help in moving the energies through this breathing meditation technique. It is very easy to follow,and you can perfect it over the course of time.

Mindful Meditation
This is a meditation technique in which you start by creating awareness in your mind. In place of trying to regulate your mind, breath, or any other process, you simply become an observer and look at the genesis of thoughts in your mind causing the clutter. You get to the root of your fears. You learn the process of overcoming the challenges posed by the mind by facing them directly.
It starts by simple observation and then you can begin training your process of thoughts. This is one of the most effective meditation methods for people who suffer from fears, anxiety, and panic attacks. You learn the process of understanding the problem and then addressing it.

Loving-Kindness Meditation
This is a meditation process that helps you in generating sweetness of emotions. It is a part of Buddhist meditation processes and helps a lot in curbing anger, temptation, guilt,

frustration, and other such feelings. If you are full of negativity about the world and don't find it fit for your mercy, you should practice this meditation first before working on your chakras.

The chakras have a very delicate balance. They can get imbalanced at any kind of surge. If you start working on your chakras with such a mentality, it can harm you a lot. The chakras can increase these tendencies to a very dangerous level. You can start having mental issues.

Before managing the chakras, it is very important that you manage your mind first. Trying to harness the powers of chakras with a poor mental state can be very dangerous for yourself.

This is a wonderful meditation practice for such issues. It helps in addressing the internal issues and makes you more grateful to society. You are able to feel the contributions of others and also able to see the areas in which you have not been able to play your part properly. It brings humility to your heart and makes you a balanced and better person. With humility in heart, the chakras can help you in becoming a wonderful person.

Mantra Meditation

This meditation practice comes from India. It uses certain mantras or recitals to raise the vibrations in your mind. The Sanskrit mantras help in touching specific energy waves which can help. Mantras for chakras are not complex ones but simple sounds. When you repeat them in sync, they cause reverberations. Even if you don't have the knowledge of Sanskrit, you can recite these mantras as they are mostly single-syllable words. If you start repeating them in continuity, they become simple sounds, and you can feel their reverberations inside you.

The process of this meditation is also the same. With a simple addition of certain sounds, you can begin the mantra meditation.

Body Scan Meditation

This is an excellent meditation technique through which you develop the ability to touch various energy points in your body through your consciousness. It can help a lot in healing various chakras and restoring the balance.

If you don't have a feeling of wellness and are never satisfied with the way you are, this meditation technique can be the thing you need.

Chakra Meditation

This is specifically a chakra awakening technique in which you learn the ways to harness the energies based on various chakras. This meditation will not only help you in restoring the energy balance, but it can also be used to open and activate closed chakras. While the lower chakras in our body are generally open and functioning, the upper three chakras remain dormant. You specifically need to follow various methods to activate those chakras. This meditation deals with those methods.

Chakra meditation requires great control and devotion. You would have to maintain certain specific postures so that proper focus can be put on the energy centers. Everything mentioned in this chakra is specifically pointed toward awakening of the higher chakras.

Third Eye Meditation

Like chakra meditation, this is also toward activation and awakening of chakras. This chakra is specifically designed to help in activating the third eye chakra. People with an interest in gaining a higher sense of perception, psychic powers, and greater consciousness can follow this meditation.

This is a top-order chakra; hence, one should be very careful while activating this chakra. The true masters of this chakra stand testimony to the fact that it is not an easy chakra to navigate through. The intensity of this chakra is so high that it can leave even trained meditators frightened at times.

This chakra also uses colors, mantras, and specific positions for faster activation.

Gazing Meditation
This is a simple meditation technique for all those people who find it very difficult to focus with the eyes closed. If your thoughts stray a lot or you get frightened due to darker thoughts, you can follow this meditation practice. As the name suggests, you will need to maintain focus at some point with your eyes open. The object of your attention could be a picture, dot, flame, point, or anything else. You will need to keep looking until your mind gets stable and then you can proceed by closing your eyes.

Guided Meditation
Guided meditations are a great help for the people beginning their journey with meditation. The sounds guide you through the whole process. Your mind remains focused with the help of imagery described in the recitation, and it helps you in visualizing the right things. This process is especially very helpful if you have fear of going into deep focus, or you face problem in building focus.

Zazen or Zen Meditation
This is a Buddhist meditation technique which focuses on the right posture and following the mindfulness as a way of life. This technique doesn't limit you to the right posture and breathing techniques only during the meditation sessions; it dictates that you have to be mindful in every step of life. Either you are cooking, playing, laughing, or taking a bath, you will have to remain mindful of everything. You can't do anything without putting your consciousness into it.

Zen mastery involves transforming life on a consciousness level. You become mindful of everything in life; hence, all desires, guilts, expectations, and regrets go away. It is the path of letting go of the unnecessary things in life.

These are some of the paths that can be followed in meditation. There are hundreds of more meditation techniques that are followed all across the globe. They may have difference in form or principle. However, one thing that's common in every technique is that they all focus on raising the level of consciousness to activate and regulate energies in the body.

Position

Some meditation techniques lay great emphasis on the postures. They would ask you to sit in a full lotus position, while others may give you a bit of relaxation and allow half-lotus position. There are even some meditation techniques that may not require you to sit at all. You can get into a meditative state while lying down on the bed or walking. It is not the form that matters but the kind of focus you are able to build. If you can reach the center of your consciousness even while walking in the park, there can be nothing better than that. You must not fret about the method, but look if it is going to serve the ultimate purpose of the exercise.

Time

It is one thing that may vary among various types of meditation techniques. However, the most important thing that matters is your ability to build the focus at the time of meditation.

The best time to begin meditation is early in the morning as positive energies are very high at that time. Your body is also well-rested; hence, it is able to summon the energies well. Another thing that can be avoided easily at this time is the burden of the day's negative influence. The whole day's functioning may have a great impact on the functioning of the mind; hence, it may take you longer to build focus at the end of the day.

However, meditation should also be done at the end of the day, as it helps in keeping the energies aligned. If you meditate at night before sleeping, your chakras are stimulated to radiate positive energy. It is especially good for your physical as well as mental health.

Chapter 9: Introduction on Chakras

The word "chakra" comes from old Sanskrit. The term means "wheel" or "round," and is, for the most part, used to reference particular energy focuses along the body's center line. By and large, there are seven primary chakra focuses. The first time that we see any mention of Chakras is from the Vedas, which structure the Hindu scriptures. There are additional mentions of energy focuses from other traditions, for example, in Chinese acupressure texts. Most spiritual frameworks that nurture the mind will also talk about energy points as well, because they play a vital role in helping the body to heal and thrive appropriately. The energy is regularly depicted as climbing from the Root Chakra to the Crown Chakra, and then up into the heavens. Energy also enters the body through the Crown Chakra, descends to the Root Chakra, and continues into the earth.

Chakra History
The history of the Chakras is one that is rich with different opinions and various origins. Many religious and spiritual belief systems contain information that relates to the Chakra system, but each has its own words, terminology, and overarching rules. What remains the same, however, is the basic understanding that contained within the body is a powerful energy that can have a wide range of effects on our mental, physical, and spiritual health.
Regardless of your own personal religious or spiritual background, the knowledge of the Chakras can have a positive impact on your own life, making it very worthwhile to take the time to understand. But before we dive into why the Chakras are so integral, we must first begin with what exactly they are.

The Meaning behind the Chakras
The word Chakra is derived from an Indian word "Chakra" which literally translates to mean "wheel". Each Chakra can

be visualized as a spinning wheel within the body that houses the energy of that particular system. In total, there are seven distinct Chakras, each controlling and maintaining a certain part of the body, as well as different qualities within us. The Chakras are both located within the physical body, as well as being a mental and spiritual focal point for us to use within meditation and other energy healing rituals.

Many of us understand that the mind and bodywork in tandem, affecting one another and influencing how each functions. But, few of us truly understand the difference between the physical body and the mental energy that sounds it, and how those two systems are integral to one another. In all traditions that incorporate the knowledge of the Chakras, it is accepted that there is an energy that surrounds and runs through the body. This energy is commonly referred to as the "subtle body", a term that helps differentiate the physical experience from the spiritual one. The subtle body corresponds to a plane of existence that is outside of the physical realm in which we exist. This plane is connected to a higher concept, a higher realm of existence, and is spiritual rather than physical. The concepts of the subtle body and various planes of existence can be extremely complicated and difficult to understand, so to avoid confusion we will focus just on the Chakras and how they impact the physical experience of all of us.

While we cannot actually see the Chakras, their influence in our lives can be felt daily. In total, there are seven different Chakras, which form a line from the foot of our spine up to the top of our head. Some religious belief systems disagree about how many Chakras there are, with some saying there are only five, and others saying there are thousands, but the most common understanding accepts the standard seven.

Working from the base of the spine upwards, you have:

- The Root Chakra (Muladhara)
- The Sacral Chakra (Svadisthana)

- The Navel Chakra (Manipura)
- The Heart Chakra (Anahata)
- The Throat Chakra (Visuddha)
- The Third Eye Chakra (Ajna)
- The Crown Chakra (Sahasrara)

Each Chakra, as you can see, corresponds to a particular area of the body and it has a great impact on each of those systems. When the Chakras are closed off or unbalanced, they can result in physical ailments and other problems which can negatively impact our lives. In order to have a healthy and functioning mental and physical experience, it is encouraged that each person learns how to open each Chakra and keep them balanced and circulating.

Now, you may be asking yourself what exactly is meant when we talk about opening or balancing your Chakras. This is something we will discuss in-depth during later chapters, but as a basic concept, it simply means being able to focus on each Chakra and ensure you are happy and healthy in that area. If you are struggling in your personal relationships, have difficulty sleeping, feel anxious, or get sick easily, then you may have an imbalance in your Chakras that are helping to cause these problems. If you can focus on each of the Chakras, you can identify where you are stuck and the underlying cause that is creating the imbalance. From here, through various exercises and techniques, you can fix the issue so that your energy flows properly once more.

Origins of the Chakra System
The Chakra system can be traced back many centuries, with the first usage of the term Chakras being seen in the Hindu Vedas. Written in ancient India, the Vedas are some of the oldest religious texts in existence and can be dated back to around the 1st and 2nd century BCE. Following the Hindu

Vedas, Chakras were again mentioned in 8th century CE inside of Buddhist texts that discussed the different energy centers within the body. In the Buddhist scriptures, only 4 Chakras are ever mentioned, but over time this was expanded to include the seven total that we know today.

Regardless of which tradition you look to regarding the Chakras, there are many parallels and similarities that exist. The concept of a subtle body is frequently mentioned, which we in the West may know as a soul. The subtle body is what leaves our bodies when we die, and is also believed to be what exists when we dream. The Chakras are connected to this part of our existence and regulate the health and well-being of our energy rather than our physical presence. While our spiritual body may be different from our physical one, the two still are interconnected and one cannot exist without the other. This is why both systems impact our well-being so drastically, as any problems in one create problems in the other.

Now, as the concept of energy centers grew and expanded, the practice of tantra also become more common. Tantra simply refers to connecting and expanding, and the most famous form of tantra practice in Tantric Yoga. Tantric Yoga is a way of getting in touch with and connecting to your spiritual energy and is one of many ways that individuals can acknowledge and balance their Chakras. The first usage of Tantric Yoga dates back to the Vedas scriptures that we discussed, but it did not become as intertwined with the Chakras until closer to 900 CE.

Moving on from 900 CE, the seven Chakra system that we know today truly began to take hold around the 17th century. It was from this point on that it began spreading to the West, and in the 18th - 19th century it was taught outside of the Eastern world in the form of books and new aged teachers.

As the Chakra system gained more traction in the West, the seven Chakras became the dominant belief system. These seven Chakras wind their way through various other spiritual concepts and traditions, and you can see their influence within Hatha Yoga, Reiki healing, meditation, tarot card reading, and numerous other beliefs and activities. Kundalini Yoga, a modern blend of various yogi traditions, is based around the concept of the Chakras and the practice involves combining yoga with meditation and chants in order to balance and open up each person's spiritual energy or Chakras.

Regardless of the specific tradition, historically and in the modern-day Chakra energy has been a widely regarded topic of discussion when it comes to spiritual health. The life energy that runs through our bodies has been called Prana in Hindu traditions, Qi in Chinese traditions, and simply our soul by others. Whatever you choose to call it, most people agree that there is something beyond our physical bodies that make us who we are, and so in that sense, the Chakras are relevant to all of us.

The Energy of the Chakras
So you may be asking yourself "how does all of this work?", and that is a great question. A lot of this information is far outside of what we come to know in school or from our parents. It isn't taught in the average classroom or in encyclopedias and instead is information that the majority of us need to seek out ourselves. You've picked up this book, so you are obviously curious and interested, but being able to understand these complex concepts can be difficult and confusing.

Spiritual energy means different things to different people, which makes it very tricky to give a broad and overarching answer to what it is and how it works. For some, it may involve a god or deity, while others feel it is something that comes from the earth itself. How you believe that it comes to be is personal to you, but what it is can be explained a bit more easily. In a sense, spiritual energy is what you feel when you close your eyes and focus on your breath. As the cool air fills your lungs, and then warm air is exhaled, you feel that true sense of your body being alive. It is also what you may feel when you walk alone in nature, when you have a heart to heart with a friend, when you look up at the stars at night, or when you simply feel positively overwhelmed by the human experience. All of those moments connect you to your own spiritual energy and are the perfect starting place for understanding the Chakras.

Working with that energy is what you need to be able to learn to do if you want to open and balance your Chakras, and your overall spiritual energy. But before you are able to work with it, you need to be able to identify and isolate it. To do this, you need to learn how to sense your own energy, and what to look for in terms of the different sensations that you may feel. One of the absolute best ways to learn about your own energy is to take the time to be alone with it, completely free of distractions. This is accomplished through meditative practice, which we will cover more deeply in Chapter 10. For the basics of meditation, however, all you need to do is sit still and close your eyes, turning off your thoughts and just focusing on yourself. Try this:

1. Find a quiet place where you know you will not be disturbed
2. Sit comfortably on the floor or in a chair
3. Close your eyes
4. Take a deep breath in and hold for 3 seconds
5. Slowly exhale and pause for 3 seconds
6. Repeat the inhale, pause, exhale, pause
7. As you breathe, think of nothing other than your breathing

8. If thoughts come into your head let them float away
9. Stay in this moment for 15 minutes
10. Repeat daily

The more you become comfortable with existing inside this space, the more you will allow yourself to connect with your own spiritual energy. Once you come to know and feel it, then you can begin working with it more closely. Some of the sensations you may feel when meditating and tuning into your energy are:

- You may experience physical discomfort such as tightness of muscles
- It may bring up emotional discomfort such as sadness of guilt
- There may be a feeling of great emotional release and relief
- Your body may feel like it has electricity humming through it
- You may feel an overwhelming sensation in your chest
- Some find they feel the temperature change and they become too cold or too warm
- Many find that a feeling of calmness will overcome them
- Sometimes people will see different colors as their eyes are closed
- Other people will feel nothing at all

Whatever your experience is, understand and know that it is completely normal. Each person will connect in their own way, and no two people will have the same spiritual awakening. Instead, it is about becoming in tune with yourself and not trying to replicate what your friend, teacher, or random person has experienced.

How Do Chakras Interact With the Physical Body?

While the Chakras are part of the spiritual body, they do have a direct relation to our physical body as well. Just like with other systems, the Chakras mimic things like our digestive system as everything impacts everything else. For example, if you were to eat something that upset your stomach, that discomfort would continue from your stomach down to your intestines and create a chain reaction which leads to some unpleasant results. The Chakra system is the same way, in that, if one of the Chakras is unbalanced it will create a chain reaction that creates more unpleasant situations. But besides interacting with itself, how does it interact with other parts of our body?

The first major system that the Chakras connect to is our Endocrine system. The Endocrine system is the glands throughout the body that work to regulate our hormones and affect digestion, our metabolisms, growth, sexual function, mood, and more. These glands run in a line from our genital area up to our heads, which is a placement that may sound familiar. Many of the Chakras are located in the same place as each of these glands, and thus they have a direct impact on how they function. These connections include:

- The Root Chakra → Adrenal Cortex Glands = How our body responds to stress.
- The Sacral Chakra → Sexual Organs = Our sex drive and reproductive functions.
- The Navel Chakra → Pancreas = Regulates our blood sugar levels.
- The Heart Chakra → Thymus Gland = Produces T Cells for your immune system response.
  - The Throat Chakra → Thyroid Gland = Affects our metabolism

- The Third Eye Chakra → Pituitary Gland = Secretes hormones and sends messages to the other glands.
- The Crown Chakra → Pineal Gland = Produces melatonin for our sleep cycle

As you can see, there is a direct link between the physical body and the spiritual wheel located at each one, and each gland affects a major part of our life. In order to keep everything in the Endocrine System working as it is supposed to, it is important we also ensure that its mirroring Chakra is balanced as well.

But, it isn't just the Endocrine System that has a direct link to the Chakras, and in fact, the Nervous System is also directly linked. The Nervous System is all of the nerves and cells in our body which are responsible for carrying messages to and from the brain. The Nervous system is responsible for interacting with our external environment, collecting all of the sensory information that we interact with in the world around us. It then takes all of that information, translates it, and sends out a message so that our body has an appropriate response. For example, if you are cooking and you touch a hot pan the Nervous System will understand that you have touched something you shouldn't have and that it is harming you. It takes that information, shoots it up to our brain, and waits for a response. Our brain says that it is hot, it hurts, and we should remove our hand, so the Nervous System signals to our hand to pull away and it signals to the nerve ending there that pain exists.

Some of the nerves that make up parts of the Nervous System all come together in a bunch at certain spots in our body and these are called plexuses. Each plexus corresponds directly its own Chakra, as you can see in this list:

- The Heart Chakra → Cardiac Plexus = Supply messages to and from the heart.
- The Navel Chakra → Celiac Plexus = Supply messages to and from the stomach, pancreas, and liver.
- The Sacral Chakra → Superior Hypogastric Plexus = Supply messages to and from the reproductive organs.
- The Root Chakra → Inferior Hypogastric Plexus = Supply messages to and from the bowel and bladder region

So, just like with the Endocrine System, the Nervous System can be directly impacted by the Chakras which are near it and can influence how our body functions. If we ignore the Chakras and refuse to balance them, then we can end up with complications that extend far beyond just our spiritual side.

The Seven Main Chakras

1. Muladhara Chakra

Located almost at the very end of the spine and touching the anus and testicles or cervix, this chakra is designated as the four-petalled lotus, whose petals represent ultimate happiness, innate bliss, the bliss of unity and bliss of courage and strength. She is considered a reflection of the crown chakra on the physical level, and therefore her petals are blissful. The nature of this chakra is identical to Brahman, the creative principle of the universe. We can assume that it preserves the material form of the body and that its underlying history and potentials of human evolution are hidden.

This is the foundation and support of the body, and its safety and self-preservation depend on its normal functioning. This chakra corresponds to the element earth, orange-red color, and sense of smell. An elephant with a black stripe around the neck is its symbol and represents earthly qualities: strength, firmness, stability and support, these qualities are represented by the yellow square inscribed in the circle of yantra or mandala depicting this chakra. It also has a triangle called Tripura and represents will, knowledge, and action.

Muladhara affects the rectum, kidneys, sperm accumulation, and the genitals, as well as bones, skin, muscles, nerves, and hair. It is associated with the occurrence of physiological disorders such as hemorrhoids, constipation, sciatica, and prostate diseases. It is associated with a sense of smell, and its vibration causes expansion or contraction of the lungs.

Mishra writes that through pratyahara (distraction of the senses), anger, lust, and greed are curbed on this chakra. Longing and depression are also considered symptoms of an imbalance in it.

Meditation on this chakra establishes control over attachments to luxury, lies, pride, envy, and narcissism. Pandit said that the Muladhara controls physical or subconscious movements or impulses. In the yantra (the symbolic image of the chakra), there is a blood-red triangle of fire that inflates the kandarpa vayu, the cause of sexual arousal, which is important for reproducing the human race. Motoyama wrote that when this chakra awakens, it releases suppressed emotions explosively, which can lead to the emergence of extreme irritability and psychological instability in a person, a violation of sleep patterns, excitability.

Meditation on the god of this chakra, Mahadeva, who sits with his face, turned back, cleanses from sins. Brahma, the god of absolute creative power, also gives this chakra the goddess Dakini Shakti, the energy of creation. If you repeat the mul mantra, while maintaining the serenity of the mind and devotion and focusing on this chakra, then you can awaken her goddess. In yoga cosmology, exactly under this chakra is the Kundalini energy, curled up in three and a half turns. Yogis believe that this is where the confluence of sushumna (nadi, carrying the stream of life), Vajra Nadi (nadi carrying the electric stream), and Brahma Nadi (sound stream or stream of spirit) merge.

2. Svadhishthana Chakra

Located slightly above the muladhara at the base of the penis, or in the center of the lower back, this chakra is associated with the conquest of water; its symbols are the crescent and the god Vishnu, nourishing the principle of the universe. Its color is usually considered red or scarlet and sometimes - white. Rakini Shakti, a dark blue goddess with three red eyes and four hands, from whose nose blood flows, carries the energy of this chakra. She holds in her hands a trident, a lotus, a drum, and a chisel. A light gray or green sea monster resembling a crocodile is an animal symbol of the chakra, it personifies dominance over the sea and indicates a connection with the unconscious. By meditating on this chakra, a person defeats the elements.

She has six petals, which represent the mental qualities of neglect, numbness, credulity, suspicion, desire for destruction and cruelty, and also represent six nerves associated with the colon, rectum, kidneys, bladder, genitals, and testicles. This chakra promotes the circulation of liquid substances in the body, their conservation, and nutrition; it is also considered a center of the heterosexual orientation of a person.

Mishra wrote that this chakra controls, controls, and nourishes the feet. By focusing on it, a person feels a magnetic pulsation, circulation, and vibration and can get rid of all the unpleasant sensations, pains, and illnesses in his legs. Other conditions associated with this chakra include sexual problems, diabetes, kidney and bladder diseases. By meditating on it, a person is freed from egoistic feelings, small impulses, and desires. The equanimity and serenity of the mind develop. The normal functioning of the Svadhishthana is associated with a sense of self-confidence and well-being, and with the frustrations in her work, disappointment, addiction, and anxiety. This chakra is also associated with a sense of taste and language. According to some tantras, in order to master it, a person must master the language.

3. Manipura Chakra

Located above Svadvishthana opposite the navel, Manipura is associated with Rudra, a god who distributes goods and creates fear, personifying the destructive principle of the universe (the world of the mind). The goddess Lakini Shakti, dressed in yellow clothes, is called the benefactress of the universe, and one of the texts describes that she loves animal meat, her chest is covered with blood, and fat is dripping from her lips. The animal symbol is a ram, an animal sacrificed, which personifies the need to sacrifice addictions, impulsive urges, and other strong emotions.

Concentration over manipura brings comprehension of feces or eternal time. Perhaps this level of openness can be associated with the return of memories of other lives or states that take people beyond the boundaries of consciousness created by time. This chakra is also associated with control of heat and directs the agni, the fiery principle, which is believed to control the creature's unbridled movements and digestive system. Manipura controls the internal organs of the abdomen, in particular, the functioning of the stomach, liver, and large intestine, and is associated with a section of the central nervous system located above the lumbar region. Some say that focusing on this center can cure diseases of the abdominal organs, especially if you meditate on the red color in it.

Ten petals that carry the qualities of shame, treachery, envy, desire, drowsiness, despondency, vainness, delusion, disgust, and fear make up this chakra. However, according to one of the tantric texts, when a yogi meditates on this chakra and pronounces a mul mantra, he is always in a good mood and illnesses cannot penetrate his / her body. Such a yogi can enter into the bodies of others and see siddhas (saints and teachers of yoga), can, at a glance, determine the qualities of material objects and see objects underground. It is clear why this chakra is so often associated with gaining power and finding a good place in the world. It is also an area of hara that one focuses

on during some Zen meditations. This concentration gives rise to a sense of stability and resilience in the being,
The opening of this chakra requires the participation of the eyes and such control over their movements so that they do not for a moment come off the center located between the eyebrows.

4. Anahata Chakra

The location of the heart chakra is usually indicated opposite the center line running between the nipples, but sometimes it is moved slightly to the right of the sternum, although not directly above the heart. It is associated with the conquest of the element of air, as well as with the heart and nada, the sound of cosmic consciousness. By meditating on this center, you can feel how the energy flows throughout the entire nervous system as if it is filled with magnetism. Many traditions of spiritual development emphasize the importance of the heart chakra as the chakra that needs to be awakened in the first place in order to experience a spiritual awakening since it is here that the energies of the lower and upper levels of consciousness merge, which symbolize two intersecting triangles. In addition, anahata, combining the energies of different chakras, also connects the left and right sides of the body, the qualities of yin and yang.
Isha is the god of this chakra; he sits on a black antelope or gazelle, which symbolizes the speed and ease of air. Isha is the supreme God, endowed with complete yogic power, omniscient, and omnipresent. It is white and symbolizes purity; it has three eyes; the third represents knowledge of samadhi. When its form arises during meditation, fears disappear, and concentration intensifies.
The yantra images of the heart chakra include intersecting triangles, inside which are a bright golden creature and Kakini Shakti, the lightning-colored goddess who radiates light and joy. Kakini is called the keeper of the doors of Anahata and meditating on it; a person learns to stabilize prana and remove

obstacles on the way to Isha. When the goddess is red, it means that her power is used to control pranic energy; when she is white, she is Isha consciousness.

The twelve scarlet petals associated with Anahata represent waiting, excitement, diligence, affection, hypocrisy, weakness, selfishness, separation, greed, fraud, indecision, and regret. Meditation on this chakra brings possession of sound, and if you say the mul mantra during meditation, you are more prepared to understand God, as a person gains control over his feelings, in particular, reducing the sense of touch. Then, as they say, not a single desire will remain unfulfilled - then a person will forever plunge into a state of bliss.

If you look from a different point of view, we can assume that, freed from attachment to all "heart" desires (as evidenced by the qualities embodied in the petals), a person gains the ability to distract the senses from all worldly things and thus acquire a state of bliss first for short periods and then forever.

The qualities of compassion, acceptance, and unconditional love are signs of the balanced functioning of this chakra. Indifference, passivity, and sadness are signs of an imbalance — some authors associate arthritis and respiratory problems with cardiac chakra, as well as cardiovascular disease and hypertension.

The opening of this chakra is considered feasible with the help of the skin; that is, you need to surpass the sense of touch, which is done by achieving control over sensory perception through kumbhaka (breath-holding). A common way to discover the energy of anahata is a meditation on it with the simultaneous presentation of light or breathing in and breathing out air from it.

5. Vishuddha Chakra

Located in the throat is the vishuddhi lotus - gray or silver (and sometimes smoky purple) and has sixteen petals. They contain seven musical notes, poison and nectar, and seven "invocations," which are used to protect against demons, during sacrifices, to light sacred lights, to give determination, to bless and glorify. Here begin the priestly or occult powers associated with the forces of projection or expression. This chakra is also associated with the conquest of the etheric state of matter (space). This chakra is usually associated with creative activity and inspiration, as well as receiving moral instruction, especially when in contact with an inexhaustible source of "grace." A person begins to feel that the inner giver and taker are one and the same.

The god of this chakra is Shiva in a half male, half female form (Ardhanarishvara), he sits on a white elephant, and with him is the four-armed yellow Shakini Shakti (goddess). He owns a variety of knowledge. She rules in the kingdom of the moon over insignificant secrets.

Vishuddha controls both hands and is the center of pratyahara or distraction of the senses. When a person focuses attention here, he loses his hands sensitivity to heat, cold, pain, pressure, touch, and temperature. Tantras say that the instruments of this chakra are ears, they are used in such a way that the noise of the world does not distract, and only one sound is heard: either nada (the sound of Ohms is of less intensity) or the name of God. Meditation on this chakra leads one to the threshold of great liberation.

6. Ajna Chakra

Ajna is located above the nose between the eyebrows is the source of two nerve flows, one of which passes through the eyes, and the other through the midbrain. There are three main nadi (sushumna, ida, and pingala). The ability to create and achieve is generated by mental waves emanating from this point. This chakra controls the inner vision and dynamic activity of the will and knowledge. This "third eye" in many cultures is associated with light, inner knowledge, intuition, and mediumistic abilities. The discovery of these abilities involves the integration of both intellectual and emotional poles.

The goddess of ajna is the six-faced and six-armed Hakini Shakti; she personifies the five principles concentrated in the lower chakras and the gifts of the ajna chakra. When its color is described as red, then the knowledge of Kundalini is fully awakened; when she is white, she represents a state of rest; when it is dark blue, it is on the verge of transitioning into a shapeless state. When seen in a combination of white, red, and black colors, she shows a mixture of three gunas: sattva (harmonious consciousness), rajas (activity) and tamas (inertia). Meditation on this center brings visions of the highest truth, yogic powers, liberation from all Sanskars, and ultimately wisdom, higher knowledge. This is the center of individual consciousness, which through pratyahara, can be expanded to universal. Ajna is often referred to as guiding all other chakras, and some yogis advise to concentrate only on it, or first of all, before awakening energies in other centers. Thus, the development of the qualities inherent in all previous chakras can be influenced, and so the student can achieve a state of nondual consciousness. It is believed that it is not possible to fully master the lower chakras before Ajna is awakened.

7. Sahasrara Chakra

According to some texts, sahasrara is located at the top of the head in the brain; others believe that it is above the physical body and is identical with Parabrahma, the supreme creator. Her lotus has a thousand petals, five of which represent all the letters of the Sanskrit alphabet. Samadhi, felt through this chakra, is a complete merger with existence, without the limits of ego-consciousness in the body. (Although there are yoga systems in which other levels of chakras are indicated, extending further beyond the physical body and to this first level of higher consciousness.)

Parabrahma governs this center, symbolized by the triangle of consciousness, which is called Vija - this is another name for the divine essence of sat-chit-ananda. It represents overcoming obstacles and merging with emptiness or the Upper Light outside the form, a state which, according to most yogic sacred books and the saying of the saints, a person cannot describe.

Meditating here, according to Bose and Haldor, a person crosses the boundaries of creation, preservation, and destruction and can taste the sweet nectar (amrita) flowing in a continuous stream from sahasrara. A person is freed, all Sanskars are destroyed, and then he is not subject to either birth or death. At this stage of awakening, individual identification disappears forever, and a person is identified with a higher consciousness. (It is important to remember that when yogis talk about the state of immortality, they usually do not mean that a person will literally never leave the body, but rather imply that conscious fusion with the infinite is achieved forever and will not be destroyed with the death of the body.)

Balancing Your Chakras

Chakras are centers of energy and power that take in energy and distribute it throughout the body. The chakras are continuously affected by the way that people interact with different situations in life and with different people in different places on an emotional, mental, and/or physical level. Both chakras collect and absorb energy. Also, they can be thought of as the medium through which the body is nourished with balance and health, or they can deplete a person's well-being, health, and vitality. It all depends on how that person lives their individual life.

As long as a person is in a state of deep relaxation, whether during meditation or while asleep, then the intelligence that exists in the forces of life will flow easily through the chakras. When people are awake, they are dominated by their ego-mind and their self-conscious, biological life force. The ego-mind creates stress and conflict that causes the life force to suffer damage during waking hours, where it had been healing in states of altered consciousness like the ones experienced during asleep. The mind is probably the largest stumbling block that prevents energy from flowing freely through the body.

It is on the emotional and mental level that most of the health issues suffered by people are created. These issues appear in the body as psychosomatic blocks. The system of chakras in the body is aligned with the endocrine glands and the nerve centers in the body, a replica of energy on a level that is very subtle. Chakras are not physical entities in the human body but instead are tied to the psychic centers of the mind and the neurological centers of the body.

The unresolved traumatic experiences create inner stress and conflict that humans experience during life. Blocked energy in the chakras is caused by emotional, mental, and physical health problems. It is fundamental to overall good health to remove energy blocks and clean and balance the chakras. This will also help to alleviate and eliminate the feeling that one is stuck in the overwhelming instances of past experiences that cause illness, disharmony, and stress. Since people can't feel the energy of the chakras radiating through the body, it is easy to dismiss this power as non-existent or not relevant. But conflict and disturbances that are felt on the emotional, mental, and physical level convert biological energy into subconscious fate. In other words, the pains that are suffering physically and emotionally become the ideas by which the body is driven, such as "I have felt suffering, and now my body must feel suffering." Living with unbalanced chakras is the basic source of all the suffering that humans endure.

When the chakras are out of balance, especially the first three, the self will go in search of things to acquire from the external world. When the energy of the chakras is sent out from the body instead of being held in to fuel the body, then negative emotions such as loneliness, despair, depression, and fear take over the mind. These are the negative emotions that will harm the physical well-being of the body. So, the body begins to search for things to make it feel better, things like work, relationships, food, drugs, alcohol, and sex. While these are temporary pain relievers, they must continuously be fed into the body, and the body will always crave more and greater amounts. This is where the addiction begins.

The chakras will become healed and balanced when one takes the time to step away from bad habit patterns and those behaviors that create internal conflicts and learn to be aware of the self and the world instinctively. That is, to not necessarily choose certain things but to accept what comes. When the mind's power does not allow dominate the innate wisdom of the body, then healing and balancing will happen. Behavior self-destructive caused the energy to flow down through the body and out into the world, instead of flowing up through the chakras to the Crown Chakra to give a better connection to the spiritual world.

Many different methods can and should be used to balance the chakras. Yoga is one of these methods. Yoga is not just about standing or lying in a certain position until the time limit is up. It is more of a way of life, a lifestyle to be developed and nurtured for optimum chakra health and well-being. The traditions and the teachings of yoga offer specific techniques that, when used correctly, will restore the power of balance to the chakras. These methods include working with the breath, poses, and exercise, learning how not to react negatively to emotions, actions, and thoughts; visualizing; chanting and mantras and meditating.

Over the last several thousand years, yogis have experimented with, studied, and learned from the power of breathing and how to use breath as a method to restore balance to the chakras and restore peace to the mind. As a method used to withdraw from patterns of behavior that create conflict and self-destructive habits, breath is a very powerful tool. Proper breathing will reverse the flow of energy from a downward flow into an upward flow that will assist in feeding the higher chakras. This, in turn, will help eliminate the patterns of bad habits that consume and eventually destroy life.

When the breath comes into the left side of the nose, it is representative of the moon, and it is cooling to the right side of the brain. The breath that comes into the right side of the nose represents the Sun and it is warming to the left side of the brain. Using the technique of alternate nostril breathing is a good way to bring harmony to the chakras as well as the spirit, body, and mind by bringing balance to the breath. This technique works to calm the mind. It also allows energy to move throughout the body freely. This will naturally give power to the body to enable it to use healing abilities that nature gave it.

To use this breath technique, sit down in a comfortable position. With closed eyes, become aware of the breath itself. Put total awareness to the breath itself. Become aware of the very top part of the head where the Crown Chakra will be located. Imagine a golden light like strong early morning sunlight radiating onto the Crown Chakra and down into the body. This bright light flows into the body and down the spine. Every incoming breath brings love, energy, vitality, and life. As the light finally reaches the bottom of the spine, imagine it collecting in a great pool, like a lake of golden sunshine at the base of the spine. Now exhale and allow the breath to pull up some of the golden glowing sunshine through the body, out through the arms and the top of the head, lighting the entire top half of the body. Push out all negativity and any other emotions that are not needed with the exhale. When this exercise is done consciously and slowly, it will bring the energy of life into the body. This technique can be used for just a few minutes, or it can be used to enter a deeper state of meditation and relaxation.

Exercises and yoga poses are necessary for properly balancing the chakras. As a method for balancing the chakras, yoga is one of the most basic. It works by creating alignment in the physical part of the body. Yoga poses the use of stabilizing and balancing methods to restore the physical balance to the human body. Returning physical balance to the body will work to rebalance the position of the chakras in the body and help toward rebalancing them. The poses that specifically work for balancing the chakras are sometimes referred to as chakra yoga and keep the body straight and aligned along the spinal column so that the path for the flow of energy from one chakra to the next remains straight and strong.

The poses done in yoga are an amazing way to balance and cleanse the chakras. The strengthening and stretching will benefit the health of the body, which will, in turn, lead to better overall health in mind and the spirit.

The yoga method known as *Kundalini* yoga is the one thought of when considering ways to use yoga to balance the chakras. *Kundalini* yoga blends the spiritual and technical aspects of yoga to achieve chakra balance. Also, sometimes known in practice as the yoga of awareness, it mixes postures, meditation, and breathing exercises to bring balance and harmony to the chakras. It is also the method used to awaken the *Kundalini* energy, which is a strong life force that is housed at the end of the spine near the Root Chakra. The main goal of this method is to send the energy from the Root Chakra through the other chakras. The method begins with awakening the *Kundalini* in the Root Chakra and using that energy to activate all of the other chakras upward along the spine until the Crown Chakra is reached. Then the chakra circuit is considered to be complete and true enlightenment is attainable.

Using affirmations is another way to balance and heal the chakras. An affirmation is nothing more than a statement of positivity and empowerment that is used for many different purposes. Affirmations are particularly helpful when balancing and healing the chakras. Using an affirmation often has an immediate positive effect on the person's vibration and overall mood. The powerful words to create the affirmation itself are used to empowering the spirit, re-program the mind, and heal the body. Using affirmations to heal and balance the chakras will help a person to work toward achieving a goal, have the power to remain motivated, and be able to create positive changes that are long-lasting in life.

An affirmation works by replacing purposefully any limiting or negative beliefs, ideas, or thoughts that have been stored internally over the years. These thoughts will be replaced with new statements that are positive and assertive that outline how life should be experienced and how life should be lived for a more positive lifestyle. Regularly using affirmations with the intention that is focused on the affirmation will work to heal and balance the complete system of chakras and will help to transform life in ever more amazing ways.

Making dietary changes is a great idea when deciding to heal and balance the chakras. Everyone has those moments where they feel emotional, frustrated, anxious, depressed, exhausted, and unsuccessful. But there is a way to remove those feelings from being a regular part of everyday life and return to the motivated awesome people hidden deep inside. Everyone has heard of the theory of eating the rainbow. The philosophy of *Ayurveda* takes eating the rainbow to an entirely new level. With this philosophy, the goal is to eat certain colors of foods realign the mind through eating foods that are good for the body.

Chapter 10: Food and Chakras

Everyone knows that the foods you eat make a difference in the way you feel. All health specialists will tell you the same thing. However, did you know that certain foods can help to heal your chakras? They can, and it's worthwhile knowing the right kinds of foods to eat. You should also be aware that drinking sufficient water is also essential. Be mindful when you eat, chewing your food, and enjoying all the tastes and textures, instead of eating on the go. Your digestive tract is the largest part of your body, and if you don't give it the respect that it needs, it can give you problems—both physical and psychological. Thus, the chakras will be affected. Take your time and get used to using all of your senses actually to get more from your food. Start thinking of your food as being your friend, rather than simply the fuel you need to keep on living. There's a difference between simply living and optimizing your health and happiness.

You have probably heard in recent health articles about the benefits of eating brightly colored vegetables. That's certainly true when it comes to chakra healing. If you can incorporate red foods and beets into your diet, you will benefit, though, don't overdo the beets as this may affect your throat chakra temporarily, taken in excess. Your Root Chakra is keen on spiced food, and a little tabasco sauce won't go amiss. You may even feel like your body craves this kind of taste. Learn to listen to it. It will serve you well to do so. You will also find that your Root Chakra enjoys lean meat, while your throat chakra is well served by a variety of fresh fruit or fruit juices. If you tend to be overweight and/or suffer from diabetes, avoid orange juice, as this concentration of fruit sugar may be detrimental to your health, and fresh fruit would be a better option.

Your Solar Plexus Chakra will find its healing source in whole wheat bread, which will help with digestion. Healing can also be found in teas that are intended to calm the stomach, such as peppermint and chamomile. You may find that you enjoy eating those foods, and rather than add unnecessary sugar to your diet, a glass of peppermint tea is the preferred option. If you don't like drinking water, why not try adding a peppermint cordial to it, as this will also help you considerably.

Green tea is the tea of choice for the Heart Chakra, and this is particularly good for many health issues, so you won't be doing yourself a disservice introducing it as a regular drink to take the place of coffee or soda. Coffee and tea are stimulants, and if you can cut down on the amount of them you drink, you will feel better. The Crown Chakra isn't a chakra that is affected by the foods that you eat. This prefers to have regular sunshine, relaxation, peace, and quiet. This chakra is calmed by meditation or relaxation exercises.

Diet in General

As a human being, you will be all too aware of your shortcomings when it comes to eating and drinking the right items. You know from normal health issues how food affects the way that you feel, but did you know how important water is to the body? The water helps to digest your food correctly, but it does much more than that, replenishes the body and the lost fluids that are needed for your movement and digestion. In sum, water is especially important for those who suffer from ailments such as fibromyalgia or arthritic conditions which often forget that lack of movement and lack of water can make their situations worse. Make sure that you drink small amounts during the day, which will help your chakras and will also help you to feel better.

If you know that you have been eating in excess and that this includes all of the wrong foods, one thing that can help you detox is nettle tea. This is a wonderful way to make sure that your body keeps up its power to clean out all of the toxins that life has let get in the way.

There are many ways that you can work on the diet that you are taking in. Most Americans are on a diet that is not all that healthy or good for them. They are used to going out to eat all of the time, picking up something quick and easy at a local restaurant, and using that to feed their families, and when they are at home, they often don't want to spend so much time making a meal so they will make up something from the freezer part at the store. This can cause a lot of bad stuff to happen to the body because all those bad nutrients, such as sodium, sugar, bad fats, and the processed carbs, are all going to wreak some havoc on the body. And if the body is not able to get some of the nutrition that it needs, it is very hard for the chakras to work properly.

This means that it is time to work on making some changes to the diet that you are eating. If the description above seemed to fit into the lifestyle that you currently have, it is important to make the changes. The first change to make is to get rid of the stuff that is so bad for the body. This includes processed foods, such as anything that you would find at a local fast-food restaurant or in the boxed and the freezer part at your local store. These are so unhealthy for the whole body and are just making you sick with all the added bad nutrients and calories.

Also, you need to be careful about the bad sugars and sodium that are in your foods, as well as the fats and the carbs that you are taking in. Sometimes these are going to sneak their way into your diet, so you need to become good at reading the labels before you purchase or make the meals for your family to eat. Watch out for the bread, sauces, all baked goods, ice creams, french fries, and more if you want to get rid of some of the bad foods that are in your diet.

Now it is time to move on to some of the foods that you should be eating to stay healthy. Here, you want to pick out foods that are healthy and whole. These are the foods that are so good for the body because they can provide the body with all the good nutrients that it needs, without having to put on all of the foods that are bad on the body and can make it sick. There are a few selections that you can go with, including the following:

Lean meats: You will want to focus on lean meats because they provide the body with some healthy protein that is so good for you and for helping your muscles to grow as strong as they need. While ground beef can work sometimes, you have to be careful because it can contain some bad fats and cholesterol than your body needs. Lean meats like turkey, chicken, and fish are great because they provide all of the protein that the body needs without the bad stuff.

Healthy fruits and vegetables: Make sure to add as many of these to your diet as you can each day. Fresh fruits and vegetables are so good for the body because they don't contain any of the bad stuff that you need to worry about, they are low in calories, and you will be able to get a ton of the nutrients that you are looking for to keep the body nice and strong.

Healthy carbs: You do not have to avoid carbs altogether, but you do need to be careful about the types of carbs that you are consuming. You do not want to focus on the processed and white carbs, such as those found in cheap bread or those in baked goods. These are going to be turned into sugars in the body, which can raise your blood sugar levels and much more. Make sure that you stick with the varieties that are whole grain and will provide some added fiber and other nutrients to the diet you consume.

Low-fat dairy: Dairy is sometimes given a bad name, but it has a lot of the calcium that you need to keep the body nice and strong. This calcium, as well as vitamin D, can be great for the brain, the muscles, and so much more. You do need to be careful about the types of dairy that you consume. For example, if you have yogurt, you should make sure that you stick with low-fat plain yogurt and then add in fresh fruit if you would like to have that added flavor in there rather than going for the yogurt that already has the fruit inside.

In addition to making sure that you are eating the foods that you should, you have to make sure that you are preparing the food properly. You should be making these meals at home, and use approved cooking methods, such as baking and steaming, rather than frying. If you are someone who is always busy and, on the run, you may want to consider working with some freezer meals. With a freezer meal, you would just spend a day or two putting together some meals, and then they are ready in the freezer for you any time that you need. They do take a bit of prep work to get all put together, but the convenience of being able to grab a meal when you need it rather than wasting money and harming your body is so worth it.

When you can follow some of the tips above about dieting and eating a diet that is full of the healthy nutrients that you need to function and feel good, you are going to notice some huge changes in your chakras. Your body will feel good, so your chakras can function the way that they should. Give it a try and dedicate yourself to eating foods that are healthier than ever, and you are sure to notice that your chakras will feel better in no time as well.

Chapter 11: Crystals to Know

Since the earliest times, recordings of healing with stones and crystals are found. Many different ways of the application were used, but all focused on the same goal - healing! The healing properties of stones and crystals are numerous, and there are too many to be named here. For the purpose of this book, some of the most popular healing stones will be used. It is always best to look for the stone that best fits your needs.

It is important to state that crystals or stones alone won't do anything to the body that the body doesn't want to be done. A perfect state of health is to maintain a perfect balance between spirit, soul, and body. As crystals and stones come from the earth and have similar minerals as what we are made of, it helps balance our bodies' energy softly and gently. Healing with stones should never be a substitute for healing in a professional manner.

Health and Healing

1. Amethyst:
Amethyst has a calming and soothing energy that helps the transmitting of neurons in the brain. It is associated with the Crown Chakra or Third Eye. As a protective stone, it naturally tranquilizes and helps to alleviate stress and anxiety. It helps the body to be rid of negative and harmful energy. It helps against insomnia. It also strengthens the immune system and helps to balance the hormones and endocrine system. With the beautiful tones of deep purple to lilac, it brings a sense of harmony and tranquility to any room, and it is very popular to have some Amethyst stones in your room.

2. Crystal Quartz:
This crystal is one of the most common stones found almost all over the world. It has an amazing ability to structure, store, transmit and control frequencies. That is why even the

electronic world uses it. For healing purposes, crystal quartz properties work like a tuning fork bringing our bodies back to a healthier state. It projects all forms of energies known to us and therefore serves as an ideal unlocker of energy in our body. Crystal Quartz opens All Chakras but activates the Crown Chakra.

3. Herkimer Diamond:

Known as an attunement stone Herkimer helps you to attune with others and your environment. It is powerful in releasing pain as the energy starts to circulate in a very short time. It cleanses the body of toxins and is also known to correct cellular disorders. The Third Eye Chakra is the primary chakra it is related to, but it is also associated with the Crown Chakra. It is very effective in re-aligning energy. This potent balancing stone sets physical and spiritual energies in order. An elixir of this stone is perfect for a weakened body. Let the stone stand overnight in clear spring water and take it in the morning to feel rejuvenated.

4. Clear Quartz

This is the best crystal to use for healing. This has no negative effects whatsoever but needs to be cleansed before you use it. You will be able to clear different types of energies in your body – physical, mental, spiritual and emotional. You will be able to align all the energies in your body. This crystal can be cleaned easily. You will find it very easy to program the crystal to balance all the energies in your body. You will be able to create a great impression on your soul.

5. Onyx

This crystal helps in balancing the opposing forces of energy – the yin and the yang. You will be able to reduce any form of stress in your body when you use this crystal. You will also be able to exercise a good level of self-control and will be able to find happiness in the smallest things. Good fortune becomes your very good friend.

6. Opal
The opal crystal is a brilliant one since it works on improving all your attributes. You will be able to enhance your creativity and imagination. A student would love this crystal since he or she would be able to improve his memory that would prove beneficial for them during the examinations. It also helps in removing any inhibitions you may have!

7. Peridot
This crystal helps in inspiring you. It will strengthen you from within and will regenerate you! You will be able to obtain great levels of protection when you use this stone. Every bit of anger or jealousy you may have will be washed off when you sue this stone.

8. Amethyst
This crystal has the ability to convert all the negative energy in your body to positive energy. You will be able to access your subconscious when you use this crystal. You will be able to access your meditative state during the healing process. It is because of this that you can use this to heal your third eye chakra! The stone is extremely spiritual and helps you access the higher self. This crystal like the clear quartz is very good for spiritual healing. You will be able to transform and heal yourself.

9. Pyrite
This crystal helps in removing any form of negativity from your body. You will be able to purge your body of any pessimism. You will find yourself becoming optimistic and also trying to understand the greater aspects of life. You will be able to improve your memory and intellect.

10. Rhodonite

This is a crystal that works best to improve your confidence and your self - esteem. You will find yourself with decreased levels of anxiety and will also be able to obtain a certain level of balance in your life. You will begin to look at the bigger picture and will be able to understand things at a greater length. This crystal helps you attain your true potential!

11. Lapis Lazuli

This is a crystal that is used to cleanse your mind and purge it of all negative thoughts. You will also be able to calm your mind when you use this crystal. You will find yourself with a free flow of thought and will be able to protect yourself from making any hasty decisions. If you place this crystal near your third eye chakra, you will be able to open the mind that will make you more knowledgeable. You will also be able to widen your horizons. If you are a student, you will find that this crystal has helped you focus on your courses and has helped you attain undivided focus on a particular task at hand. This crystal works wonders when you use it at work too. The best part about this crystal is that it helps you remember all your dreams, hence the name dream-catcher.

12. Tourmaline

This stone is called the protection stone since it creates a protective shield around your body and your mind to ward off any negativity. You will also be able to remove any amount of fear that you may feel. You will be able to enhance your inspiration and will also be able to learn on your own. Your confidence will be given a great boost!

13. Hematite

This crystal is the perfect friend for your mind. This crystal works towards purging your mind from any negative thoughts. These thoughts are terrible for you since they bring you down mentally and emotionally. Your mind will begin to open itself up to learn more and will start observing the world around you more. The advantage of this crystal is that you will be able to remove any inhibitions you may have with respect to the different aspects of your life. If you use this crystal along with clear quartz, you will be able to regain the balance of your mind. Your blood will be cleansed too when you use this crystal.

14. Moonstone

This is a crystal that women often use since it always keeps them calm during pregnancy and during the menstrual cycle. The energy is always balanced and so are the thoughts in the mind. It is because of this crystal that clairvoyants find their capabilities increasing and sharpening. You will also be able to balance certain areas in your body using this crystal. You will also be able to keep any negative emotions at bay.

15. Pyrite

Students often use this crystal to help them perform well during any examination. Professionals also use this crystal when they are looking for different ways to improve their work ethic. When a person possesses this crystal, he will find a boost in his self - esteem. The properties of this crystal work best when it is worn on the body like an ornament.

16. Smokey Quartz

This crystal is a wonder since it always finds a way to absorb any pain you may be feeling. It acts as the neutral wire in an electric cable and will help you remove any negative energy in your body through the process of grounding. The earth absorbs all the negative energy in your body. This process leaves you with a sense of security and will help remove any depression you may face.

17. Rose Quartz
This crystal is one that depicts every aspect of love. You will find that this crystal works best with your heart chakra. You will be able to understand your heart better and will be able to understand all your feelings. You will also be able to increase your trust and faith in the people around you. You will be able to love yourself unconditionally which will help in introducing you to your inner self. You will also be able to remove any depression and grief. The love that you have for yourself will help you overcome any negative thoughts you may have about yourself. Any resentment that you feel towards the people around you will vanish when you use this crystal. The best combination of this crystal is amethyst.

18. Agate
This is the strongest stone and it leaves you with a lot of courage. It strengthens your body and your mind. You will be able to perceive the environment around you in a better fashion. You will begin to be precise. The crystal also helps in grounding you and leaving you with immense energy. The best part about this crystal is that the energies in your body, both the yin and yang, will be balanced soon.

19. Amazonite
This crystal is another delight! It helps in creating a balance between your physical body and the astral body. It also helps in aligning the energy in your body. The crystal helps in calming you down and also helps in enhancing your creativity by giving you the power of imagination.

20. Aquamarine
This crystal has the power to provide you with emotional support and intellectual stability. It has the power to clear your mind and is often used by people when they are meditating. You will be able to express yourself easily and will be able to develop a certain level of tolerance towards the people around

you. You will also be able to strengthen the image you have of yourself and remove any phobia you may have.

21. Aventurine
This crystal is a wonder since it has the ability to balance all the opposing forces in your body. You will be able to find yourself thinking positively and will feel independent. You will begin to work on projects you had never thought you would opt for before. All your anxiety will be washed away if you use this crystal.

22. Azurite
This is another crystal that can be used to cleanse the mind and the soul. You will be able to awaken your third eye and will be able to perceive numerous entities around you when you begin to use this crystal. You will find yourself beginning to change! The other advantage of using this crystal is that you will be able to find inspiration in the littlest of things thereby enhancing your creativity.

23. Bloodstone
This is a stone that works wonders when it used in the healing processes. The crystal helps in revitalizing and rejuvenating the mind and the body. You will be able to keep yourself happy and calm throughout your life. You will find yourself wiser than ever before and will be able to sense your ultimate self or your inner soul very often. You will then be able to make the right decisions throughout your life.

24. Turquoise:
This is a truth stone and master healer. As a communication stone, it helps public speaking but also verbalizing your own problems. On a physical level, it helps to release stress and is a regenerator. It is good for headaches and circulation. This helps in viral infections and lung problems. It is related to the

Throat Chakra and it also helps to absorb nutrients and strengthen the immune system.

25. Carnelian:
This stone is an active stone that removes blocked energy. It is associated with the Sacral Chakra. Wearing it increases vitality and positive thinking. On the physical side, it helps with blood circulation and problems with the kidneys, bladder, spleen and liver. It is also known to help allergies related to pollen and neuralgia. As a creative stone, it augments a fighting spirit to reach and fulfill goals.

26. Bloodstone:
As a grounding stone, Bloodstone is excellent in calming difficult situations. It releases blockages and is very helpful in emotional traumas. It is related to the Root Chakra and also cleanses the Lower Chakras. It is used to treat anaemia and blood-related illnesses. It can also be used to treat diabetes and post-surgical treatment.

27. Lapis Lazuli:
It is a stone that acts as a protector against psychic attacks and brings inner-peace and self-knowledge. It relates to the Throat Chakra and Third Eye Chakra. It furthermore boosts the immune system and purifies the blood, and soothes areas of inflammation. It helps treat the respiratory system, especially the throat and thyroid.

28. Black Tourmaline:
This is a powerful protection stone against negative energy and also acts as a grounding stone. A very popular stone for metaphysical purposes. It absorbs negative electromagnetic energy and helps the body to restore the electric field. It is related to the Root Chakra. It is a purifying stone and very helpful to have in all the areas of your home or office.

29. Fluorite:
This stone is associated with the Heart, Throat and Third Eye Chakras. It cleanses and absorbs negative energy. It helps with concentration and brings balance to us. It is a regenerating stone that helps with the restructuring of cells and DNA and strengthens the respiratory tract. It is very good to use when you have shingles or other nerve-related diseases as it eases the pain going with it.

30. Jade:
As a balancing stone, it offers wealth, health, and love. It opens the Heart Chakra and brings inner peace. It is very soothing for the nerves and is relaxing and calming overall. It furthermore brings healing energy into the gallbladder, liver, bladder, and kidneys. It is a regenerator stone too. Throughout centuries, Jade is used to helping with depression. Wearing it in the form of a bracelet is very soothing and brings a lovely calmness.

Caring for the Crystals

When a crystal is obtained, the first important thing to do is to cleanse the crystal. Crystals are natural energy absorbers, and to cleanse them means to remove previous energy from them. The process of cleansing is important not only in the beginning but after every time the holder uses the crystals. Stones need to be revitalized and recharged in order to work.
There are many different ways to recognize when a crystal needs to be cleansed. Some stones such as quartz tend to become cloudy. Some crystals lose their brightness and clairvoyance, while others manifest other physical changes, for example, they become heavier. The crystals that are placed in the house or used as accessories have to be cleaned often, and that also depends on how much are they used. This kind of stone, when charged, doesn't emit any special energy, it just provides the feeling of willpower and the decisiveness to

succeed. When this happens, cleanse the crystal, and the crystal will feel just as brand new as before.

There are a few methods for cleansing crystals, here are some of the most common ones:

The first one is to cleanse the crystal using the energy of the holder. This kind of cleansing is achieved through clear intention and a focused mind. The holder needs to visualize that the crystal is immersed in the white light while holding the crystal, and keep visualizing the purification of bad energy as well as its recharge. This process should last for a few minutes, and when completed, the energy inside the crystal will have transformed into a positive and pure one and that the crystal now has its full potential.

Another way is to cleanse the crystal is with water. The crystal should be put under a tap, and it should be washed with cold water. For the process to work, the holder must visualize that the negative energy is dissolved in the water and that it is washed away from the crystal. The visualization should continue by imagining the transformation of dissolved negative energy into the positive, healing one. When the water has washed away this visualized energy and transformed it into the positive one, the impurities of the crystal should have disappeared and the crystal is once again, ready to use. If the crystals, however, are washed in the rain or somewhere else in nature, it is important to keep in mind that the stone must be dried naturally - the best way would be to put them in a sunny spot.

There is a third way to cleanse the crystals, and it is mostly used by dedicated practitioners who enjoy exotic scents and understand the importance of crystal care. The crystal is cleansed by using the smoke of herbs that are considered to be sacred. In this case, those herbs can be lavender, sage, cedar, and so forth, and their smoke is used to smudge the energetic matrix of crystals and consequently, cleanse them. Smudging the crystals using white sage removes negativity away from the crystals. In essence, smudging is a process of lighting these sacred herbs and burning them. When the flame of these plants dies, the embers stay, burn, and they create smoke. The crystal is put through this smoke with the intent to be purified.

Crystals can be put on a rock salt bed for 48 hours and cleansed by the purifying rock salt. They can also be cleansed slowly by being buried into the soil. This process lasts two to seven days.

Crystals should never be washed with hot water. Water should always be from a tap and washing under water is not recommended for crystals such as opals, pearls, or turquoise since they can be damaged in the water due to their structure. It is also recommended not to use chlorinated water since it can also damage the crystals.

There are many ways to cleanse the crystals. However, after they are cleaned, they need to be recharged. Here are a few ways to recharge the crystals:

The first way is to place the crystal in sunlight for a few hours. This technique is used to recharge most stones. After leaving it for some time under the sun, the crystal will have a brighter color. For a full and complete recharge, the crystal should be placed on the earth so it can connect with the sun, the moon, and the stars.

The second way to recharge a crystal is to leave the stone under the moon, ideally a full moon. The moon has a great influence on the stones and gives them an even greater charge.

Crystals can be charged if they are put out in some dynamic weather conditions. If the crystal is charged during a thunderstorm, for example, it would give the stone a strong electromagnetic charge.

Crystals are fragile so it is important to treat them with care. They can chip and get damaged so it is recommended to have a separate bag for them if you are traveling. If the holder wants to unlock their full potential by using the crystals outside, stones should be handled with care and put on some silk or satin material. The location must also be carefully selected. Use the crystals in a dry area; there should not be moisture or you should not be in conditions that could damage or break the stones.

If the holder has crystals that are really expensive and hard to obtain, they should use boxes built from materials that are acid-free, otherwise, there is risk of a chemical reaction. Small fragments that are fragile should be kept in separate containers - an economical way would be to use egg cartons for storage. It is important to keep the harder and softer stones separate as the harder stones could damage the soft ones.

All crystals are unique. They should be handled with care because they represent one point in time and one stage of earth's geological development. Some gemstones are more expensive than others, but that doesn't mean that their spiritual worth is lesser. They are all a part of the process and should be treated as such.

Different Colored Crystals and Their Significance

It might all be quite fascinating if you're using crystals for the first time. They not only offer spiritual healing powers, but are also a great way to build a connection with the energy given off by the crystals. There are several types of crystals, and each of these crystals means a different thing. Each crystal is unique, and their powers are unique too. The color of the crystal is one of the factors that must be taken into consideration while selecting a crystal. The power of the crystal, when combined with the frequency of the color, tends to create a certain effect. It is quintessential that you understand this before you start selecting crystals.

Since you're just getting started with learning about crystals, understanding the colors and the significance is a great way to start. Also, don't forget that when it comes to crystals, trusting your intuition matters more than the color, shape, or even the type of the crystal. If you know what you are seeking, you will find that you are not drawn to the crystal. So, a little awareness will certainly come in handy. The colors of different chakras tend to resonate with one of the colors of the seven chakras or the energy centers in your body. Each of these energy centers is responsible for your physical, or will, and emotional well-being. In this section, you will learn about the significance of different colored crystals.

White-colored crystals
White crystals are said to signify purity and peace. White or clear crystals tend to emit energy, which is believed to be cleansing and purifying. For instance, clear quartz can be used for amplifying the energy of other crystals, whereas selenite can be used for cleansing any space. Likewise, moonstone can be used for removing any tensions or negative emotions from an individual. Apart from this, white crystals or clear crystals are quite easy to work with and connect with. They promote an overall sense of peace and serenity. They are also a great tool to be used while meditating or doing any sort of energy-cleansing work.
The different examples of white or clear crystals include moonstone, selenite, clear quartz, white chalcedony, and apophyllite.

Black-colored crystals
Black crystals are considered to be extremely powerful when it comes to offering protection. If you want to banish negativity from your life and your surroundings, then using black crystals is a great idea. Whenever you need to protect yourself and safeguard your mental health, then these crystals are helpful. Safety and security are the two things provided by black stones or crystals. They can quickly dispel your fears and start creating a sense of security and safety. Security and safety are not just related to your physical health, but your mental and spiritual health too. Since they shield you from so much negativity, they are referred to as barrier crystals. Not only do

they offer these protective abilities, but barrier crystals also help improve the wearer's focus while amplifying their efforts to keep away any negativity.

White stones tend to help reflect purifying light, whereas black-colored stones can absorb light. It can also be used for unlocking any hidden talent or potential within an individual. Black is said to be a solidifying color. It is believed that black crystals have tremendous power stored within them, and you need a little patience to unlock it. The different examples of black crystals include obsidian, shungite, black tourmaline, and black kyanite.

Red-colored crystals

If you're looking for a crystal that will make you feel energized and pumped up, then these crystals will do the trick. Do you every use the clever drink red bull or any other energy drink? Don't you feel revitalized or unauthorized? Likewise, red crystals perform the same function. Red is a color that is associated with our life force, the planet Mars, and the root chakra. Our life force, or blood, and the planet Mars are associated with war, passion, and sex. The root chakra guides our basic animalistic instincts. So, it is no wonder that the energy given out by red-colored crystals is raw and intense. It is believed that red crystals will give you the determination and the motivation that's necessary to keep going. So, if you need to boost your energy or get actively involved in something, then opt for red stones.

The different examples of red-colored crystals include garnet, ruby, red jasper, rubellite, and vanadinite.

Orange-colored crystals

Orange crystals help to combine energy with focus. Therefore, these crystals are believed to promote creativity as well as artistic skills in an individual. This color is also associated with the sacral chakra. So, orange is believed to be associated with creativity as well as sexuality. These crystals can provide a source of energy and inspire creativity. If you feel like you need to make things a little more interesting for yourself, then these crystals will certainly come in handy. Also, these crystals are believed to be quite helpful in general as they act as catalysts or supporters of any major life changes. So, if you're looking for swift decision-making, then you can start working with these crystals.

One of the most popular orange-colored stones is carnelian. Carnelian is believed to project warmth and there are various instances throughout history about how carnelian was favored by the pharaohs of ancient Egypt. Different examples of orange-colored crystals include amber, sunstone, carnelian, orange calcite, and sunset aura quartz.

Pink-colored crystals

The energy radiated by pink crystals tends to feel like a warm hug for your heart. It's gentle, soothing, warm, and loving energy can make anyone feel good. Pink crystals tend to promote feelings of calmness and compassion. It is believed that these crystals bring love and kindness into the life of its wearer. These crystals can be used for matters related to love, forgiveness, kindness, self-love, emotional healing, or anything else along these lines. If you want to open up your heart and let others in or connect with others, then start using pink-colored crystals.

Emotions and sensitivity, along with subtle and gentle energies, can be incorporated into your life by using crystals of this color. One of the most popular pink-colored stones is the rose quartz. Any suppressed or unexpressed emotions can be quite a hindrance to your personal growth and you can use rose quartz to prevent this from happening. By using pink crystals, you can unleash or let go of such suppressed energies. These stones are also associated with unconditional love and self-love.

Pink tourmaline, rose quartz, pink opal, rhodonite, and rhodochrosite are all examples of pink crystals.

Yellow-colored crystals

The color associated with the solar plexus chakra is yellow. The energy given out by yellow-colored crystals is quite similar to the energy of the solar plexus chakra. Yellow is also associated with the color of the sun. Just the way a sun shines brightly and gives off energy that can fill anyone with warmth, yellow-colored crystals tend to do the same. It is also believed that these crystals are associated with your digestive system, nervous system, and the immune system.

The energy of these crystals is bright and optimistic. Apart from this, it will also help you find your true self. The solar plexus chakra is related to your sense of self, so yellow crystals can inspire self-confidence. If you want to feel good and experience a boost in confidence, then yellow crystals can help. Sulfur quartz, citrine, golden onyx, yellow jasper, and honey calcite are all examples of yellow-colored crystals.

Blue-colored crystals

The color blue is associated with two chakras in your body. Light blue is associated with the throat chakra, whereas indigo is associated with the third eye chakra. The throat chakra is representative of all forms of communication, and therefore, light blue is representative of the same. Your senses of touch, taste, smell, sight, and the ability to feel are all related to the color blue.

Apart from this, all of your internal communication processes, such as the way you talk to yourself and express your thoughts, are influenced by the energy of these stones. Peace of mind, intuition, perception, and the ability to understand are associated with indigo. The way the ocean or the sky tends to have a soothing and calming effect, blue-colored crystals also have that same effect on your body. Blue crystals can bring about clarity and enable you to be your most authentic self. You can do all this while staying calm, composed, and collected.

Lapis lazuli, aquamarine, azurite, blue lace agate, and larimar are examples of blue-colored crystals.

Green-colored crystals

Green is the color of nature as well as money. If you're looking at making a fresh beginning and want to enable the growth of your spirit, then connecting to a green crystal is a good idea. Green crystals like jade are often used for attracting prosperity, wealth, and money. They are considered to be sacred stones in Asia.

Green is also associated with the heart chakra. Green colored crystals can be used to establish balance as well as stability in all relationships and an individual's emotions. It is representative of your personal growth and serendipity. Apart from this, green crystals can also help in getting rid of any feelings of anxiety or stress while inciting happiness and joyful attitude towards life. If you want to break free of any toxic relationships or harmful behavior patterns, green crystals can help. By bringing about stability to matters of heart, it will certainly improve your overall sense of well-being.

Moss agate, green aventurine, jade, and malachite are examples of green-colored crystals.

Purple or violet-colored crystals

Violet is the color associated with the crown chakra or the seventh chakra. Violet crystals can help you tap into feelings of inspiration, empathy, and also give you a sense of service to those around you. These stones can help bring balance in extreme situations. Also, you can use them whenever you are unsure of the nature of the problem that you are facing in life. Purple crystals are believed to be quite spiritual and can help in bringing about balance to your spiritual side. They can not only help you find inspiration, but also enable you to tap into the divine forces of the cosmos. If you want to find your true purpose in life, then these crystals are the ones to use. Purple or violet colored crystals and stones are often used for practicing meditation.

Amethyst, sugilite, lepidolite, charoite, and spirit quartz are all examples of purple crystals.

Chapter 12: Chakra's Meditations

Root Chakra Guided Meditation

The root is where you touch the soil of all life and energy and how you begin your journey of healing. In the concept of Kundalini Awakening, your dormant life force is stored here and it is where you begin to rise up to enlightenment.

It is the first chakra and is located at the base of the spine where your pubic bone ends and where your tailbone or coccyx is located at the bottom of your sacrum. The color of your root chakra is red and its energy is a throbbing life force that has all of the initiation, potential life force, vitality, security and power that your whole life needs for forward momentum. The element associated with this chakra is earth.

The physical attributes of this chakra are connected to the legs, feet, large intestine, and the coccygeal plexus. Your gonads or sexual glands are also affiliated with this chakra and have a lot to do with your desire to procreate or not. Even if you have a desire to procreate, you can still have a blocked or deficient root chakra. The kidneys are also affiliated with this chakra and kidney health could be linked to issues in your root chakra.

The major quality of the root is the concept of survival. When your root chakra is in a healthy, balanced life flow then you will likely feel grounded, prosperous, physically healthy, robust, vital, stable and within your right life path. This is where the right to have lives and breaths and when you have a deficient or blocked root then you may feel like you don't deserve what you truly want.

There are a lot of significant forms of malfunction when the root chakra is blocked and it can often be represented by some of the following issues: eating disorders, obesity, irritable bowel syndrome, constipation, sciatica, bone and joint issues, knee problems, general illness that occurs frequently, fearfulness, lack of focus, fidgeting and more.

When you are presented with your root chakra healing techniques, you may find that some of these issues could flare up, even if they were only experienced in your past or early life. Energy blocks in your chakras can last a lifetime and so when you are in need of regaining a healthy energetic flow, you may be poking the hornet's nest, so to speak. This will be a good indication that you are on the right path and to keep doing the healing work you are intending to do on this chakra. The same will be true of all of the other chakras which will all have different types of issues arise during opening and cleansing.

The root is the beginning point of your chakra healing journey. It can have a major impact on all of your other chakras and although it leads to other places, sometimes it is the biggest block for someone. You may find as you start working in your root that it will lead you to a different chakra higher up from the root, like the heart or the throat, guiding you to engage with clearing these chakras first before you can fully heal the root chakra.

When you begin your journey of healing each chakra, you may notice that you are guided by your own chakra system to follow the right path of opening. You do not have to go in order from root to crown and you will need to trust your intuition and follow the signals from your body, mind, and spirit to move in the best healing direction. Cracking open traumas in your root chakra could point directly to the issues you have held in your brow chakra for years and you may be asked by your body to work more directly with your brow chakra first.

The path is unique to you and will guide you as you begin with the first step of introducing yourself to your roots.

How the Root Chakra Gets Blocked

The root chakra can be blocked by many experiences, but life during your childhood has a large impact on the root chakra. When you are a small child, you are very tuned into the feeling of safety. If you had loving parents who were stable and who provided a stable home life, then as a child, you felt completely safe. This is likely to carry over to adulthood, but of course, there can be events throughout your life that can disrupt the root chakra.

One of the ways that the root chakra can become blocked is that during childhood, a child may experience erratic care. Having their needs met only on a sporadic and unpredictable basis, the child will soon have a blocked root chakra. Any abuse during childhood will certainly lead to a blockage of the root chakra. Inconsistent treatment during childhood can also block the root chakra. A moody caregiver can have a negative impact, as the child never knows when the parent is going to be angry, leading to feelings of fear and insecurity.

Any negative experience that significantly impacts your ability to feel safe, or to trust other individuals, can also block the root chakra. Sexual assault and rape are major reasons that many people, especially women, have a blocked root chakra. This is one way that a root chakra can become blocked in adulthood. Another event that can lead to a blocked chakra at any time is a break-in in the home. This leaves people feeling unsafe and violated, even if they were not at home during the break-in.

Foods to Heal the Root Chakra
As a part of healing the root chakra, you can spend some time eating foods that are specifically helpful for this purpose. Begin by considering root vegetables. As they grow in the earth, they contain foundational energy vibrations that can help heal your root chakra. These include potatoes, carrots, radishes, onions, and garlic. You can also focus on consuming foods that have a red color. Tomatoes are an excellent food to consume while working on your root chakra. Beets are an excellent choice because they have a reddish color, in addition to being a root

vegetable. Sweet potatoes and pumpkin seeds can also be helpful.

Essential Oils for the Root Chakra
When using essential oils to help you heal the root chakra, consider using oils that are calming. A good example of essential oils for the root chakra is sandalwood. This essential oil can help you to calm the nervous system, which will help to release the negative energies that are associated with the anxiety and feelings of fear. Myrrh is also a good essential oil that can be utilized when working with the root chakra. It also has a gentle, calming effect on the nervous system.

Colors for the Root Chakra
You can use colors to help heal the root chakra. The main color to use when healing the root chakra is red. In order to use colors, there are many things that you can do during your healing period. The first thing is to wear red-colored items of clothing. This can be done at any time, but a special situation to consider is when you either do yoga or engage in meditation. You can also fill your home with red-colored items. This can include pillows, sheets, throws, and drapes. The goal is to constantly surround yourself with the energy of the root chakra. This energy vibration is strongly associated with the red color.

You can also place red flowers throughout your home or in your office. Paintings that have a lot of red in them can also be hung on the walls. If you are in need of healing of the root chakra, surrounding yourself with as much of this red energy as possible can be very beneficial.

Crystals for the Root Chakra
Crystals can play a central role in healing your chakras. For details, please see my book on *Crystal Healing*. For the root chakra, the crystals that you want to use are those that are red

or black in color. The energy of the crystal, more so than the specific color, is important for its function. Four crystals that are strongly recommended include garnet, hematite, black tourmaline, and obsidian. Ruby is also an excellent choice. If you feel unsafe in your living space, consider using four stones of black tourmaline, and place one in each corner of the room. You can also place crystals in your car, or wear them to help heal the root chakra, reduce your anxiety, and increase your sense of safety. Try holding hematite in your hands, either just for calming or during meditation. It is said that simply holding this crystal can help you feel centered and secure.

Meditations for the Root Chakra

- Lie, or sit, in a comfortable position.
- Bring your attention to your breath and begin by inhaling and exhaling slowly to increase your relaxation.
- Let your mind wander and allow your thoughts to come slowly to your root chakra.
- Spend some time visualizing what it looks like. See its color, size, health, etc.
- On your next inhale, breathe air all the way down to your root. Feel this part of your body fill with breath. While you are here, continue to take breaths like this as you consider this chakra.
- Explore any thoughts, images, ideas that come up. Do your best not to avoid any intense feelings, repressed memories, or thoughts that emerge.
- Continue to breathe for a while as you explore anything that "happens here." Don't be afraid to let any deeper feelings surface and come out. Pay attention to what the feelings are and create awareness of them.
- Now, prepare yourself to release these energies. Using your inner eye to see this release, it can look however you want

it to when you let it all go. It can shoot out of you like a rocket, or pour out of you like a river.
- Visualize this release of unwanted energies as you take several deeps inhales and exhales.

Sacral Chakra Guided Meditation

The second chakra is known as the sacral chakra because of its location in your body, just below your navel and parallel to your sacral bone (the bone that joins your hips at the base of the spine). This chakra has the color orange and is one step above the root color red. This chakra has an association with the element of water and is considered the seat of your emotions, desires, passions, sexuality, and creativity.

The organs associated with this chakra are the genitals, and it is also linked to the lower back hips and sometimes the knees. The second chakra is also associated with the adrenal glands in your endocrine system, which regulate immune function and metabolism. This chakra is also associated with the ovaries, uterus, spleen, gallbladder, prostate, bladder, bowels, and kidneys.

Blockages, excesses or deficiencies in this chakra can be linked to adrenal fatigue, metabolic issues, and immune deficiencies. The physical association with certain organs can lead to any number of issues directly associated with each organ, such as infertility issues (ovaries), irritable bowel syndrome (bowels), urinary tract infections (bladder), and so forth. Some of the other issues correlating with the sacral chakra are stiffness in personality (stoicism, lack of passion), sexual addictions, or conversely, frigidity, numbness of feelings, or emotional roller coasters.

This chakra governs sexuality and emotions and is the place where your right to feel is located. So many people struggle with suppressing and bottling their emotions for months and years and it can lead to a lot of distress and imbalance in the overall health of a person's life and ability to experience joy. There are a variety of ways that these types of situations can arise in life and many of them start in childhood and as you age you continue to choose relationships that keep this chakra blocked and avoidant of the true flame of passion and creative desire that lives here.

Often times, when you start to release your sacral chakra, you also begin to release the throat chakra. Since the sacral chakra has to do with emotions, a block in this area can be directly associated with your inability to express or communicate your feelings, which is a block in your throat chakra.

There is a lot of life force in the second chakra and looking for an opening here can be the gateway to living the love life you have always wanted, making the art from within your soul, and expressing your deepest desires and emotions in a joyful and passionate way.

How the Sacral Chakra Gets Blocked?
There are many ways that the sacral chakra can become blocked. Any type of sexual abuse, rape, or assault is an obvious cause of a sacral chakra blockage. If this is the cause of a blockage, a long and intense process of working on the sacral chakra is going to be necessary.

A blockage of the sacral chakra can also happen when an early relationship goes sour in dramatic fashion. If it is a person's first sexual relationship, and there are issues of betrayal or other emotional abuses, this can lead to a blockage of the sacral chakra.

Many other things can lead to a blockage of the sacral chakra. For example, if parents have strange aversions to a healthy view of sexuality, they can cause the sacral chakra to become blocked in childhood. Often, this is something that is passed down from generation to generation, and puritan views of sexuality have, in many cases, led to a cultural-wide phenomenon with problems related to the sacral chakra. Even now, although sexuality is more open and accepted in western cultures, puritan heritage is still influential. The puritan view of life also goes beyond the expression of sexuality. It also discourages the enjoyment of pleasure generally. We are often not conscious of how the puritan view is influencing us, but it is still a large factor in American culture, leading people to *feel* that pleasure is "dirty." When something is felt rather than believed logically, it has far more power, and it gets ingrained in the subconscious mind, and a blockage of the sacral chakra can happen.

The explosion of pornography is an important thing to consider and a difficult thing for people to talk about. With free pornography available all over the internet, people are getting the sacral chakra blocked. This does not mean that people should not look at pornography, but it is very easy to do so and then end up with a blocked or unbalanced sacral chakra. The first danger that comes out of it is that it can lead to an obsession with sexuality. Second, it can drive a person to become too prone to fantasy. When you are living in a fantasy life, this can prevent you from having real sexual relationships, and you might develop "high standards" that are unrealistic as a result of spending too much time fantasizing with pornography.

Pornography, paradoxically, can dull the sacral chakra. After too much pornography, a person may actually lose interest in sexuality or pleasure-seeking. Nothing seems to satisfy. Care must be taken if you are going to expose yourself to this material.

Foods for the Sacral Chakra
Eating the right foods can help balance and heal the sacral chakra. Fortunately, the natural world is full of foods that can assist you when working with the sacral chakra. Also, these foods are often beneficial for the root chakra, so you can heal and balance both simultaneously. Not to mention that many of these foods are extremely healthy. Keep the color orange in mind when seeking out foods for this purpose.

Foods that can help both the root and sacral chakra include carrots and sweet potatoes. This is because they have deep orange colors, while also being root vegetables that promote grounding and security.

Other foods that help balance the sacral chakra include oranges, orange juice, orange peppers, mangos, orange cantaloupe, peaches, and apricots. Salmon is an excellent protein source that can help with both the root and sacral chakra. Eating beef steak can also help to heighten sexual energy. Almonds and walnuts are also reported to help heal the sacral chakra. Since the element of the sacral chakra is water, drinking adequate amounts of pure water to stay hydrated can help maintain the sacral chakra. You can also consider taking vitamin C supplements.

Essential Oils for the Sacral Chakra
The sacral chakra, associated with sensuality and pleasure, can benefit from the use of spicy essential oils. Sandalwood, which is useful for the root chakra, is also beneficial for the sacral chakra. You can also use orange oil. In order to stimulate sexual energy, many people swear by ylang-ylang, which is also reported to have a calming effect. This will help you relax and open up to pleasure. Clary sage is mildly spicy and found to be relaxing so that you will open your sensuality. It is particularly useful for older women. Also, consider using essential oils and lower back massage.

Colors for the Sacral Chakra
The sacral chakra is closely associated with deep, bright orange color. You can elevate your sensual energies by surrounding yourself with orange. Consider adding orange sheets, pillowcases, or bedspreads to the bedroom. Use orange pillows in your meditation space. You can also heighten your sexual energy by wearing bright orange-colored clothing items.

Crystals for the Sacral Chakra

The main crystal preferred for the sacral chakra is carnelian. This amazing stone, when polished, has the exact bright deep orange colors that activate the sacral chakra. Consider filling your bedroom with carnelian stones. Hold them in your hands, just for the sake of doing so or during meditation, and feel the energy and absorb it. Get a carnelian pendant or necklace to wear on your body to heighten your sensuality.

Amber is also a good crystal to use for the sacral chakra. It also overlaps with the solar plexus chakra, and you can use amber by purchasing jewelry items made of amber and wearing it on your body.

Goldstone is a dark orange crystal that can also help with the sacral chakra. Sunstone, tiger's eye, and citrine can also be used. However, note that these crystals are primarily yellow in color and have more impact on the solar plexus chakra. In summary, the carnelian stone is the primary crystal that you probably want to use to work on the sacral chakra.

Meditations for the Sacral Chakra

- You can start this meditation as you started the root chakra meditation. One great way to do this meditation is in the bath. This is the chakra associated with water and you can add another layer of connection to your chakra healing by connecting to the water.
- Connect to your breathing in a comfortable, seated, or lying position. With this chakra, you will want to explore your feelings a little more deeply. Be open to crying, laughing, or other things coming up that need to be released.
- While you are breathing in and exhaling out, spend a lot of time focusing on the orangey hue of your second chakra.

Picture the energy as a whirlpool of orange water and see it spinning in your lower abdomen.

- Focus your breath in this area. With every inhale, breathe into your sacral chakra and feel its watery nature. Continue this breathing focus and attention to the color and feel of this chakra for several minutes.
- As you see the water of this place, what emerges? Can you see any people, places, objects coming up to the surface of the water? Are you having any feelings surface, or ideas and thoughts about anything in particular?
- Pay attention to your senses as you breathe into this chakra. What do you hear all around you? Can you smell anything? What are you seeing in your mind's eye? What are you touching right now that you can feel? Go through each of your five senses to connect with the energy of the second chakra.
- Bring any issues to the surface of the orange water and imagine all of your issues, fears, repressed energies, and emotions. Imagine a boat of some kind arriving on the water of your sacral chakra. See all of the negative issues or emotions climbing into the boat.
- With a deep, long slow inhale, breath all the way down to this chakra and hold your breath for ten seconds. As you exhale, watch the boat sail away from your body and out of sight.

Solar Chakra Guided Meditation

The solar plexus is the third chakra coming up from the root and is a bright yellow sun of vital energy and life force. A balanced solar plexus chakra means that you are living in your power and your truth. It is the element of fire and is like a ram charging full steam ahead at all of life's ups and downs.
This chakra is located above the navel and sits just below the sternum of the rib cage. It is the color yellow and has

everything to do with the strength of will and purpose, effectiveness in life actions and choices, vitality and a strong sense of I AM ME. This can be a place of many excesses, deficiencies, and blockages, especially in a culture that demands fame, glory, popularity and perfection.

Examples of having an overactive, or excessive solar plexus chakra might look something like this: demand to be in control; never stopping, slowing down or resting; anger management issues; overpowering others; possible stomach ulcers; heaviness around the waist and middle.

Examples of deficiencies in this chakra can be represented in the following ways: shyness or timidity; submissiveness in life; lack of energy; chronic fatigue syndrome; trouble with digestion and processing foods for energy; addiction to alcohol or drugs in order to stimulate a false sense of life force or vitality.

Several of these issues in the solar plexus chakra can also be created by blocks of energy flow in other chakras in the body. It is never just one chakra that has an issue or a block; they work together as a whole system, cogs, and wheels in the machine of your life. The energy from this chakra has a lot of connection to the first and fifth chakras, so when you are looking into your own energy centers to help yourself heal, consider how much of your energy may be blocked from either of these two places as well.

How the Solar Plexus Chakra Gets Blocked?
Events that sap our confidence in childhood can lead to a blocked solar plexus chakra. In many cases, it can be a guardian or teacher, who while meaning well, use harsh language and put-downs trying to motivate children to work harder. Often, instead of helping the child, they sap the child's self-confidence, leaving them with low self-esteem and taking away their natural can-do attitude.

Of course, you don't have to be a child to be affected by this. Anytime someone important to you engages in put-downs or doubts your abilities, you might start to feel a lack of self-confidence. The energy that is associated with this kind of self-doubt is going to lead to a blockage of the solar plexus chakra.

Depending on the overall balance of the chakras and the makeup of the person, the inevitable failures that happen in life can have a large impact on the solar plexus chakra. If you are coming from a place of strength, to begin with, you can bounce back from failures easily. If all three of the lower chakras (root, sacral, and solar plexus) are open, and in balance, a failure on a major project is going to lead to analysis and planning to recover from the failure and learn lessons that can be applied next time. But if you are already suffering from blockages or imbalance, a failure on a project can serve to fully block your solar plexus chakra.

Also, the reactions of those around us can determine how we respond to failure, whether it is on a work project, something in the home, or at school. There are many negative people in the world who will use the failure of someone else to put them down. If you are the recipient of this kind of behavior, it can help to block the solar plexus chakra.

Apathy and Lack of Purpose
Two qualities that are often associated with a blocked solar plexus are apathy and lack of purpose. The degree of apathy will vary from person to person, but when the solar plexus chakra is blocked, you can become pretty apathetic about having to work and your work life in general. While in school, you might find yourself unable to see anything satisfying or something you could get passionate about. People with a blocked solar plexus chakra that go to college often jump around from major to major. They do so because no matter what they try, they feel apathetic about it, and they also lack

the discipline to stick to something and take it to completion. Don't be surprised if they fail to graduate. If they do graduate, it will be from muddling through, not because they have found something that engages their passions.

This is coupled with a general sense that there is a lack of purpose in life. This can also be accompanied by blockages at the spiritual levels. However, when the solar plexus chakra is blocked, there will be a lack of purpose that relates to a sense of occupation or career. This will be accompanied by a lack of caring for work or efforts at work, and the person will do what is necessary to get by and avoid getting fired, but nothing more.

An Overactive Solar Plexus
Just like we've seen with the sacral chakra, it is possible to be out of balance and have an overactive solar plexus chakra as well. In this case, the workaholic personality comes to mind. Some people have an overactive solar plexus and so devote too much time to work and earning money. They will put in excessive hours at the office and won't balance that out with meeting their normal human needs for pleasure and relaxation. They will always find an excuse to stay late at the office. If they have a partner or family at home, this is going to be the person who neglects their family. They may also neglect their health, working so much that they develop ulcers, digestive problems, and even serious health problems like heart disease and cancer.

Surprisingly, people with an overactive solar plexus chakra are penny pinchers. Since the solar plexus chakra can be associated with a mentality of wealth and abundance, when it is overactive and out of balance, this can lead to valuing money for its own sake. The person becomes unwilling to spend any money, even for reasonable expenses. Despite a high income, they become obsessed with saving a penny at every turn. They will use coupons, refuse to lend anyone money, and drive an old, beat-up car. They will be severely judgmental of people who enjoy luxury items or take vacations. This is the type of person who, if they never heal, will take their money to the grave with them.

Food for the Solar Plexus Chakra
Yellow, brightly colored foods can help heal the solar plexus chakra. Start with squash. Flavor your foods and your drinks with lemon. Add yellow peppers to your salads. Eat corn, tacos with yellow corn shells, or corn chips. Golden apples will help to open the solar plexus chakra. You can also help the solar plexus chakra by eating pasta, lentils, and oats. Regular potatoes can help as well, and use lots of butter, especially grass-fed butter that will have a strong, deep yellow color.

Essential Oils for the Solar Plexus Chakra
The top essential oil to use for healing the solar plexus is lemon oil. Many other oils can be helpful, however. These include chamomile, ginger, and cinnamon oil. Some practitioners that use essential oils also advise clove oil for the solar plexus chakra.

Colors for the Solar Plexus Chakra
Of course, bright yellow colors are good for healing the solar plexus chakra. You can also combine yellow and white. Fill your life with these colors, and let as much sunshine into your living space as possible, especially in the mornings, late afternoon, or early evening as sunset approaches. Use yellow sheets on your bed and yellow pillows and consider painting a room bright yellow to use for meditation on the solar plexus chakra when necessary.

Crystals for the Solar Plexus Chakra
There are several yellow-colored crystals and stones that can be used to help you heal the solar plexus chakra. Among the most

popular is a crystal called citrine. Some stones used to heal the sacral chakra overlap with the solar plexus chakra, and utilizing them can help you to heal both at the same time and bring them into balance. Try using amber for this purpose, and the tiger's eye also works well for both chakras. Other stones that can help you heal the solar plexus chakra include yellow jasper and yellow topaz.

Meditations for the Solar Chakra

- This is a great meditation to perform in the sunshine if you can.
- Begin by relaxing your body in a comfortable position, either sitting or lying down.
- Bring focus and attention to your breathing. Long, slow, and deep breaths to start.
- After you have connected to yourself in this position, engage in a breath of fire to ignite your solar plexus energies. The breath of fire is quick bursts of inhales into the nose and out through the nose, pulsing the abdomen (like panting with your mouth closed.) Make sure that your belly is moving in and out and your diaphragm is going up and down.
- Practice the breath of fire for a few rounds and return to deep and relaxed inhales and exhales.
- Begin to visualize the sunny yellow color of your solar plexus. Bring your breath to this space as you watch the energy churn here. If you want to you can visualize your solar plexus as being a small sun.
- Offer yourself some time with this visualization. As you spend time here, notice what thoughts, ideas, and feelings come up. They may not always be exactly what you would think, or specifically regarding the qualities of the chakra. You might think about your boss or your relationship. You

might have images pop up of an argument you have with a grocery clerk. Anything that comes up here has something to do with this energy and as you meditate on it, consider how this chakra has been involved in any of these people, places, or things. (Example: thinking of your boss while clearing this chakra could relate to wanting to be the boss one day and not feeling adequate, or having a disagreement with how your boss makes you feel like you don't know what you are doing or talking about, etc.)

- Whatever energies have come up to be healed and cleansed, allow them to be brought into the light of this chakra. See the fiery heat of sunlight setting fire to these energies to purify them and release them. Let the sunshine of yourself ignite your power and let go of any negative beliefs you may hold about yourself here.

Heart Chakra Guided Meditation

The fourth chakra says what it is: heart. The heart chakra has everything to do with love and relationships. It is not only romantic love that lives here, but also familial love, platonic love, the love you feel for your pet, or even a place you like. It is also greatly about love for the self and when you have blocks, excesses or deficiencies here, you may have struggled or are currently struggling with the issues surround self-love. There is an old saying: if you can't love yourself, how will you truly love another? This is the heart chakra's question more than any other. Looking outside of yourself for love has a detrimental impact on the energy of your fourth chakra and is often the cause for why people have difficulty in their love relationships with others.

The heart is located in the center of the chest and your heart chakra is exactly where the heart is. The thymus gland, which is associated with immune system regulation, is connected to this chakra. The organ of the heart, as well as the lungs, are the physical organs connected to this chakra.

It is the color green and has the element air linked to it. Here is the right to love and it goes without saying, or it should, that we all have the right to love and be loved. When you have a balanced, clear and open heart chakra you experience compassion and self-acceptance on all levels. You will also have harmonious relationships and feelings of love and self-worth. All of your heart chakra energy is devoted to the love of all things and all life and leaves you ready for all manner of joyful and heartfelt experiences in your life.

The heart chakra is a notorious place for blockages, excesses, and deficiencies. We can be so easily wounded here because of another's lack of love for others and for themselves. There are a lot of childhood moments that become heart chakra blocks that lead to long term excesses and deficiencies.

For example, if you have a deficient heart chakra you may have feelings of melancholy or sadness in general, low self-worth and lack of self-love, fear of loving another or opening up to friendships, difficulty breathing or a feeling of heaviness in your chest. You may also have a lack of desire to create the life you want because you are unable to love the truth of what you want and who you are truly meant to be. So many people end up living lives that they are not content with because of a lack of self-love from a blocked heart chakra.

There can also be excessive energy here, just like with all of the other chakras. You might think that it is a good thing to have an overabundance of heart chakra energy, however, it can present in other ways that are unhealthy. For example, an excessive heart chakra could look something like this: clinging behaviors in relationships; codependency; care-taking of others to the point of exhaustion; narcissism.

We all have a heart and we all want to love and be loved. The heart chakra is an important place to find balance. As the fourth of seven chakras, it is in the direct center of your tower of energy and is the area where the lower and upper chakras connect. The heart separates the mind from the body and when this chakra is balanced, your whole system has an ability to feel light. Connecting the mind to the body so that you can know spirit is the ultimate work of the heart chakra.

How the Heart Chakra Gets Blocked?
There are many ways that the heart chakra can become blocked. When love is sporadic or withheld in childhood, this can block the heart chakra. Children can develop a blocked heart chakra if one parent abandons the family. While a divorce can be a traumatic experience for a child, it will not have lasting damage on the heart chakra if the other parent remains loving and involved in the child's life.

Any type of rejection throughout life can block the heart chakra. The younger and less developed you are, the more likely a blockage is going to occur. Rejection by friends can have a major impact on the heart chakra, especially if this occurs between the ages of 6-13. Of course, a failure to be accepted in the teenage years can also block the heart chakra.

When there is a rejection that is based on betrayal, the impact is especially important. At any age, when there is an experience of betrayal, the heart chakra can be blocked. This is something that occurs in romantic relationships, of course, but it can also happen in work relationships or among friends. Anything that removes the ability to trust others and, hence, limits the possible connectivity between yourself and others can block the heart chakra.

Again, the general pattern is that the younger you are when you experience betrayal, the more likely the heart chakra is to be blocked. However, this can happen at any age, as we have noted.

Like the other chakras, balance is very important when discussing the heart chakra. An out of balance heart chakra can lead to dysfunctional behaviors, and this can be just as important as a blocked heart chakra depending on the circumstances.

An Overactive Heart Chakra

Previously, we have seen that an overactive chakra can be as damaging as a blocked chakra. In the case of the sacral chakra, we saw that an overactive sacral chakra could lead to problems, such as sexual addiction, drinking, drug use, and gambling.

An overactive heart chakra can also be damaging. When the heart chakra is out of balance, like the sacral chakra, we can see the aspects of the heart chakra expressed at an excessive level.

Let's think about the emotion of love and caring for others. There is a balance that is achieved between the ego/self and the other person. This is true, no matter what type of love we are talking about. In a healthy relationship, you do not only care about the needs of the other person, but you also care about your own needs. Assuming that you have appropriate levels of self-confidence, you will make your own needs known to your partner or friend. We also know that there is a balance, and compromise is an important part of healthy relationships.

This boundary between the self and the other can melt away and vanish when the heart chakra is overactive. In severe cases, people lose their entire sense of identity. When this happens, you may not work to satisfy your own needs at all, and instead, you will be completely attending to the needs of others. You can loosely think of this as being completely selfless, or having a "Mother Theresa" complex. While many people admire those, like Mother Theresa, who devoted their lives to giving to others, the truth is, for most of us, it is an unhealthy way to approach interpersonal relationships. Loving humanity at the complete expense of yourself is not a way to contribute either.

Others with an overactive heart chakra are not quite that dramatic. But they will find that they are constantly getting involved in co-dependent relationships. Healthy adults do not base their relationships on co-dependency, and instead, both contribute to the needs of the other, and each can take care of themselves independently. A relationship that is healthy is bringing together two independent souls to form something that is greater than the sum of their parts. In a co-dependent relationship, you essentially have a needy child and a person with an overactive heart chakra who ends up playing the role of a parent figure. A large part of the relationship will be based on the person with the overactive heart chakra, supporting the needs of the other person, without having their own needs satisfied.

Another symptom of an overactive heart chakra is being too willing to trust people. We have seen that a blockage can result when trust is betrayed, and trust plays an important role in establishing connections with other people. But the reality of the world is that there are a lot of people out there who are not worthy of trust. They will steal, cheat, and hurt other people. When you lack proper discernment, you will find yourself getting into relationships of this type, and it will cost you in many ways. Often, a person with an overactive heart chakra is going to be too willing to trust and accept people, and they will suffer as a result when people not worthy of trust get intimately involved in their lives and end up taking and destroying.

This brings us to another aspect of someone with an overactive chakra. When your heart chakra is overactive, you are going to say yes to everything. You might find that you are always giving other people money, even when it ends up hurting you. Or you might never properly meet your own needs for health, exercise, and *me* time because you are always saying yes to anyone. Although this can affect people of both genders, women tend to be the "yes" people more often than men do.

Another indicator of an overactive heart chakra is that you are constantly and easily getting involved in love relationships. You might find yourself "falling in love" frequently and then jumping from person to person. When the heart chakra is open but healthy and balanced, you should not fall in love easily. You will be open to love, but you will also be discriminating and careful.

The bottom line with an overactive heart chakra is that it is going to be associated with the complete erosion of the ego and self.

Foods for the Heart Chakra
Green colored foods are very helpful for the heart chakra. You can eat green vegetables, including spinach, broccoli, and green beans. You can also use olive oil and eat avocados. Green olives are also good, along with green peppers. Basically, any green vegetables can be included in your meals for this purpose, and kiwi is a green fruit, along with lime, which can help heal the heart chakra. Think of innovative ways to incorporate lime into your diet. Highly energetic foods can also help, including types of meat that are pinkish. With this in mind, consider salmon. Pork can also be consumed for this purpose, and you can also eat prime rib.

Essential Oils for the Heart Chakra
When thinking about healing the heart chakra, think about igniting compassion and connection. Rose oil can be used to help you expand and develop the heart chakra. The pleasant scent of rose oil will help to open up the heart and bring about feelings of joy and empathy, as well as promoting a feeling of calm. Neroli oil with its citrus scents will help you establish a fundamental baseline for the heart chakra, helping to open it

while keeping you from losing your sense of self. Marjoram, with its green colors, is also a good essential oil to use for healing when traumatic events may have blocked your heart chakra.

Colors for the Heart Chakra
The colors you want to surround yourself with to heal the heart chakra are shades of green. You can use various tones of green, and it can be helpful to wear green items of clothing and green crystals (see below). You can use green pillows, drapes, and sheets to promote the green energy that is associated with the heart chakra.

Crystals for the Heart Chakra
Many crystals can be used with the heart chakra, including the green emerald and jade. The choice of color can be based on what aspects of the heart chakra are giving you the most trouble. If the problem is general in nature, stick to naturally green-colored stones. If it is primarily romantic love giving you problems, you can use rose quartz to promote healing.

Meditations for the Heart Chakra

- This meditation will open your heart chakra, and as with the sacral meditation, you may feel some intense and powerful feelings arise. Open to your feelings and let them come. Try not to hold anything back that you might be thinking or feeling. We hold a lot of pain and trauma in our hearts and oftentimes, even when we feel like we are healthy in this area, there is always something that is deeply hidden that needs some love and attention.
- Begin seated comfortably, in a chair, or on the floor in a lotus pose.
- Focus on your breath. Take some long inhales and exhales to the ground and connect you to your meditation.

- Breathe into your heart space and see its energy. Picture the emerald green color and notice how it feels. Big? Small? Quiet? Tight? Expansive?
- Continue to breathe into this place and explore the energy of the heart chakra. What images are popping up? What thoughts and ideas? Do you already feel enough love in your life? Are you feeling like you love yourself enough?
- As you get closer to opening to these ideas and feelings, spend time with each one. Is there one that pops up the most? If so, then the idea, image, or emotion wants you to spend some quality time looking at it. Where does it take you? What, or who, do you see when you follow that feeling? How is it making you feel?
- Connect to these realities and meditate on each part of your heart that is asking for you to connect to the information. You may notice a shift in your energy as you look. You may feel like crying out loud, followed by a sense of inner peace and calm after you have given yourself release.
- Move your hands to your heart and place your hand's palms down over your heart center. Breathe into your hands and feel the green light and energy of this chakra as you breathe.
- With your hands over your heart, you can say quietly in your mind, or out loud, these words, or something similar: "I am love. I have the right to love and be loved. I am capable of giving and receiving love to others and from others, as well as myself. I choose to create a loving attitude in my life as I embrace all people and all of my experiences with them. I am practicing self-awareness through love. I am connected to my heart as a sensitive, tender, and receptive person. I love to learn how to work with loving energy in my life. I release any past hurts about my heart that has caused me to stay closed off here. I know it is okay to protect myself and my heart from being hurt, and I am

also open-hearted at the same time. I will connect more fully through my heart and feelings as I experience life. I am ready to offer love to myself and others."

- After you have said or thought these words, return your focus to your breath for several moments. As you feel ready to close out your meditation, remove your hands from your heart and wrap your arms around your body in a hug. Hold yourself for as long as you like and really give yourself an opportunity to feel held (at least a few minutes.) Continue breathing deeply as you embrace yourself.

Throat Chakra Guided Meditation

The fifth chakra is how we speak the truth of our life. When you are in alignment with the fifth chakra you are able to communicate openly about what must be said in order for you to stay in alignment and balance with your life as a person and a soul. The fifth chakra is the color blue and is connected to the element known as ether. Ether is where you begin to leave the earthly realms. It is beyond the atmosphere of air and it is here that the world of sound is open to our lives.

Here is the right to speak and communication is the main energetic reality of the throat chakra. The thyroid gland is connected to this chakra, and it regulates body temperature and metabolism. If you have any thyroid issues, either excessive or deficient production of hormones here, then you may have had or still have issues with communication or speaking your truth. There are other factors that create chemical imbalances in the body, so it is important to examine all angles, but having a blocked throat chakra can lead to problems with the thyroid.

This chakra is also connected to the bronchial tubes, vocal chords, respiratory system, tongue, mouth, and esophagus. The health of these organs is directly linked to the health of this chakra. If you are a chain smoker and you have no intention of

quitting cigarettes, then you will likely never heal this chakra, which will lead to a lot of issues in the rest of chakras as well.
When you have a balanced and open throat chakra you are good at communicating your feelings, thoughts, ideas, creativity, emotions, and understanding of yourself. It is good communication and resonance with yourself and with other people. Self-expression is the main issue of the throat chakra and when it is blocked there can be strong issues with identifying the truth of the self.
Blockages in this chakra relate to repressed or blocked emotions that cannot be released, blocked creativity, and issues with listening to others due to an overabundance of unreleased thoughts and feelings. Physically, it can manifest as sore throats, tight neck and shoulders, and a residual cough. A deficiency in this chakra would appear as someone who rarely speaks up at all, even when called upon to talk. Excesses in this chakra are the opposite: someone who cannot stop talking but isn't really speaking the truth. This can be an issue of the self as well in the sense that if you cannot stop talking, you cannot listen to others or yourself to find the truth.
The ability to communicate your truth is the sign of a clear and balanced throat chakra. It will take a lot of time to truly identify what causes issues in this chakra because of how it connects to others more than other chakras because it is how we communicate and talk to people. There are always reasons for having a blocked throat chakra and you will have to find the source of that energy by digging through all of the chakras together.

How the Throat Chakra Gets Blocked?
Experiences that are negative with respect to communicating your truth or ideas can result in a throat chakra blockage. Again, if this happens in childhood or adolescence, the impact is going to be strongly felt. If parents or guardians mock a child when the child comes to them with ideas or the truth, this can be very damaging and work to block the throat chakra.

As you get older, the throat chakra can become blocked if people mock or disregard your thoughts and ideas. That can be a potent weapon used by those who are abusive.

Physical Symptoms of a Blocked Throat Chakra
Physical symptoms of a blocked throat chakra are typically centered on causing difficulties speaking. Laryngitis is a common problem among those with a blocked throat chakra. Sore throats often that cannot be traced to a specific cause are also tied to a blocked throat chakra. A scratchy or dry throat often manifests when there is a blocked throat chakra, and you might feel like you always have to clear your throat. Neck pain or oral problems can also take place as a result. Recurrent biting of the tongue, creating discomfort, and soreness can be related to a blocked throat chakra. Dental problems, including toothaches, are also a possible symptom. Sometimes, the problem may not be in the immediate area, but rather in chronic sinus problems or allergies that can make communicating more difficult. You might even have pains in your hands or wrists, as these can make it difficult to type on a computer or send text messages.

In general, any problem that makes it more difficult to speak or to speak with a voice loud and clear enough for others to understand what you are saying, especially if this is a chronic or recurrent problem, is probably a symptom of a throat chakra that is blocked. When serious physical problems manifest, you should consult a medical doctor to take care of the immediate problem, but then you should work on the throat chakra to deal with the long-term energetic problems that are leading to the blockage and then causing these issues to develop in the first place.

Foods for the Throat Chakra
There are many foods that are useful for healing the throat chakra and maintaining its health. You are going to want to

look for foods that are bluish in color, but purple-colored foods work as well. Blueberries and blackberries are excellent foods that can help to heal the throat chakra, besides the general health benefits that they provide. Dark-colored grapes of any shade can also help to heal the throat chakra. There are also purple varieties of potatoes that can be included in your diet as a part of the healing process for the throat chakra.

Essential Oils for the Throat Chakra
When using essential oils to heal the throat chakra, choose varieties that are calming and helpful for sore throats. You should also choose varieties that can help maintain and enhance your sense of well-being. Geranium is a good choice, as this citrusy oil is often used for sore throats. Jasmine oil can also be a good selection. Jasmine has been known to help with problems related to a hoarse voice. Many people have problems with hoarseness when they have a blocked throat chakra. Consider using jasmine oil if you have chronic problems with a hoarse voice.

One consideration with essential oils when working on healing the throat chakra is that you should take into account the fact that the throat chakra is a spiritual chakra, with a relatively high level of energetic vibration. Frankincense is a good oil to use with healing the throat chakra due to its elevated energetic frequency and its role as a spiritual and holy oil.

Colors for the Throat Chakra
Blue and aquamarine colors are associated with the throat chakra. Turquoise is also an excellent color that will help you to heal the throat chakra. When you are working on healing the throat chakra, you can decorate your home in varying shades of blue, from light to darker blues. The darker the shade of blue and the lower the level of green components in the coloring, the more spiritual the energy is. So, you might want to choose your shades appropriately, using darker colors

if you feel that a blocked throat chakra is manifesting more in character issues like gossiping, lying, or not keeping your word. If your blocked throat chakra is manifesting in insecurities while speaking, or keeping things to yourself that you want or need to communicate to others, opt for more light shades and include colors of blue that are mixtures of blues and greens, such as aquamarine and turquoise. For most people, when you are working on healing the throat chakra, a mixture of these colors is preferred so that you can have a healing energy that will help with all aspects of your consciousness related to the throat chakra.

You can also wear blue colors while working on healing the throat chakra. Wear blue colors when meditating or doing yoga, and you can also wear blue colors throughout the day.

Crystals for the Throat Chakra
Many good crystals are available for helping to heal the throat chakra, and due to their vibrant and pleasing colors, they make good jewelry items that can be worn to help promote the energetic frequency of an open throat chakra. As with the colors that you wear or fill your home with, you can select different varieties of stones and crystals to impact the energy vibrational range of the throat chakra.

Turquoise is a stunningly beautiful stone that can be used when healing the throat chakra. It can be worn and is a common stone used in jewelry. You can also spend time looking at and holding large turquoise stones, and feel the calming energy as it surrounds you and flows through your body.

For truth, use lapis lazuli, a stunning stone with darker blue colors that are not expensive to obtain. You can also use a blue sapphire for this purpose. These stones will help you speak your truth and help you avoid problems related to gossiping or talking badly about others. They will also help you to hold the truth in your dealings with other people and keep your word.

Meditations for the Throat Chakra

- You can begin this meditation either in a chair, sitting on the floor, or lying on your back.
- Place yourself in a comfortable position and focus on your breathing. Connect to your body and allow yourself to become grounded and relaxed.
- The throat wants to make noise and so you may want to arrange to be in a space where it is okay for you to be loud, or verbally expressive.
- Continue your breathing by performing the alternating nostril breath technique you learned about. Try a few rounds of this to get you more closely connected to your upper body with your breathing technique.
- If you are in a seated position, try doing a few neck rolls and stretches to open up your neck energy.
- Focus on your breath and keep it relaxed and deep.
- Place your tongue on the roof of your mouth. And take a long, deep breath through your nostrils. As you exhale, begin to intone an "L" sound, like you are about to say "La." Intone this sound for 3 breath cycles on inhaling and then intoning as you exhale. Try to draw out the sounds as long as you can through your breath.
- Following the same breathing instructions from step 7, you will make a humming sound. Start by intoning "hum" and when you close your mouth to make the "M" sound, keep your lips together so that you can feel them vibrating. Keep your mouth relaxed. Repeat this intonation 3 times, through your inhales and exhales.

- Next, you will make a "Ha" sound. Let your tongue and jaw relax and drop as you open up to let the "Ha" come out through your exhale. Repeat 3 times.
- As you begin making these noises and finish the L, Hum, Ha cycles, allow yourself to improvise noise. Make any noise that feels normal to you, or like it has the urge to be released. Relax into it. Try not to control what comes out.
- Pay attention to your energy here. Are you trying to control the sounds coming out of your body? Do you feel connected to your voice, or does it sound foreign to you?
- When you are finished making these sounds, return your focus to your breathing and relax. You can say the following affirmations, preferably out loud, to keep your throat chakra awakened and open: "My voice is my own and I want to be heard. I have things to say and that is okay. I am willing to experience other words from other people as much as I am willing to experience my own voice. I communicate well. I am able to speak the truth of myself and what I know. I am a powerful instrument of sound and vibration. I have honest thoughts, feelings, and words that I would like to say. I have the right to talk openly, as much as I have the right to not talk when I don't want to. I am capable of understanding my own words of truth."
- Feel free to alter the words to reflect your personal experience with this chakra energy. Continue to breathe deeply for several minutes before moving forward with your day.

Third Eye Chakra Guided Meditation

The brow or Third eye chakra is located between the eyes just above your eyebrows. This location is where we place the "third eye", the all-knowing, all-seeing eye of light. There are several cultures that honor this area of the body. You may have seen people with a painted eye on their forehead, or even a small, red dot painted at this chakra center. There is a long history of knowing this place in the self and it comes from a human desire to "see" all that is and to witness what is beyond our knowledge of the universe.

The sixth chakra is the color indigo and is connected to the element of light. Here is the right to see. This means that you see beyond what is available to your organic eyes on the third dimension. This is the place of intuition and clairvoyance, dreams and visions, and perceiving visually that which is not directly in front of your eyes. The eyes and brain are connected to this chakra, as well as the pituitary gland which regulates and governs the hormones of all the other glands in the endocrine system.

When you have a balanced brow chakra, you are aligned with another dimension of reality and you can see what others cannot. This is the landscape of other energies that you can connect with and tap into and have the knowledge to perceive it as a reality and not a made-up fantasy. Many people have trouble unlocking this chakra due to skeptical beliefs about what is possible and what is not. It is especially a challenge for those who have harsh or severe critical judgements about other people's lifestyle choices, living circumstances, and attitudes toward their own lives. Many people behave in a negative way when they are not aligned with this chakra due to a lack of trust on the inside and an inability to truly "see" the truth.

Sometimes, blockages here can manifest as strong headaches, low energy in the eye leading to visual perception issues, such as poor eyesight, nightmares, and hallucinations. Although you will be seeing things from the dimension connected to the third eye, a hallucination comes from an excessive amount of energy around this chakra and is linked to the crown chakra being hindered or closed. When both are open then you will be more aligned with the truth of what you "see".

After the throat chakra, you enter the realm of the perceiver and the psychic realms of knowing. Many people live in their heads, overthinking every detail of life and the day and the future. All of that wasted energy ends up blocking the natural cycle of connecting to the energy of the universe through the third eye. Limiting beliefs live here as well as a lack of compassion for all other life and others. The thoughts and perceptions that you have lain here and if you have inherited limiting beliefs from your family members or society, then you are looking at a blockage in your brow chakra.

The energy of this chakra is closely connected to the crown chakra and the realms of magic and mystery. Opening this chakra means opening your life to what seems impossible but what is actually a reality and always will be.

The Unbroken Whole of Reality
Western thought tends to want to breakdown the world into discrete things and steps. You can think of this as the "mechanical" view of the universe that our culture shares. We view the universe and everything in it as being distinct and individualistic.

The true nature of the universe is a duality. The universe does contain discrete individual things and beings within it, but the view that they are independent and completely individualistic is an illusion. At once, while there are individual things and beings, there is also an unbroken whole and totality. You are an individual inside the universe, but you are also the universe itself, a small discrete corner of it that is able to be an isolated individual while also being connected to the unbroken whole.

The third eye is the first chakra that has an aspect that is holistic. The third eye connects you to the fabric of reality beyond. By opening the third eye, you will enhance your ability to see and experience the unbroken totality of all that is. The third eye will help you to connect with your inner wisdom and also the spiritual wisdom that exists as a part of the Higher Self and the Universal Consciousness.

Some people can develop rapidly in their spiritual growth, and you may find that in addition to lucid dreaming, you are able to experience astral traveling. Do not worry if these abilities do not come to you right away. Everyone will develop their spirituality in unique ways and at their own pace. You may be experiencing astral traveling while in the dream state, and not even be consciously aware of it. Many people dismiss those experiences as "dreams." Try to look at things in a different way and then see how that changes your perceptions of the world.

The third eye chakra can also open up communication with spirit guides. In short, think of the third eye as opening a gateway to the spiritual and the divine. The third eye is the way that you can readily access information and knowledge that comes through means other than the five physical senses.

Wisdom and Ethics
The third eye is also the seat of wisdom. It is through the third eye that you can fully integrate the creativity of the sacral chakra, the self-confidence and leadership characteristics of the solar plexus chakra, and the expressive abilities of the throat chakra. As we have mentioned before, not all ideas are good ideas. But by developing and opening the third eye chakra, you can add a touch of wisdom to the creative forces that originate in the sacral chakra, and turn your ideas toward the good of humanity and of all life.

Opening the third eye will also help you become more balanced, tolerant, and open-minded. A strong connection to your own inner wisdom, as well as the collective wisdom of the Universal Consciousness, is a benefit of a third eye awakening.

There are different aspects of psychic awareness that different people will tune into two different degrees. Lucid dreaming may be stronger in some people as compared to others. Some will become clairvoyant, which means you are "clear seeing," and able to receive visions. These visions may be visions of the future, or they may provide knowledge of information and events that you could not be aware of through normal means. Others will develop a strong sense of clairaudience, which means "clear hearing," where information is revealed in the form of sounds or voices. *Claircognizance* is simply clear-knowing, which means you will suddenly "know" something.

All of us have these gifts to one degree or another, so they are not mutually exclusive. Don't worry about having one or the other or getting bogged down in focusing on the individual definitions. Instead, let yourself experience things as they come to you. Simply being open will reveal the experiences to you in due time.

The third eye is also closely associated with your direction in life and your sense of purpose. Often, this is going to be experienced as a higher sense of purpose. It will be a sense of purpose that transcends mere career or material aspirations. It may also take the form of a sense of purpose that goes beyond individualism and is communal, spiritual, and ethical in nature.

How the Third Eye Chakra Gets Blocked?
The third eye can become blocked when your experiences are discounted. For example, many of us have spiritual or psychic experiences but are mocked when we share them with others. When you are younger, especially in childhood, having your experiences discounted or mocked can have a large impact on the third eye, causing it to become blocked.

Our larger society also causes many people to have a blocked third eye. The larger society has adopted a viewpoint that is materialistic in outlook. The larger society believes there is nothing beyond the physical world and that science is all that there is and the only way of knowing. It discounts psychic experiences and writes off intuition as wishful thinking or coincidence. Belief in spirituality is seen as quaint, and spiritual experiences are deemed to be illusions, the product of an overactive mind, or even the product of mental illness.

We are not consciously aware of it, but when these attitudes are all around us, constantly expressed and pervasive, they infuse and train the subconscious, making it more difficult for us to open the third eye and to doubt any psychic or intuitive experiences that we have. Without realizing it, we may even adopt a skeptical attitude steeped in materialism and scientism that prevents us from experiencing the full richness of the world that is around us.

The third eye can also become blocked as a result of traumatic experiences. Any experience that leaves you with post-traumatic stress disorder or lingering effects of abuse that occurred during childhood can work to block the third eye.

Nightmares
This symptom deserves special mention. If your third eye becomes blocked or overactive, you might find that you suffer from extremely vivid and unpleasant dreams or nightmares. Often, these dreams will entail a spiritual component that feels like an evil presence. You may wake up from these dreams feeling threatened and uncomfortable. If these types of dreams become recurrent, this is a definite symptom that you are having problems related to the third eye chakra. Immediate attention should be devoted to meditation, affirmations, and the use of crystals to help direct the correct energy.

The Pineal Gland
The third eye is said, by some, to originate from the pineal gland, a small organ that is closely associated with the brain. Many in the medical community will assert that the pineal

gland serves no useful purpose, but in fact, it is a relay station of sorts when it comes to the reception and transmission of psychic energy. The pineal gland can become calcified, and one of the most important factors in the calcification of this important organ is the consumption of fluoridated water. If you can eliminate the use of water with fluoride in it from your body, then you will go a long way toward healing and decalcifying the pineal gland. By itself, for some people, this is enough to open and awaken their third eye. There are many supplements and tonics you can take to detoxify and decalcify the pineal gland.

The pineal gland is closely associated with our sleep-wake cycle, and when the pineal gland is calcified, you may find that your sleep-wake cycle is impaired. Your circadian rhythm may not be properly tuned to the daylight cycle our bodies are naturally designed for, and you might find that you are a so-called "night owl." You might have trouble getting a full night's sleep and have to take naps often.

Excessive calcium intake can lead to calcification of the pineal gland. To get appropriate levels of calcium, avoid supplements, and get calcium from natural sources instead. There are many natural sources of calcium that can help you get adequate levels, including whole milk, cheese, and leafy green vegetables, like spinach. Avoid synthetic calcium, if possible.

Many people worry about fluoridated toothpaste, but in truth, it is fluoride in the water that is the main concern. If you can eliminate the consumption of fluoridated water, then toothpaste should not be an issue. Just avoid swallowing toothpaste, and the amount of fluoride you will be exposed to, in that case, will be minimal and inconsequential.

In order to decalcify the pineal gland, there are many supplements you can take. The primary substance that people turn to, for this purpose, is iodine. You can take iodine supplements or drops for this purpose. You can also increase the amount of iodine that you are consuming by eating sea kelp. Consider adding dried seaweed to soups, broths, and meals.

Turmeric is also believed to help decalcify the pineal gland by inhibiting the toxic effects of getting too much fluoride in the body. If you continue to use fluoridated toothpaste, a turmeric supplement can help keep you healthy and in balance.
A supplement known as Activator X is also considered helpful when it comes to the pineal gland. Activator X contains the vitamins K1 and K2, which are important for overall health, in addition to assisting with the pineal gland.

Third Eye Awakening
If you start meditating on the third eye, do not be alarmed if you notice unusual symptoms. You might start to feel a pressure sensation in the center of your brow. This is entirely natural, as there is energy flowing through the third eye as it begins to open. You might also experience ringing of the ears, and other unusual symptoms as the third eye fully opens, maybe for the very first time in your life since childhood. You might also be awakened by vivid dreams. Do not be alarmed by this unless the dreams that you are experiencing are of a negative character. Again, as mentioned before, if you have dreams that are negative and extremely vivid or heavy nightmares, then use third eye meditation to rectify the problem. When your third eye is awakened, you are going to have lucid dreaming, but the dreams are not going to be frightening in any way. Rather, the dreams will serve to inform, convey, and enlighten. The dreams that you have when the third eye has been awakened may be so vivid that they are indistinguishable from reality. This is because, in a sense, they are real. Prepare yourself for his possibility by meditation and other techniques.

By healing the heart and throat chakras, you can help to ensure that your experience of a third eye awakening will be positive in nature. Often, the experiences that we have while moving into the more spiritual aspects of the chakras are going to depend on the overall level of spiritual development and growth that you have had up to this point. If you are unprepared, you might find that you are unleashing energies that you are ill-equipped to deal with. That can lead to nightmares, bad visions, and other problems. So one thing to consider if you find yourself having negative experiences, such as bad dreams, is to take a step back and work on the heart chakra first. Then work on the throat chakra.

Think about the impact of opening up spiritual and psychic energies when you are steeped in negativity, and possibly lacking love, acceptance, empathy, and truth. This is why it is important to work on the lower chakras before attempting a third eye awakening. All of the chakras should be involved in this process. For example, you need to have a healthy root chakra so that you have an overall sense of safety and security. You also need to have a healthy solar plexus chakra because that chakra is involved in self-confidence and self-assurance, and both of these are going to be important for the ability to accept and manage powerful, intuitive, and psychic energies.

It is also important to recognize that evil does exist in the world and in the universe. That is one reason that awakening the third eye without a basic grounding can lead to problems. Don't misinterpret this. We are not saying that you are a bad person, only that these energies are out there, and they can be stirred up when a person is not properly prepared.

This is why working on the heart chakra is so important. Evil energies can be nullified with love and understanding. By fully healing and opening up the heart chakra, you can maximize the love energy in your spirit. Doing so to the point of attaining higher levels of development is necessary. You will be able to recognize when you have reached this point when you feel and experience unconditional love, empathy, and forgiveness for all humankind.

From here, it is important to ensure that the throat chakra is fully open and healed. Remember our discussion of the throat chakra and how we discussed the impact of gossip or speaking for untrue or bad purposes and the importance of keeping your word. These may sound like basic values, but in fact, they also go straight to the heart of spiritual coherence. The foundation of the good begins with truth. In fact, you can say that truth is central to the concept of good, as opposed to the concept of evil, which finds a friend in deception and lies. From this perspective, you can start to appreciate how important it is to heal the throat chakra, in addition to healing the heart chakra, before you attempt a third eye awakening and connect yourself at a spiritual level to worlds beyond our physical universe.

Foods for the Third Eye Chakra
When you are working on healing and opening the third eye chakra, think in terms of dark-colored and purple foods. Grapes (red, purple, and black), blackberry, and blueberries are excellent foods to include in your diet when you are working on the third eye. In addition, consume eggplant, purple carrots, and purple potatoes.

The idea of mindful eating is also important for the third eye chakra. Remember that with the third eye chakra, we have completely entered the realm of the spiritual. Therefore, your intention and purpose while eating can have an influence on the opening of your third eye. Also, use your intuition. Sometimes, the third eye makes itself known through small signs, and we might not really be aware of them. You can heighten your intuitive abilities by paying more attention to the slightest intuitive impulse. Intuition often makes itself felt when you are making food choices. When you notice that your intuition strikes when it comes to a food choice, rather than overthinking it or worse, doubting the intuition, follow it instead, and consume the foods that your third eye is directing you to consume.

Other foods that help with the third eye are those that are rich in omega-three fatty acids. Try bluefish, salmon, and mackerel. Walnuts are also good for the third eye, and the role that omega-three fatty acids play in protecting brain health is a more practical way that the third eye and the pineal gland can be enhanced.

Essential Oils for the Third Eye Chakra
Aromatherapy and essential oils play a more important role for the third eye and crown chakras than for the lower chakras. Look for powerful holy oils like frankincense and myrrh. Clary, which is made from a purple flower, is also useful for the third eye chakra. Juniper is also helpful. Use aromatherapy to help awaken the third eye and for balance.

Colors for the Third Eye Chakra
The third eye chakra is associated with indigo, which is a bluish-purple color. You can use dark blue colors, along with purple colors when healing the third eye. Due to the spiritual nature of this chakra, I like to involve the use of candles when working on opening it. Use purple or, if you can find them, blue colored candles together. You can light the candles at any time and breathe in the aromas to help unlock third eye energy. It can also be helpful to use purple candles during meditation sessions. You can also decorate your meditation space with dark blue and purple colored items, and wear purple clothing.

Crystals for the Third Eye Chakra

Purple amethyst is a favorite crystal when it comes to the third eye chakra. Typically, this crystal will manifest multiple colors, including white and sometimes, bits of gold. This is a powerful crystal that can channel spiritual level energies. Use it while meditating or as a touchstone, when you are interested in unblocking the third eye. You can also use lapis lazuli with the third eye. This dark blue stone is able to channel energies for the third eye and for the throat chakra, and it is more attuned to the higher vibrational states of the throat chakra and is, therefore, more spiritual in nature. It can be helpful to use it because keeping the throat chakra open and healed is an important part of a third eye awakening.

Meditations for the Third Eye Chakra

- There are a lot of ways to connect to the seat of your higher sight and intuition. This is a simplified form of meditation, but as you become more advanced in your chakra work, you can intuitively transform this meditation to be more appropriate for your present needs.
- Lie on the floor or in a comfortable place where you will not be disturbed. Relax here and become focused on your breathing.
- Spend several minutes focused on your breath. For some people, they will already be guided through their third eye of where to go and can just intuitively follow a meditation from this point.
- If you are not naturally guided through your "sight" then you can work on getting closer to that energy here. Picture your brow chakra. See its color, indigo.
- With your eyes closed, move your eyes to "look" at the place in your head where your third eye is (up and inward.)

- With your eyes focused like this under closed eyelids, spend some time with your deep inhales and exhales. Continue to picture the light and color of your chakra.
- As you look at this energy, see it begin to elongate, like a pole or shaft sticking out of your forehead. Extend it as far as you can. It can go to the roof of your room, house, or apartment building, into the clouds, into the cosmos.
- As you engage with this vision, what do you see? Where are you going? Pay attention to the details. Feel the energy of this connection outside of yourself. You can relax your eyes if they become tired of looking up and in.
- After you have extended your third eye energy up and out of you, relax into your breath and pay attention to any images that come up. You may experience thoughts and feelings as well, and oftentimes they are accompanied by visuals.
- Let your mind reflect on this as you take your "inner journey."
- Spend as long as you need to in this space until the images have ended. Connect with your third eye energy, back down in your forehead, and say in your mind the following words, or something similar: "I can see more than what is in front of my face and eyes. I can see beyond what is here on Earth. I have infinite wisdom and the capacity to look deeply into the great unknown. My sight extends beyond what is normally seen, and I am proud of my openness to the spirit and the beyond. I am not afraid of this gift and look forward to using my intuition regularly. My soul is ancient and wise, and I am ready to heal any past realities that have prevented me from connecting to this truth. I am grateful for my capacity to see."
- Take some time to reflect and breathe here. You may fall asleep in this state, and that is okay. It is rather common when working with this chakra.

- Enjoy the effects of this experience as you go through the rest of your daily activities.

Crown Chakra Guided Meditation

The final chakra is at the crown of the head and is so named. It has the color violet and is associated with the element of thought. This element is beyond the reality of space and time and has no physical form. It is where you expand your consciousness to truly comprehend the reality of all that is in the universe.

Here is the right to know and expanded consciousness is the main goal of this chakra. At the top of the head and located at the cerebral cortex, this chakra is aligned with the spinal cord, brain stem and pineal gland, which regulates biological rhythms and cycles (ex. Sleep/ circadian rhythm).

When you read about or hear people discussing the concept of enlightenment, they are talking about opening the crown chakra. This is the place where you allow all life to shine through you from all around you and how you begin to truly know, not just see. The connection between the brow and the crown chakra is strong because of that very concept. In order to know, you must first see, and a lot of people have a challenge bringing the two together.

Deficiencies in this chakra can look like this: feelings of alienation, depression, boredom, confused by things easily or lack of comprehension, learning difficulties, apathetic nature, overly quizzical about unproven concepts of reality. Excessive energy in this chakra can manifest as being overly intellectual without room for other ideas or thoughts, headiness, arrogance in ideas or mannerisms, unwavering beliefs about a certain idea or concept.

In order to fully come alive to the power of your energetic life force, you have to be able to comprehend a reality beyond what is on the Earth plane. There is no way for you to understand that reality until you become awakened to your own energy through your chakra system. The light inside of all people comes from this chakra and beams down through all of your being, all the way back to the root to give you the clarity of life and purpose that you need to exist fully and openly to the self. It may seem like a long journey, but it has to happen if you want to make yourself see and know the truth of who you are and why you are here in this life.

The crown chakra is the end and the beginning of all that you need to accomplish to ascend into the truth of your soul identity. What this means is that you will begin at the root and start to uncover all of your energy blockages and as you release, clear and unblock, you will find the answers you are looking for in your crown chakra. By that point, you will be ready to end your lack of faith and trust in your energy and begin a new life as a soul alive to the energy of your own being. You will walk in a new way and talk from your point of knowing.

The lessons in the rest of this book are designed to guide you through some ascension processes to help your chakras open and align more with each other, your whole being and your life. The energy that you put forth in these pages will be an answer to your life and help you find what you are looking for from within.

How the Crown Chakra Gets Blocked?

Many things can serve to block the crown chakra, including blockages of lower charkas. In fact, this will surprise many due to its lower location, but a blockage of the heart chakra can cause a blockage of your crown chakra. The reason is that the heart chakra is closely associated with our connection to other people and living beings. Although the heart chakra is associated with our connection to physical beings in the here and now, any connection to a conscious, living entity is associated with a spiritual connection. If you are unable to make a basic connection between yourself and other living, physical beings, this is going to inhibit your ability to form connections with the spiritual world that exists beyond.

As a result, shallow and disconnected or dysfunctional relationships in your physical world can cause your crown chakra to become blocked.

An overdeveloped or hyperactive ego can also lead to a blockage of the crown chakra. While we emphasize the development of a healthy solar plexus chakra, when considering the building and development of the lower, matter-based chakras, we can actually block the crown chakra if we overemphasize the solar plexus chakra and it becomes unbalanced. This is because the solar plexus chakra is associated with the development and elevation of the self or ego, which causes a hyper-development of the self if this is carried too far. In contrast, the crown chakra emphasizes the communion of the self with the Universal Consciousness. It is important to realize that this communion of the self with the Universal Consciousness does not involve the obliteration of the self. Rather, it involves the joining of the self with the larger, and pervasive, universal consciousness. That is, although it may be difficult for you to understand now, it involves the retainment of the self while simultaneously joining your consciousness, together with the unified whole that represents the universe.

Foods for the Crown Chakra
When thinking of foods for the crown chakra, think broadly. White-colored foods like white or yellow carrots and white cauliflower are additions to your diet that can definitely help heal the crown chakra. Moreover, you can include purple foods like eggplant, blueberries, and purple potatoes that we have discussed in conjunction with other chakras. For the crown chakra, it is beneficial to make meals that consist of a mixture of the colors purple, white, and gold, into a single meal. With this in mind, consider mixing together blueberries or blackberries for purple, white potatoes or cauliflower for white, and corn and butter for gold, in order to build a complete meal

for unblocking the crown chakra. Other yellow or golden foods can be helpful for the crown chakra, including yellow squash, carrots, parsnip, almond, walnut, and sesame seeds.

Essential Oils for the Crown Chakra
When it comes to essential oils for the crown chakra, the spiritual or holy oils are the best oils to use. Frankincense is an excellent oil to include when healing the crown chakra. It will help you to attain a state of meditative contemplation, spiritual connection, and openness. Vetiver is a good essential oil to use with aromatherapy or in conjunction with other essential oils to promote the healing of the crown chakra. Moreover, this oil can be used to work with the third eye because it promotes vivid dreaming. It will also help you to recall your dreams, which is an important way to promote spiritual awareness. This oil also promotes grounding and relaxation, so it can help you to open your crown chakra. To elevate the frequency of vibration, consider adding helichrysum. This less well-known essential oil is also known as everlasting oil. This essential oil contains energies that are of a higher frequency of vibration and, hence, more spiritual in nature. This high frequency of vibration can help you to unleash the power of your crown chakra.

Colors for the Crown Chakra
The main color for the crown chakra is a deep purple. Pure white, representing the mixture of all the colors of the rainbow, is also an important color associated with the crown chakra. Gold is also associated with the crown chakra, due to its elevation as a spiritual concept. You can wear all of them together when you are working to heal the crown chakra.

Crystals for the Crown Chakra
There are several crystals that are useful for healing and opening the crown chakra. Purple amethyst, which is also used with the third eye chakra, can be of great assistance when

healing the crown chakra. This stone vibrates with high frequency, and it can store, receive, and transmit large amounts of energy. White-colored stones are also useful, including clear quartz and plain quartz. If you have access to it, pure gold is also helpful for work with the crown chakra.

Meditations for the Crown Chakra

- Begin this meditation in a seated position, on the floor, or in a chair. Start with your breath to get grounded in your practice.
- As you focus on breathing, ground your root energy to the place you are sitting. Imagine you have roots growing out of your root and into the floor and through the soil underneath your space.
- As you continue to take slow, relaxing breaths, see your entire chakra system, awake and alive. Picture the energy flowing freely through your whole body.
- While you are picturing this energetic flow in all of the chakras, bring your hands together, palm to palm, and hold them in front of your heart chakra.
- Continue to breathe in and out as you feel your energy flow through all 6 chakras and as you get to the 7th at your crown, see the light of your being shot out of the top of your head, like a colorful rainbow.
- Allow this rainbow of light to be a sustained shaft of energy that connects to the Universe. Feel it connect to the cosmos and beyond.
- See your tree roots holding you to the Earth as you breathe, while the rainbow of light flowing out of your crown connects you to the stars.
- Hold this image in your third eye while you speak, or think the following words, or something similar: "I am one with all energies. I am made of vibration and light, and I

am here to become more in tune with all that is around me. I am a source of positive life-force energy and I witness the whole Universe with my wholeness. I am releasing any fears, doubts, or beliefs I may have carried in my life that I am not one with everything and everyone. I am ready to release any pain and suffering that has held me back from knowing my infinite nature. I am ready to walk through my life path with purpose and the energy I know as my whole self. I trust that I am here for a reason and that we all have a unique and important purpose. I am alive to the energy of creation."

- Visualize any fears that you may have about your energetic potency flow out of the rainbow light from your crown to be released into the cosmos for transformation. Accept your life force as you bring your hands down from your heart.
- Lay your hands, palms up on your knees, and breathe in this state for a while. Smile and enjoy the relaxation of being grounded to Earth and connected to the Universe around you.

How to identify your blocked chakras

What Causes Chakra Blockages

Chakra blockages are caused by several factors - ***belief system, career, living situation, financial situation and relationships.*** Traumatic experiences such as abuse, accident, and loss of a loved one may also cause chakra blockages. Negative emotions such as anxiety, anger, stress, and fear may also put your chakras out of balance.

For example, being physically and emotionally abused by a former partner may cause heart chakra imbalance. You might have ended up closing yourself out to potential romantic partners. You may also tend to feel empty most of the time.

Your root chakra represents the foundation of your being. So, if your parents do not have enough money when you were growing up and they failed to provide enough for you, you'll most likely experience root chakra blockage. You may constantly fear that you do not have enough. You may also constantly worry about money.

Opening and Closing the Chakras
The opening and closing of your chakras work a lot like an energetic defense system. When you experience something traumatic or negative, the associated chakra will close itself to keep the negative energy out. If you are clinging to low frequency feelings such as anger, guilt, or blame, you'll experience chakra blockage.

Holding on to the following low frequency emotions for a long period can cause chakra blockage:

- Anger
- Pain
- Resentment
- Jealousy
- Covert hostility
- Grief
- Apathy
- Hopelessness
- Sadness
- Apathy
- Regret
- Pessimism
- Worry
- Blame
- Discouragement
- Shame
- Powerlessness

- Depression
- Disappointment
- Frustration
- Despair
- Guilt

The following positive or high frequency emotions can raise your vibrations and help open your chakras:

- Love
- Joy
- Acceptance
- Eagerness
- Optimism
- Passion
- Hopefulness
- Contentment
- Faith
- Belief

So, to keep your chakras balanced, you must let go of egoism. You must choose to act with love.

Chakras and Empaths
Many people have open chakras. These people are called empaths. They are highly sensitive people. They easily pick up other people's energy so they find public places overwhelming. They also know when someone is not being honest with them. They are creative and they have a strong need for solitude. They feel weak when they are exposed to toxic people.
Empaths should keep their chakras guarded and balanced. They should carry protective stones such as rose quartz, black

tourmaline, amethyst, and malachite. These stones help balance emotions and remove anxieties and negative energy.

Symptoms of blockage

Chakra blockage can wreak havoc in your life. It can lead to weight fluctuations, health problems, financial problems, and relationship problems. It can lead to crippling phobias and physical issues. It can also lead to depression, anxiety, and other mental health issues.

When your chakras are blocked, you'd feel that something in your life is off. You'd have persistent worries, such as money problems, career difficulties, and fear of intimacy. If you feel that your finances, relationships, career, and everything else in your life is crumbling down, it's time to act.

Here's a guide that can help you determine if one or two of your chakras are blocked.

Crown Chakra Blockage

Your crown chakra is the gateway to wisdom and enlightenment. It connects you to the universe and everything in it. A blocked crown chakra can lead to spiritual connection, it can also lead to a number of symptoms including:

- Loneliness
- Lack of direction
- Inability to build a genuine connection with others
- Inability to set and maintain goals
- Nerve pain
- Learning difficulties
- Indecisiveness
- Lack of inspiration and joy
- Confusion
- Over intellectualism
- Dominance

- Nightmares
- Epilepsy
- Brain tumors
- Amnesia
- Delusions

Having an underactive crown chakra leads to confusion, spiritual addiction, catatonia, and over intellectualism. This means that if you're a "know-it-all", your chakra may be spinning too slowly.

Overactive crown chakra leads to dominance, depression, greed, headaches, and disconnection from reality. This is the reason why you should make sure that your crown chakra is balanced. There are many ways to do this, which we will discuss in the later chapters.

You can also say the following affirmations to help balance your crown chakra:

- I am complete.
- I am one with the Divine Energy.
- I am a spiritual being.
- I have faith in God.
- I believe.
- I go beyond my limiting beliefs.
- I am aligned with the Divine Energy.
- I am wise.
- I am open to questions
- I trust God.
- I understand.
- I am open to enlightenment.
- I am open for pure bliss.
- My consciousness is growing and expanding.

- God's love heals me.
- I let my fantasy run free.
- I am open minded.
- I accept myself totally.
- I am enlightened.
- I feel pure joy.

Root Chakra Blockage
The Muladhara chakra governs your ability to connect with the world. This chakra is extremely sensitive. This chakra represents security and stability.
When this chakra is blocked, you'd experience the following symptoms:

- Kidney infections
- Tumors in the rectal area
- Reproductive health issues
- Laziness
- Addictive behavior
- Anemia
- Circulatory issues
- Bladder irritations
- Anxiety
- Depression
- Low self esteem
- Leg pain
- Lower back pain
- Fear of change
- Materialism
- Anxiety attacks
- Lack of energy and motivation

- Insecurities

When you feel a lot of these symptoms, take time to sit down, breathe, and say these affirmations:

- I am grounded.
- I am safe.
- I am powerful.
- I am wealthy.
- I have enough.
- I am brave.
- I have enough.
- I am centered.
- I trust myself.
- I am open to possibilities.
- I am safe.
- I am loved.
- I am not afraid to change
- I am not afraid to trust people.
- I nurture my body with clean water, food, exercise, and water.

Sacral Chakra
Your sacral chakra is the center of your feelings and emotions. It is also the center of your sexuality and creativity. When your sacral chakra is balanced, you radiate sincere friendliness and warmth, without being too clingy. When you have a balanced sacral chakra, you have strong intuition, energy, and a strong zest for life. You're also compassionate and emotionally stable.
But when this chakra is off, you'll also feel that something's not right in your life. It could lead to various symptoms such as:

- Guilt
- Lack of motivation
- Infertility issues
- Low back pain
- Low libido
- Inability to orgasm
- Depression
- Low self-esteem
- Jealousy
- Detachment
- Fear
- Lack of vitality
- Fear of change
- Diabetes
- Sexual dysfunction
- Lack of flexibility
- Diarrhea
- Weight loss
- Loss of appetite
- Chameleon personality
- Depression
- Menstrual issues
- Lack of focus
- Poor boundaries
- Bipolar mood swings
- Immobilized by fear
- Aloofness

When your sacral chakra spins too fast, you often experience jealousy, mood swings, and sexual addictions. You often consider people as sex objects and you may be overly dramatic. If your sacral chakra is underactive, you may have digestive disorders and sexual issues. You may be oversensitive and shy. If you're overly shy or you've been acting like a drama queen lately, then you should say the following affirmations daily:

- I am confident.
- I am comfortable with my sexuality.
- I accept myself.
- I am at peace.
- I am radiant.
- I listen to my own truth.
- I respect my emotions.
- I have the capability to provide for my own needs.
- I trust my instinct.
- My sexuality is sacred.
- I am enough.
- I am graceful.
- I am creative.
- I am grateful for everything in my life.
- The universe is filled with beauty.

Solar Plexus Chakra
When your solar plexus is balanced, you have complete control over your thoughts and emotions. Your small mind or ego won't influence your actions. You fully accept your place in the universe. You love and appreciate yourself and others. You can also easily see the uniqueness and importance of the people around you.
When this chakra is balanced, you have a healthy self-esteem. You have good relationships.
If this chakra is unbalanced, you're overly critical and judgmental. You'll easily find fault in others. You may be

demanding and may have extreme emotional problems. You may be rigid and stubborn. You are also more likely to engage in a codependent relationship. You'll also experience the following symptoms:

- Diabetes
- Binge eating
- Constipation
- Lack of self-control
- Gallstones
- Hepatitis
- Inability to lead others
- Stomach ulcers
- Self-esteem issues
- Allergies
- Pancreatitis
- Reflux problems
- Obesity
- Inability to reach goals
- Stomach ulcers
- Growing addiction

When your solar plexus chakra is not balanced, you can say the following affirmations:

- I am strong and powerful.
- I am empowered.
- I make my own choices.
- I treat myself respectfully.
- I trust myself.
- I am worthy of love and kindness.

- I am authentic.
- I direct my own life.
- I am at peace with myself.
- I am responsible for my life.
- I release my desires and appetite to the universe.
- I accept my responsibilities.
- I make my own choices.
- I am successful.
- I am in control.

You can also do yoga, color therapy, and other chakra balancing tools that we will discuss later in this book.

Blocked Heart Chakra

Holding a grudge or a traumatic event may block your heart chakra. Repressed feelings can also negatively affect the function of your heart chakra and can lead to:

- Heartlessness
- Fear of getting hurt
- Loneliness
- Social anxiety
- Shyness
- Holding grudges
- Inability to give or receive freely
- Fear and suspicion in romantic relationships and friendships
- You are extremely self-centered.
- You feel unworthy of love.
- You feel embarrassed of your failures.
- You easily lose patience.

- You have difficulty breathing and you have allergies.
- You have heart and lung issues.
- You may experience insomnia.

When you have an overactive heart chakra, you are unable to say no to others. You try your best to please others and you are desperate for other people's love and appreciation.
When you have an underactive chakra, you feel like you're cold, shy, and resentful.
The heart chakra controls most of your emotions. So, if you want to achieve emotional stability, it is important to keep this chakra balanced. If your heart chakra is not working well, you can say these affirmations:

- Love is all there is.
- I am worthy of love and respect.
- I love myself just as I am.
- I forgive myself and I forgive others.
- I trust in the power of love.
- My heart is filled with love.
- I open my heart to unconditional love.
- I love my life.
- I am compassionate.
- I openly receive love.
- I am not afraid to love.
- I am compassionate and forgiving.
- I am grateful.
- I embrace love.
- I open my heart to love.

These affirmations will help heal emotional wounds. If you have problems giving and receiving love, say these affirmations in the morning after you wake up and at night before you fall asleep.

Throat Chakra

As mentioned earlier, this chakra governs our ability to tell the truth. So, habitual lying is not just a character flaw, it is also a symptom of blocked throat chakra.

Throat chakra blockage has also a number of other emotional and physical symptoms such as:

- Extreme shyness
- Social anxiety
- Inability to express thoughts
- Inconsistency in actions and speech
- Social anxiety
- Detachment
- Stubbornness
- Inhibited creativity
- Detachment
- Chronic sore throat
- Laryngitis
- Frequent headaches
- Mouth ulcers
- Thyroid problems
- Neck pain
- Hoarseness

People with blocked throat chakra are deceptive, manipulative, domineering, anxious, and insecure. So, if you're constantly insecure or envious, take time to say the following affirmations:

- I have a voice.

- My opinions matter.
- I speak the truth.
- I uphold the truth.
- I am free of all delusions
- I claim my voice.
- I am speaking my personal truth.
- I let go of the chains that are holding me back.
- I have a beautiful voice.
- I am not afraid to speak my feelings.
- I listen to others with others.
- I am content and truthful.
- I value honesty.

Important.

- I am not afraid to speak up.

Third Eye Chakra Blockage
Third eye chakra blockage can wreak havoc to your health. It could disrupt your day and it could lead to serious mental issues. It's normal to feel crazy on some days. But, if you're feeling crazy too often, then you may have a blocked third eye chakra.
This chakra governs your psychic abilities and intuition. So, if you feel that your intuition is out of whack or you get deceived easily, you may be experiencing third eye chakra blockage.
If your third eye chakra is blocked, you'll experience these symptoms:

- Poor vision
- Seizure
- Migraines

- Sciatica
- Inability to focus
- Oversensitivity
- Delusions
- Depression
- Paranoia
- Anxiety
- Fear of success
- Lack of clarity
- Paranoia
- Cognitive problems
- Psychotic behavior
- Severe retardation
- Lack of discipline
- Pride

If your third eye chakra spins too fast, you're proud, dominant, manipulative, and you may be living in a fantasy world. If it spins too slowly, you're often confused, undisciplined, afraid of success, oversensitive, and unable to focus.

So, if you have an imaginary fiancé or you're experiencing other third eye chakra blockage, then you must take action by saying these affirmations:

- I see clearly.
- I have a strong intuition.
- I have an open sixth sense.
- I am important.
- I am intelligent.
- I am open.
- I am ready to see the truth.

- I am wise.
- I trust my intuition.
- I forgive myself for my past mistakes.
- I accept myself.
- I am open to bliss and inspiration.
- I am at peace.
- All is well.
- I release my past.

When you feel that something is off in your life, one or two of your chakras may be unbalanced. Later on in this book, you'll learn tips on how to heal and balance your chakras.

Your healing journey starts with a lesson in how to help your chakras shift into awakening after many months, years, or a lifetime of not working with this energy consciously. When you are preparing to work with letting go of blocks in your chakras and you are ready to finally allow your healing process to begin, you can follow many of these simple steps and guidelines for each chakra.

When you are looking at them, keep a journal handy and some other tools I will share with you in the following list. You don't have to use all of these tools however they are an added benefit while you are working with healing your chakras.

- Clean, pure water for drinking
- Palo Santo, or sage incense for purification
- Candlelight
- Crystals or gemstones
- Yoga mat, or pillow for comfortable sitting or lying down. You can also lie down on a bed or couch.
- A blanket for warmth

Each of these simple tools can have a powerful impact on your ability to effectively clear, unblock and balance your energy. The use of each of them is not required to do this work, however, for a better and more powerful result, these tools are an excellent way to impact the healing process.

Having a glass or bottle of clean, pure water handy is helpful because you will want to flush your system of toxins in your purification process. Even though you will be clearing old and unwanted energy from your person, it can shift the chemical balances inside of your various internal systems, releasing stored toxins into your bloodstream. Flushing out these toxins with clean, pure water is detoxifying and will help your energy release and flow out of your body.

Certain types of incense are purifying to the energy in and around the body. Many cultures have used incense to help clear energy or to provide a clear environment for ritual purposes. Clearing your chakras is a kind of ritual; it is a ritual of healing. Having Palo Santo incense (wooden sticks) or dried sage bundles will help you begin the process of cleansing your auras and your chakras as well. The lighting of incense is also a signal to yourself that you are preparing to work on your energy and healing and it has a way of preparing your mind and spirit for the process.

In addition to igniting your ceremonial energy clearing with incense, you can also light a candle to represent a chakra. Candles come in a variety of sizes and colors and it can be a fun part of the experience to find candles that are colorful like the chakras are. For example, while working on your root chakra energy, you may want to light a red candle, or when working on your throat chakra, you can light a blue one. Having a candle isn't a necessity, but the warmth of light and the ritual of lighting the fire energy is like lighting the flame of your chakra energy, bringing it into the light so it can be regarded and cared for.

Crystal and gemstones are incredibly powerful tools. The bigger they are, the stronger their energy. There are hundreds of different kinds of crystals and stones and many of them are perfect for use in clearing your energy. You may already have some that you are using, or that you feel a connection to and you can use these stones in your healing practice. You can also purchase them on line or from a local retailer of crystals and gems. There are many shops that provide a wide range of these tools and are easy to find with a little bit of searching. Find the crystal that feels right for you. They all have an energy and as you are looking for the right one, pick it up and your hand and see how it feels. If you don't feel any energy from the crystal or stone, that's okay, too. It can take some practice to connect with this energy and as you open and clear your chakras more you may find yourself more capable of sensing this kind of energy.

Setting up your environment for a healing experience is important to the process. You will need to find a quiet space to enjoy the benefits of connecting to your energy. Sitting in the living room while people are walking in and out while you try to focus is not an ideal situation. You will need to find a time and a place that gives you some solitude and privacy so that you can fully engage with your senses and feelings without being disrupted or disturbed. You can use a yoga mat to sit or lie down on the floor and having a pillow under your knees, or head can provide additional comfort. These items are not required and you will simply need to find the best position of comfort for your own body and its needs.

You can also lie down on the sofa or bed if it feels better for you. Keeping a blanket nearby is a good tool for you during a healing journey due to the shifts that can occur in your energy. When you are clearing blocks or sensing your chakra's energy, your body temperature can shift from hot to cold and it will feel better to have something close at hand to keep you warm if your temperature drops.

All of these items are helpful to the process. You can use some, none or all of them to help you connect with your energy and clear your chakras. I recommend using as many of them as you can during your first several experiences to provide yourself with the beauty of the ritual of healing yourself. As you progress, you may not need to light the candle every time, or burn the incense, however as you establish your first experiences with chakra clearing, make it a special experience for yourself by creating the warm and loving environment you need to heal.

Lesson 1: Preparing to Clear
The first lesson begins the process of clearing your energy. In order to prepare to clear your chakras, you will have to provide yourself with the right intentions mentally, emotionally and physically. It isn't just about lighting candles and burning incense; it has a lot to do with your mental approach to your experience.

While you are getting ready for your journey it is important to listen to your inner feelings. Are you skeptical? Do you feel silly or uncomfortable with these ideas? Are you fully engaged with the concept of chakras and healing them? Are you listening to the voice in your head that is telling you it will be a waste of time?

All of these questions are worth asking and need to be addressed before you start to work with your energy clearing. If you enter into a cleansing ritual with a skeptical heart, you will resist the unblocking and energy clearing. If you are not willing to sacrifice the time required to spend alone time in meditation and concentration on your energy, then you might not be ready to start the process.

The lesson to prepare to clear your chakras is that you spend quality time asking yourself what you are wanting to gain from this experience. Try the following questions to help you prepare to clear. Use your journal or notebook to write down your thoughts and answers. Be prepared to listen to your intuition and instinct as you prepare for healing.

1. What am I wanting to get out of this healing journey?

2. Am I ready to spend time with myself listening to my inner energy and life force?

3. Am I uncomfortable with this idea and if so, why?

4. When will I feel ready to do this energy clearing work, if not now?

5. What am I doing that makes me feel ready, or not ready to clear my energy?

6. Are there any people I am afraid will notice my healing process and make me uncomfortable about it?

7. What can I do to help myself feel excited about this journey if I am not already?

All of these questions are designed to help you align with your process of opening. To open to your emotions about what you are about to go through is the beginning to opening and clearing your chakra energy. It causes a softening and preparation to allow your mental and emotional self to prepare the body and spirit for the work ahead.

Many of our blocks come from our thoughts and beliefs, so showing yourself how you think and feel about the energy cleansing you are about to go through will help you be more mentally able to reflect, emote and receive insights and inputs about your chakras as you engage with them.

Lesson 2: Connection
In lesson 2, there is the phase of connection. This phase includes the ritual of preparing your environment and the energy of the self for the focus and meditation of your chakra cleansing experience. Connection to the space, yourself and

what's to come is a very helpful way to begin this process after preparing mentally.

Set up your space, or environment to make it as comfortable for yourself as you can. Prepare either your floor mat or area where you can lie down. You can also sit cross-legged on the floor if it is more comfortable, or in a chair, if that feels best. Standing, however, will not be an affective stance or position as it will require too much physical effort and your body needs to be totally relaxed to engage properly in this healing.

Once you have the environment prepared you can follow these next steps to help you connect with your chakra cleansing journey:

1. Light your candle in a safe space.

2. Light your incense and as it smokes, waft the smoke around your whole body from head to foot. Direct the smoke around the areas of your chakras and intentionally open yourself to each one. Think of each chakra's name and color as you pass the incense across the area of each one. Set the incense aside, or near your candle.

    3. Position your body however you have chosen to rest and relax. Lying on a mat or on the bed; sitting cross-legged or in a chair.

    4. Once you are comfortable, take a nice, long inhale and count for 10 beats as you breathe in. Hold your breath for 10 beats and then exhale for 10. Repeat this cycle 5 times to help yourself fully relax.

    5. Once you have relaxed with breath, continue to breathe deeply and normally, allowing all of your muscles to relax. Find all of your tense places and release them with an exhale.

6. Picture your chakra system in your head, from the root to the crown. Imagine each swirling circle of colorful energy in its place and see it all connected to you. Give yourself several moments of this activity of seeing your energy circles.

7. As you connect to your chakra system as a whole, begin to connect with each one individually. Start at your root and visualize its color, its quality, and its properties. Consider what ideas might be coming up in this area and if it feels open, blocked, or foggy. Add your crystal or gemstones into this portion. As you connect to each chakra, move and place your crystal on the position of the chakra you are connecting to. Leave it in place until you are ready to move to the next one.

When you are a beginner working with energy, you may not feel anything right away. It may take a few times of practicing this Connection Lesson in order for you to open to the energy sensations more and more.

8. As you begin to connect to your chakras one at a time, notice any feelings, sensations, memories, thoughts, patterns of thought, and so forth, that come up. No need to write it down now; just feel it. You may get stopped in a chakra for a while because your energy has guided you to this area to concentrate on healing it first. One of the essential lessons to consider is that your energy is intelligent and knows how to guide you. Opening yourself to the quality of energy you are feeling an allowing it to guide you can improve your ability to clear and heal blockages. Remain relaxed and let your chakras do the talking.

9. Once you have considered each chakra individually, you will need to go back to any that stopped you or that

you felt a more significant sensation in. This could simply mean that your mind started saying a lot of things when you spent time connecting to your heart chakra, or that your body started to feel colder while you were connecting to your solar plexus. These are the areas that will take you into the next lesson.

Lesson 3: Consideration
This next lesson continues the cleansing journey. When you sense or feel an area or a specific chakra that has a more noticeable sensation or "attitude" you can return to this chakra for Consideration. The lesson of consideration simply means that you pause in this area longer so that you have more time to adjust to what you are sensing, feeling, hearing, or noticing and have time to consider everything that comes up. Keep your crystal in the area you are wanting to consider for a longer period, allowing for your chakra to align with the crystal energy to give you a more open energetic response. It is almost like using a magnifying glass or a loud speaker to better hear your chakra's energy.

Consideration is the gateway to unblocking and healing. It is in this step that you might have unwanted thoughts or emotions surface that you have been hiding from yourself. You may also have repressed memories rise up for you to recall and face again. This is the step that asks you to spend time considering all of the energy that is stuck in this chakra, blocking it from flowing fully. Look at the following list of things to consider when you are digging more deeply into a specific chakra:

- Feelings of sadness, sorrow, grief
- Sensations like pulses, twitches, tingling, itching, burning
- Old, forgotten memories from childhood or adulthood
- Aches or pains in the muscles or joints in the surrounding areas

- Thoughts and ideas that suddenly switch on that sound like a negative or deprecating voice
- Specific words, phrases, or thought patterns that repeat
- Images of people, places, or things
- Anger, frustration, agitation
- Sudden crying or emotional outburst
- Deeply uncomfortable feelings that are not easy to vocalize or express with thoughts or imagery

Starting with these types of considerations can help you get an idea of what to consider while you are spending quality time with each chakra. An important thing to remember is that as you are working in a certain chakra, your energy may guide you to another, expressing a link between the two and that they have a strong connection to what needs to be unblocked or cleared. Giving yourself time and space to go through each chakra can have a more impactful energetic healing, as opposed to focusing on only one chakra. If you are feeling a connection between two chakras from your considerations of what could be blocking you, then it will help you to heal both at the same time.

Lesson 4: Letting Go
In this lesson, you will take your considerations from Lesson 3 and prepare to let them go. Consideration is how you identify the cause of your blocks and chakra imbalances. They surface as memories, thoughts, self-perceptions, insecurities, and fears, feelings of neglect, shame, guilt, and sorrow. All of the considerations that you find and unravel in each chakra must be released.
The release of these ideas, thoughts, and emotions are what step you out of your old energetic platform and into the lighter, clearer energy of your original chakra balance. It doesn't happen right away, and it can take several years to fully clear all of the energy that needs to be cleansed, depending on your

life journey and experiences. Beginning with these lessons is the beginning of letting go of what is ready to be released and as you continue the practice of loving yourself and tending to your energy, the more you will connect with that needs consideration and eventually, release from your chakras.

To practice letting go of these unwanted energies that appear in the form of thoughts, memories, and emotions, you can follow this set of steps to give you the intentional release you are looking for:

1. Place your hands on the chakra you are working with and leave them there.

2. Ask yourself to become open and free to release by saying, "I am ready to open my heart chakra and release the wounds, sorrows, pain, and loss that I have felt here. I am open to receiving positive love and light in my heart chakra from now on. I let go of all of the hurts and sorrows that have affected my life so far. I am ready to love now." (This works as a specific example for the heart chakra. Ahead in Chapter 8, you will uncover more examples of words and phrases to help you release energy from each individual chakra).

3. Continue holding your hands over your chakra and repeat the breathing exercise from before (Inhale 10 beats, hold 10 beats, exhale 10 beats, repeat x5).

4. Sense the energy of the chakra and notice how it shifts or feels. How has the quality changed? Does it feel lighter, different, and more open? Did letting go of blocks in this chakra make you more aware of another chakra to work on?

5. Follow your energy to the next chakra, or decide that you are ready to end your cleansing ritual and prepare to return to your daily life.

When you are ready to let go of the healing process, you can give yourself some time to relax before returning to your day, or evening. Connect again to your whole chakra system by picturing it in your mind, from root to crown. See all of the colors lined up. Do any of your chakras look or feel different? Are the ones that you worked on clearing or releasing feeling or looking bigger, or clearer? Spend time noticing the quality of how you feel before getting up. To close the experience, blow out your candle and refresh your environment by putting away your tools and preparations.

Be sure to enjoy a glass of water or two following this experience to help your body feel flushed and cleansed. Drink plenty of water for the rest of the day following a cleansing time.

Lesson 5: Writing It All Down
After engaging in Lessons 1-4, it is important to give yourself some time to reflect. A major part of the healing and cleansing process is the time you spend honoring your emotions, thoughts, and memories that surface. Having your journal ready right after you practice clearing rituals is an incredible step in the right direction.

While it is all still fresh in your mind you can use your time after the energy clearing to make some notes about what you experienced. Write down some of the following ideas or thoughts:

- What chakra you were drawn to the most
- How it felt differently from other chakras
- Sensations you may have felt
- Specific feelings, thoughts, and emotions that surfaced

- Memories that cropped up
- Sounds or senses of voices you may have heard
- Mental images or pictures that appeared
- Physical feelings like aches, pains, tingles, itches, body temperature shifts

All of these things and more can be written about in your chakra healing journal. I recommend keeping a separate notebook just for this journey so that you can easily document your experiences and connect the dots between your chakras. As you connect more in this way to your healing process you will be better able to identify what is blocking or clogging your chakra energy from flowing fully and clearly so that you can be your truest, most vibrant self.

Repeating these lessons regularly will help you the most and give you the best results. Give yourself a few days between each clearing ritual so that your mind, body, and spirit have time to adjust to the changes. It may feel subtle at first, but the more you practice energy clearing, the greater your energy will feel and the bigger the impact on your life. It takes time, patience and above all, love for yourself and your experience. Practice these lessons often and you will find the life you are hoping to live as you're most balanced and joyful self.

Purging and Cleansing the Chakras: Side-Effects

Waking up to your energy sounds beautiful and like a wonderful, blissful experience that will bring you glittering joy and peace of mind; and you will eventually feel all of those things...one day after a whole lot of healing and going through the necessary purging and cleansing of all of the old wounds, emotional or physical traumas, and all of the damage you have done to yourself through thoughts of low-self-esteem and poor health and lifestyle choices.

There is no room for regret when you approach your healing journey. All of your life lessons are an important part of your journey along your path to finding your true self and although much of what you collected energetically along your life journey doesn't belong to you, you are still a whole person on a journey of self-love and healing. All of your experiences are a vital component of how you align properly with your energy as you heal and the work that you do to release the energy you have sorted from your chakras will require some assistance from your heart and mind.

Compassion, patience, and love are all you need to walk the path of chakra healing and when you allow yourself the assistance from your own heart to embrace the life story you have already lived, then you can heal well. If you hold onto regret and tell yourself that you could have, would have, or should have, then you will impede your journey from moving forward. It is important to love yourself through the darkness as you heal and be ready for the side effects of purging and cleansing your chakras.

The possibilities are endless when it comes to your own quest and journey through your energy, memories, thoughts, beliefs and life choices. This chapter will provide some examples and descriptions of how energy blockages might feel within your everyday life, as well as how they can feel when you begin to release or purge energy that is ready to be unblocked and release. Some energy is not only blocked; it can also be deficient or excessive, meaning that it has a low quality of energy, or an overabundance of energy, which can be just as detrimental to your balance as a blockage.

To be clear, all of these concepts (deficiencies, excesses, and blockages) are not related to the original Upanishads and Vedic texts from the Hindu belief systems that described chakra energy and healing. These ideas and concepts have been uncovered as we have evolved our understanding of chakras and our own energy systems. In our culture, we often refer to these concepts through the language of psychotherapy or counselling, but as we achieve more understanding about the whole human system, we can apply the concepts and language of therapy to how we unravel all of our chakras and heal ourselves more wholly.

Purging the chakras sounds exactly like what it is: a great flushing of old energy that has become a stagnate plug to your full life force flow and beautiful potential for harmony. Think of it like having a clogged kitchen sink that won't come unblocked. A lot of buildup in the pipes over time and a lot of other food scraps and trash get in the way of the drain flow and prevent clear water from running through. Living your life with a clogged system creates a lot of issues. Some of these issues include, and are not limited to the following:

- Depression
- Anxiety
- Fear
- Compulsive disorders
- Dementia
- Alcoholism
- Obesity
- Eating disorders
- Insomnia
- Anger issues
- Paranoia
- Pathological disorders (ex: lying)
- Chronic illness
- Chronic pain
- Chronic disease
- Fibromyalgia
- Gastrointestinal disorders
- Infertility issues

- Heart conditions
- Allergies

All of these issues and more actually stem from severe and chronic chakra energy blockages, excesses and deficiencies. Modern Western medicine has not yet incorporated the science of our energetic system into the way we treat our health issues and so in order to achieve the true balance, we must decide to heal our chakras on our own.

AS you look at the list, how many of these things have you suffered from in the past, or are currently suffering from? How many of your caregivers, partners or friends have suffered from any of these ailments? We are all learning to live with our problems instead of treating them from the source: energy blockages. The chakras are the beginning of where you start to accrue the issues listed above, and others that are not listed.

When you begin to release and purge your chakras from their blockages, excesses, and deficiencies, there will be a variety of possible side-effects that are the result of letting of old energy from wounds, traumas and early life programming. If you are an adult, then you have had a lot of these experiences and will, therefore, have a lot to work through and clear as you spend quality time cleansing, purging and healing each chakra and the system as a whole.

The list below illustrates several possible side-effects from cleansing your chakras. Keep in mind that all journeys are different and you may experience some, none, or all of these possibilities.

- Excessive crying for no apparent reason, and out of the blue
- Excessive giggling or laughter for no apparent reason and out of nowhere
- Soreness in your muscles, joints, and tissues

- Night sweats
- Cravings for certain foods that you may not normally like to eat
- Extreme thirst for water
- Change in weight, either gain or loss
- Exhaustion
- Loss of appetite/ gain in appetite
- Excessive sleep/ tiredness from energy purging
- Dreams and visions about your history or past lives
- Change in attitude from negative to positive
- Rashes, hives or "allergic reactions" on the skin
- Disinterest in usual hobbies or activities
- Memories surfacing, especially the most painful or traumatic
- A desire to write and journal often to purge thoughts and feelings
- A desire to speak out loud more often to purge thoughts and feelings
- Rushes of electrical pulses or energy throughout the body
- Tingling in the body in areas of the chakras
- Psychic abilities/ clairvoyance
- Hearing spirit guides

Once you begin to align your energy through your whole chakra system, you begin to let go of years and sometimes decades of clogged emotions, pains, feelings, and experiences. Remember that clogged sink? Imagine clearing out your chakras in the same way that you clear the clog. You won't be using a chemical or a plunger, of course, but you will be using tools and techniques to help you release the old and unwanted energy from your system so that you can thrive.

Many of the side-effects listed above are directly linked to specific chakras and don't come all at one time. For example, your root chakra opening can cause a lot of excessive crying or laughter because of how long you have held onto to pain around your childhood security, or rather insecurity. So many people have insecure attachments from the way they are parented and letting go of that energy releases a lot of emotions. Becoming open to your psychic abilities comes further along in the process and occurs when your crown chakra can open fully after you have successfully released a significant number of blocks in your other chakras.

It all takes time and it all takes the practice of aligning your energy through your knowledge of how to work with your chakras. Allow yourself time and space as you heal so that if you begin to experience any of these side-effects you can provide proper time for healing after releasing and purging.

Chapter 13: Questions That Arise on the Healing Path

Ascension is what you call the process of aligning with your true energy as a soul. Working towards ascension brings you into direct contact with how to heal your chakra energy and what must be done in order to align your energy with the light of your whole life purpose. As you begin to heal and balance your energy system, you will have to go through a long quest for information from yourself and through your inner emotions, feelings, thoughts, and experiences from your life up to this point.

The questions you need to ask are the kind of questions a therapist might ask you in a healing session. They are designed to guide you on the right path to helping yourself heal and clear all of the blocks from within you. If you think about it, working with a "talk" therapist in a counselling session is exactly like the work you do to heal your chakras through the lessons and meditations you have already learned about. You are your closest counsellor and ally and have the power to begin answering your own questions about how you feel, what you think and what is lurking under the surface of your existence as a person in society.

In this chapter, you will answer the questions outlined for you as though a therapist is asking you how you are feeling about your life. The questions will be directly associated with each chakra to help you concentrate on the specific energy of each one. As you practice your clearing and balancing techniques, you can start to incorporate these questions into your meditations, connections, and considerations. Open your journal and answer the questions for the chakra you are currently working on. You don't have to do it in the order they are listed here.

Root Chakra

1. When do I feel the most at peace with myself?

2. When do I feel the security I need the most?

3. How long has it been since I have felt financially secure?

4. When was the last time I had a good cry?

5. How long has it been since I felt good about my life purpose or my path?

6. What happened in my early life or childhood that could have made me feel less secure?

7. How many minutes a day do I devote to myself alone?

8. When are my most joyful moments about my security and my financial situation?

9. How hard do I try to set aside time for the things I truly want and desire to have in my life?

10. How do I set myself up for a better home life that fits my basic needs?

Sacral Chakra

1. How long has it been since I let myself feel my whole body from head to toe?

2. When do I feel the best in my body and my sense of sexuality?

3. How often do I allow myself physical or emotional pleasure?

4. What sensations make me feel the most alive and free?

5. How long has it been since I have done anything creative?

6. When was the last time I danced or moved my body to music?

7. Are my feelings about my life something that I deny and ignore, or embrace and explore?

8. Are there any times when I feel afraid to be naked with myself and my body, or with other people?

9. When do I give myself the time to truly embrace, hold, and love myself?

10. How often do I let myself sense all of the things in my life by touching them? (Ex: petting a cat, feeling the fabric of your sofa or living room furniture, carefully feeling the vegetables or fruits you are going to chop to eat for dinner, caressing your house plants, feeling water coming out of the faucet and enjoying the sensation).

Solar Plexus Chakra

1. Do I allow myself to show off my talents in front of others?

2. Am I only okay with subjects that make me look good in front of other people?

3. Do I have a history of alcohol/substance abuse or addiction?

4. Are there times in my life when I have felt weak around other confident people?

5. Am I allowed to give myself the time to openly act as my true self, even when I am afraid of other people's judgments?

6. Do I have the ability to stay focused on my goals and intentions?

7. How many self-help lessons have I taken to try and improve myself but have not succeeded in the way that I am hoping?

8. When I am my most honest with myself?

9. When do I feel the proudest of my life?

10. Am I able to let other people be as strong and powerful as I am?

Heart Chakra

1. When was the last time I truly felt loved by anyone?

2. Am I giving myself the love that I want, or am I asking it to come from other people more often?

3. Am I open to receiving love and friendship from other people, or do I have a hard time feeling open with other people?

4. Am I able to love someone unconditionally, or do I have strict parameters about how love should be?

5. When was the last time I said: "I love myself"?

6. How long has it been since I gave myself a loving embrace and gave myself a pat on the back for all of my hard work as a mother, father, friend, employee, partner, etc.?

7. Have all of my relationships ended in a negative way or left me feeling a lot of heartache and sorrow?

8. When was the last time I had a relationship with someone that had a positive feeling of love?

9. Where am I the most vulnerable in my relationships with others? (Ex: jealousy, self-confidence, communication, sexuality, etc.)
10. How well do I know my own heart and the truth of what I actually want to have in love and relationships?

Throat Chakra

1. What are my least favorite words and why do I dislike them so much?

2. When was the last time I shouted out loud or screamed because I needed to release something?

3. How many times in my life have I wanted to say something but then decided not to?

4. What did I do in my childhood to express myself and was there a time that I was told not to by my parents, teachers, or friends?

5. When was my last attempt at singing for fun and pleasure?

6. How long has it been since I told myself, or someone else, a lie?

7. What kind of sentences do I use to describe my feelings? Are they long and elaborate, or short and uninformative?

8. When someone asks me about myself, am I able to easily talk about my life or do I quickly change the subject?

9. How often do I tell myself that what I am saying is stupid or dumb?

10. When is my favorite time to talk to someone? (Ex: after a crisis, over a casual meal, right before bed, all of the time, etc.

Brow Chakra

1. How many times have I felt myself thinking a thought and then telling myself that it is stupid or impossible?

2. How well do I know my real thoughts, attitudes, beliefs, and values?

3. Are my ideas a question of the reality that I live in, or do I just decide to follow what everyone else is thinking or doing?

4. When am I the most content with how I think and feel about my life?

5. Are my ideas good enough for me, or are they supposed to fit into what other people want and desire?

6. Do I believe in my psychic abilities, or do I think that these things are impossible?

7. Have I ever told myself a certain word or phrase over and over again to train myself to think a certain way? (ex: "I am not smart enough." "I am not good enough." "I don't have all the things I need to accomplish anything I want." "I am a failure.")

8. Have I ever seen objects, lights, visions, or other energies that are not usually perceived by other people, or with the naked eye?

9. When was the last time I had a dream I could remember?

10. What is the most intense dream or vision I have ever had and how did it affect me?

Crown Chakra

1. How long has it been since I felt a flower petal and enjoyed its beauty?

2. When was the last time I gazed at my own reflection and saw a beautiful light in my eyes?

3. How many years has it been since I had faith in something bigger than myself?

4. How long ago did I let go of my love for life and all of the people, places, animals and things in this world?

5. Have I ever allowed myself to be truly open to my own personal spirituality?

6. Have I allowed myself to be brainwashed by other people's ideals about religion or faith?

7. How long ago did I give myself permission to leave my whole light and live as something less than my true self?

8. What was my first major experience with spirituality?

9. How long ago did I feel like there was nothing in the universe and that we are all alone, or did I feel like we are not alone, but felt like there was no point in knowing it anyway?

10. When do I allow myself time to appreciate the beauty and magic of all life on the planet and in the universe?

Whole Body, Mind, Spirit

1. When do I fell the most aligned with my whole self?

2. Where do I hold the most tension in my being: physical body, emotions or feelings, thoughts, and ideas, or faith?

3. What lives have I lived before this current life that may have affected my whole energy system? (ex: past life karma, patterns of behavior from another soul life)

4. Where so I look for guidance for my whole being: inside of myself, or outside of myself?

5. What is the nature of my greatest wound and how does it affect my whole self?

6. How well do I know my true feelings from all of the experiences I have had in my life so far, and how do they relate to my current state of feeling and behaving?
7. When was the last time I gave myself a chance to ask for help from someone or something (spirit guides) else?
8. What is my purpose and am I already living it?
9. When I am alone, do I feel happy, sad, doubtful, fearful, or another emotion, or emotions?
10. How well do I trust the answers I have given to all these questions, from the root to the crown?

All of these questions are a great beginning to digging deeper into the true source of your energy blockages in your chakras. Healing yourself means communicating with yourself on all levels. It is not just about how you meditate or perform your rituals or visualizations; you must also talk to yourself, ask yourself important and probing questions, even when you fear the answer. The truth of you is always better than a lie, and so it becomes the object of healing your chakras to seek out the truth of who you truly are underneath it all.

Ask more questions of yourself and develop your own methods about how you connect and communicate with your energy. It is only the beginning of a lifelong bond with your whole chakra system and the energy of your life.

Chapter 14: The Quest for Self-Discovery through the Chakras

We all have a journey. Every one of us is a totally unique creation. You will always only have your truest self to guide you on your path to healing. You will find many ways to support your growth as you open your chakras. You can see a counsellor, and go to yoga. You can take a painting class, or join a book club. You can take a holiday with a friend or your partner to the place you have always wanted to go to. In the end, your chakra healing journey is something only you can truly experience and understand.

All of the ways that you support your journey (therapy, vacation, healthy lifestyle, hobbies, and activities) are all wonderful ways to keep your chakras open and balanced. In reality, though, you will have to explore this healing path on your own. It is a great journey of self-discovery and it aligns you with your whole self. How can you be your whole self if you are asking others to participate in your path of healing?

Support from friends, family, partners, and co-workers is always appreciated and helpful and you will likely get it when you communicate your story of chakra healing to all of the important people in your life. We are all in need of support and help on our journeys and living with all of our heart means letting other people in to help us when we need it and being available for others as well.

Only you can take the journey through your chakra system and only you can be responsible for the language of healing yourself. As you begin to travel this path, you are going to have to find ways to enjoy your experience on your own without anyone else's interference. There are sometimes practitioners who can help you with your chakra journey, like a Reiki Master or practitioner. Having a Reiki session is an excellent way for you to bond with your own energy and to continue to heal and open. What happens after that session those in your hands and it is up to you to decide how you want to face all of the issues, emotions, feelings, fears, and lessons from your life journey.

Be brave and allow yourself the opportunity to face YOU. All you have to do is trust your ability to hear your own energy and to find your way through all of the chakras in the way that feels best for you. It takes time. It takes space. It requires love and patience from yourself. All of the ways you engage with this journey should be a reflection of your own needs, wants and desires and not anyone else's.
Sometimes on the healing journey, as you release traumas, anxieties, self-doubts, and outworn beliefs and thought patterns, your life can start to shift in big ways. As you heal your chakras, you might begin to realize that the person you have been dating for the past 2 years is no longer a good match for you as you grew more fully into the truth of who you are. It can be a very upsetting time as you struggle with how to open to your own truth and maintain a life with someone else that is no longer a part of that truth.

Other times on the healing path you may be opening and balancing and get to a point where you have to leave your current job because it feels so out of tune with who you are becoming and how you now feel about yourself. It is a great opportunity to start to work towards the life and career your soul actually wants. Our hidden desires and purposes begin to surface during our chakra healing and cleansing journey and when you stay in a profession or job that is not in alignment with your energy and who you actually are or how you feel, then you can remain blocked in your energy system.

How we spend our time has a massive impact on our energy. You may also discover as you heal that you no longer want to watch TV all of the time or futz around on social media for several hours. When your energy shifts and balances, so does your life. You may start to take more pleasure and new activities and hobbies you were always wanting to engage in. You may even pick up and move to another city, or country, depending on your personal journey of self-discovery.

The main thing to note when you are going through a chakra cleansing and healing journey is that it is a special and unique experience for you. Other people in your life may question your choices and decisions as you become more aligned with your energy, and it can be blocked to your energy to have an outside voice telling you what you should or shouldn't do.

Keeping your chakras clear and balanced can help you avoid backtracking when other people put their two-cents in about your healing process. It is not for anyone else to decide how your journey should be. When you open your chakras, you open your whole life up to what you want, who you truly are, how you want to live and where you want to be. It is the most empowering thing you can do for yourself and it is a beautiful journey of self-discovery that only you can know.

Moving forward, make sure that you are listening to your own voice of reason and intuition when it comes to your "right path". Your chakras are talking to you and giving you all of the information that you need to heal and get where you want to be. Embrace the journey and accept your power of knowing: this is your story and you are the one in charge. Let your chakras be your guide.

Part 4

Breathing Meditations

Chapter 15: Concentration and Breath Meditation for Chakra Healing

When you are working on healing your chakras, it is an invaluable tool to have a good grasp on breathing techniques and exercises, as well as powerful concentration. Both of these concepts are the basis of meditation, and this chapter will open you up to understanding what that means and why concentration and breath are imperative for the chakra healing process.

Your energy will always need a place to go and relax and when you can stop, focus on your feelings, and breathe, then you are able to connect with your energy centers in a way that will essentially block unwanted energies from causing a disruption in your balance, as well as helping your return to your center.

The world is full of upheaval and things out of our control, and these types of things are what throw us off course when we are finally just feeling aligned again. Breath and concentration will act as a shield from these outside forces so that you are regularly calling upon your own strength to fight for your own energy more.

You may have already learned a variety of yoga breathing techniques or tips for concentration and focus, and you should always continue finding new and exciting practices that work well for you. In this chapter, we will use a very simple, step-by-step activity to help you understand the power of breath and focus on your chakra system.

If you are new to meditation, then this will be a perfect entry point for you. If you are already practicing meditation techniques, then you are welcome to skip over this section.

Meditation for Breath and Concentration to Heal the Chakras

1. Find a space where you will be undisturbed. Silence your cellphone and put a do not disturb on your door, if desired (you can play meditation music if you prefer to start with some music to help you relax).
2. Find a comfortable seated position. You can sit on the floor with your legs crossed or on a cushion, and you can also use a chair if it is more comfortable.
3. Sit and take a few moments to adjust until you feel fully comfortable. Make sure your spine is straight. If you are in a chair, be sure to keep your feet flat on the floor.
4. Place your hands comfortably on your knees, palms up.
5. Take an inhale in through your nostrils for a count of 5 seconds.
6. Hold the breath for 5 seconds.
7. Exhale for 5 seconds.
8. Repeat. In for 5, hold for 5, out for 5. Repeat this step 5 times.
9. After you have finished this round of breaths, concentrate your attention on your body starting at your feet. Begin scanning your feet, ankles, and toes for any tension.
10. When you find some tension in this part of you, take a deep breath in for 5 seconds and as you hold the breath for 5 seconds, picture the tension preparing to release from your body. As you exhale for 5 seconds, release the tension from your feet, toes, and ankles.
11. Move up to your legs (knees, shins, thighs, etc.) and scan for any tension. Perform the same action on the legs that you did in the previous step. Breath in for 5, collect the tension as you hold for 5, release the tension for 5 on the exhale.
12. Continue this activity through your whole body and use your chakras as markers of where to concentrate on releasing the tension. When you have made it to the top of

the head at the crown chakra, and you have completed the tension release in all of the chakras, end the tension scanning in the shoulders, arms, and hands.

13. Breathe in for 5, collect the arm, hand, and shoulder tension while you hold for 5, and then exhale for 5.
14. Now that you have released the tension from your body, you can practice deeper breath within each chakra. The next series of steps will be repeated for each chakra, starting at the root and going up to the crown.
15. Take a long breath in for a count of ten. Hold the breath for ten. Then, release the breath in an exhale for ten.
16. Focusing on the root chakra, picture it in your mind as you take in the next breath for a ten count. See its color, light, shape, and size inside of your body.
17. Hold the inhale for a count of ten, and while you do, see the root chakra preparing to grow in size and clarity. See it getting ready to release any tension.
18. As you exhale for a count of ten, see your root chakra enlarge slightly as it pushes out any tension and unwanted energies.
19. Repeat steps 16-19 with the root chakra at least three times before moving up the spine to the sacral chakra.
20. Once you are ready to move to the sacral chakra, you can perform the same actions you did with the root chakra (steps 16-20).
21. You will continue these steps through every chakra, steps 16-20, moving up one more chakra after you finish your breath and concentration meditation for the one before. For the most effective results, perform steps 16-19 for each chakra at least 3 times or more.
22. Return your focus to your whole body once you have finished your breath and concentration meditations. Spend a few moments taking several inhales for 5, and release for 5. In for 5, out for 5.
23. When you are ready, you can return to your daily activities.

Using a breathing and concentration meditation like this one is a powerful tool to help you reorganize your energy and help you maintain all of the possible levels of basic chakra methods for awakening, healing, balancing, strengthening. It is simple, effective, and easy and won't take up a lot of time.

You can modify this practice and incorporate other, more yogic styles of breathing if you are familiar with some of those methods. Anything you do to bring additional breath and focus to the experience will be beneficial to you.

Chapter 16: Keeping Balance: Breathing Practices to Keep Your Chakras Open

Breath is significantly important to the quality of your energy and your chakras. Breath is life and the force that engages the flow of energy through your chakra system. The final chapter of this book offers you a series of breathing exercise for each chakra, designed to help you keep balance as you practice living with your energy. Each of these exercises may be added to your lessons and meditations from previous chapters.

I strongly encourage you to commit to using these breathing techniques on a regular basis. You can do them in the morning before work, or at the end of the day to clear all of the energy from your daily life or work schedule. They can be used in place of your yoga or fitness routine and can be a good way for you to practice your energy clearing techniques on a regular basis.

Bring breath to your chakras and awaken your energy within!

Breath for the Root Chakra

1. Sitting on the floor, stretch your legs straight in front of you. Be sure to keep your back straight.

2. Place your hands to your shoulders and push your elbows out to the side in line with your shoulders.

3. Breath slowly in through your nose. Lift your arms overhead and pull your knees up to your chest so they are pointing upward toward the sky. Make sure your feet stay flat on the floor and keep your sacrum planted to the ground while you reach up.

4. Begin to release your breath and lower your legs down, back into a straight position. Keep your spine straight while you bring your hands back to their original position on your shoulders, elbows pointed to the sides.

5. Repeat this cycle several times. If you feel comfortable, you can gain momentum, but be sure to keep in your comfort zone.

6. Remember to practice seeing yourself rooted to the Earth as you practice this exercise.

7. Ending this exercise, pull your legs into a cross-legged position. Sense the energy of your root chakra and consider it for as long as you need.

Breath for the Sacral Chakra

1. Sit on the floor and draw your knees into your chest. Place your hands on the front of your knees. Your knees do not have to be against your chest, just slightly out from you, feet flat on the floor.

2. Breathe in through your nose and pull your sacrum forward, tilting your pelvis to make a curve in your lower back. Use your hands against the front of your knees to support your back.

3. Open your chest upward to the sky as you are pulling yourself forward and arching your back.

4. Breathe out and reverse the action to push the curve back, drawing your navel toward your spine and reversing the curve of your spine.

5. Repeat this cycle several times.

6. Bring your legs into a cross-legged position and shut your eyes. Return to a normal breath cycle. Meditate on the energy stirred and awakened in your sacral chakra and relax here for as long as you need.

Breath for the Solar Plexus Chakra

1. Position your body in the same position you did for the second chakra. Place your hands gently on the front of your knees keeping them pulled close to your chest with your back straight.

2. Arch your back and pull your abdomen forward pushing your navel forward. Keep your back supported by keeping a hold of your knees with your hands.

3. Roll your torso from over to the left side, continuing all the way around. Pull your navel back into your spine and continue rolling back around to the front with your navel pushed forward. The idea is to create a smooth, circle roll.

4. Repeat this circle roll around starting from the front to the left side, and then back to the right side. Repeat several times.

5. Repeat again going in the opposite direction, several times.

6. You can gradually pick up speed but only if it feels comfortable for your spine. Don't overdo it and keep it slow if you need to limit your spinal movement.

The importance of this exercise is that you maintain focus on your breathing. Try to breathe in for the belly forward position, and then breathe out as you reach the navel-back position. Breathe in from the front to left to side, and breathe out from the back to right side, breathe in front...and so on.

Breath for the Heart Chakra

1. Sit with legs crossed on the floor or sit in a chair. Place your hands on your shoulders and push your elbows out so they are pointed to the side.

2. Take a slow and deep breath in. Twist your body to the right and lengthen and straighten your spine as you twist. Keep your abdominal muscles engaged.

3. Slowly breath out and twist your body all the way over to the left. Remember to keep your back straight and long. Engage your abdominal muscles engaged and chest wide open. Try not to arch your back.

4. Keep the breaths in and out slow and deep.

5. Repeat steps 1-4 several times.

6. Bring your back to normal resting position. Drop your hands down to your knees and breathe normally, keeping your eyes closed

7. Consider the energy of your heart and reflect on the feelings, thoughts or emotions that come up for as long as you need.

Breath for the Throat Chakra

1. Sit with your legs crossed on the floor, or in a chair keeping your spine long.

2. Lace your fingers together and clasp your hands together. Keep your elbows pointing down towards your navel and touching together at their points. Place your clasped hands under your chin.

3. Inhale long and deep and push your elbows out to the side. Keep your fingers under the chin and woven together.

4. Letting the breath out, lift your chin and push your elbows back together. Keep your fingers as they were under your chin. Open your mouth and tilt your head back. Stick your tongue out for an extra stretch.

5. Make an audible sound while you breathe out. Any sound will do. Let it come naturally to you

6. Repeat this cycle of breath and motion several times.

7. Bring your head back to a normal resting position and breathe normally. Rest your hands in your lap, or on your knees. Consider the energy pulled into your throat chakra and listen to the energy of your throat chakra for as long as you need.

Breath for the Third eye Chakra

1. Sit on the floor with your legs crossed or upright in a chair with your eyes closed Focus attention to your breath.

2. While breathing, envision opening a curtain or drapes hanging in front of your third eye to let light in. Imagine

the drapes from your living room or bedroom if it helps you find the image you need.

3. Breathe in through your nose and then reach your hands out in front of you. Stretch your fingers wide and then open your eyes as wide as you can.

4. Reach your arms to the side while you hold your breath. Imagine as you reach your arms to the side that you are throwing the curtains open in front of a window. See a light, image, or color as you "open the drapes".

5. Breathing out, bring your hands to your face and cover your eyes. Picture in your brow chakra the image, shape, color or light that you envisioned with your eyes opened.

6. Repeat this cycle several times.

7. Return your breath to a normal pace for you. Rest your hands on your lap. Keeping your eyes closed, focus on your visualization. Practice seeing with your eyes closed.

Breath for the Crown

1. Sit in a chair or on the ground with legs crossed. Keep your spine long and chest open. Place your hands on your knees. Begin to concentrate on your breathing.

2. Places your palms together with your fingers pointed toward your chin and placed in front of your heart chakra.

3. Draw in a long, deep breath and then reach your arms and fingers up toward the sky with your palms still pressed together.

4. Breathe out and reach your hands out to your sides in line with your shoulders.

5. Place your hands back in the prayer position in front of your heart. Begin your next breath in and start the next cycle over.
6. Repeat this exercise several times.

7. To finish this breath exercise, place your hands back in your lap, or on your knees and breathe normally. Keep your spine straight. Reflect for however long you need to be silent and still.

Part 5

Positive Thinking Meditations

Chapter 17: One Breath at a Time

Learning to meditate can be a little bit like walking into the dark without a flashlight. If you have read or heard people say that have to prevent yourself from thinking about anything, let that go. The idea of meditation is not to block the flow of thoughts, but to channel them, to learn how to not attach to every thought that floats through your mind. It is like going to the market for apples. There are a host of other fruits that look tempting, but you remind yourself that you are only there to buy apples. When thoughts barge their way into your consciousness, you can very nicely say, "No thank you," then return to clarity of your mind. Meditation quietly trains the mind to focus. You learn to concentrate with a clear vision.

Breath awareness is one of the first steps you learn in meditation or any mindful practice such as yoga or tai chi. You are not forcing anything. Rather, you are simply making a conscious choice to not create a story out of thoughts that pass through your mind. You cannot stop thinking, but you can learn to bring your awareness and your attention, to where you want it to go. This process takes time, so be patient with yourself!

There is an interconnectedness to the body, the mind, and the breath. When you bring awareness to your breath, it naturally begins to slow down. And when the breath slows down, the mind and the body relax. Think about when you have been anxious or frightened, your heart pounds, your breath becomes rapid and shallow. When you begin to practice purposeful breathing, meditation becomes easier. It is a preparation for the practice of meditation. Be aware though, even long time meditators sometimes struggle with focus. It is normal to find your mind wandering off, particularly in the beginning. Meditation is about kindness, you simply repeat to yourself internally to come back to your breath.

To prepare for your meditation session, choose a time that will not be interrupted for at least ten to fifteen minutes. Carving out a set time to meditate and sticking to it (when possible) helps to establish your practice. Early mornings or late evening may be ideal for you, or perhaps you have time in the afternoon that would work. Everyone has unique schedules and circadian rhythms that influence when you sleep, when you are most alert and engaged, or when you are fatigued or have low energy. Choose a time that works for you. Remember, too, it is better to meditate for ten minutes five days a week than to meditate for an hour once a week. Consistency is what helps you establish your new meditation practice.

Where should you meditate? You can practice meditation anywhere, but in the beginning, you want to establish your sweet spot. Try to find a space where you will not be disturbed. The space needs to be a relatively quiet place free of noise that you can control. That said, if you are in your house or apartment and there are children outside playing, dogs barking, etcetera, do not worry. In modern life it is challenging to find a space that is absolutely silent. You just don't want to meditate with a television on, or where there are a lot of distractions, especially in the beginning. During nice weather you may meditate outside, or on a porch or deck. The point to finding a place is again, making it consistent, familiar. When you go to that spot your mind and body recognize it as a place to meditate. It is like doing yoga, when you step on your mat, you step into a place for practice.

If you live in a lively household with a lot of people and finding a space is challenging, there are creative ways around all of that. Try wearing earplugs or headphones. Or, maybe you rise earlier before everyone wakes up in order to get your meditation in. Some people meditate first thing in the morning, which if possible is highly recommended as it can set the tone for the day. If that is not possible, maybe you meditate before going to bed in the evening, letting go of the day's events. The crux of meditating is the actual practice, which can literally be done anywhere or any time that you can find where you will not be disturbed. Perhaps the only time you have alone is after work in your office or at lunch. Let those around you know that while you are meditating, you don't want to be disturbed. It is your right to ask for space and time. You are not asking for anything outlandish, remember that. Don't be deterred by people who don't understand your desire for improving the way you navigate through life. It is your life, and meditation will only enhance it.

There is a ritual nature to meditation Think about special holidays you celebrate, whether they are part of a spiritual practice or not. You prepare for them, make particular food or wear certain clothes. Because you are choosing to make it part of your life, a practice with intention, it is good to make preparations. Some people like to build an altar of some sort, others may decorate their meditation space with nature; rocks, or stones, flowers or plants. You may like to light candles or have the lights off. Paying homage to your meditation time and space is another way to honor it, to connect to it and make it important to you.

When you meditate it is important to be able to have your spine straight. Along the vertebrae are nerves that connect to your body; they need to be aligned. Imagine a hose with running water, the water being your energy flow. If you kink that hose or bend it, the flow of water diminishes or stops altogether. You spine is like that hose. Sit on a comfortable chair, making sure your feet touch the ground. Or, sit against a wall (which is great for back support). You can even try lying down. There are also meditation cushions you can buy, but they are not essential to your practice. If you are extremely tired, lying down may be challenging to stay awake. Meditation is not napping, it is a practice in focused attention and as you progress, it will grow in meaning. Wear comfortable clothing that breathe. It is difficult to meditate in tight fitting clothes that cling to you as they impede the breath. In other words, you want to be comfortable when you meditate, and you don't want to be distracted by clothes that are pinching you.

In the beginning, it is best to use a timer. Start with ten to fifteen minutes. A timer will help you relax and you can let go of thinking, "How long have I been meditating?" It is one less thing to distract you. People often ask if it is okay to listen to music while meditating. This will ultimately depend upon the preferences of the individual. If you are playing soft nature tunes such as rain or birds singing or ocean sounds this may help you focus. If possible, try to establish a meditation practice that isn't dependent on music though. Some people prefer a soft background of classical music when they meditate. You definitely don't want to play songs with words, unless it is chanting or a soft repetition. If silence is hard to find, put on headphones or wear earplugs to block the noise.

Remember that meditation takes time and practice, much like learning to play an instrument or learning any new skill. The more you do it, the more proficient you become. What is unique about meditation is that the subtle changes will be incremental, and not necessarily overt or obvious. They are internal as opposed to going on a diet and seeing the weight loss when you put on your jeans. It is the consistency of your practice that over time will have a profound and far reaching impact on the quality of your life. Because of the very nature of meditation, in the beginning it may feel like you are not accomplishing anything. It may even feel like you are wasting time. If that happens it is simply the mind looking for excuses. The reptilian aspect of the human brain will want to slip back into what is comfortable, familiar. Let old thoughts pass and practice anyway. All new healthy habits come with a bit of struggle, but soon enough, you will begin to openly look forward to your meditation sessions.

Setting clear goals for when and how long you meditate will help you establish your meditation practice. For example, you commit to setting your alarm for 6 am to meditate for 15 minutes during the week and for 8:30 am on the weekends. Rather than an ambiguous promise to meditate in the morning. Dr. BJ Fogg, a behavioral scientist, found that there are three elements of habit. Cue (triggers, prompts), routine, and reward. Establishing a defined time and place will remove the guesswork. The alarm is your prompt, and the routine will cement your commitment. Then you are rewarded with your progress as you notice a growing sense of mastery over being able to calm down easier, to achieve a subtle serenity, to be present. You can also incorporate milestone rewards, such as treating yourself to a massage after a month of meditation, or whatever feels like a reward to you. Maybe you incorporate a short reading of something that inspires you into your practice over a cup of tea or coffee. Set yourself up for success. Make it a pleasurable experience from the get-go. Pay attention to the particulars, then choose a date to begin and stick to it. There is no room for judgement in meditation. When you start, be easy on yourself, allow room for kindness and acceptance. This practice is new to you, give yourself time.

Meditations to improve breathing technique
It's important that you have experience with basic and mindfulness meditation before you begin this chakra meditation. Let's begin.

Sit in a comfortable position, either sitting cross-legged on the floor, or in a chair with your back straight. Let your eyes close and lower down into your breathing, relax your belly, and soften your mind.
Notice and feel how you are supported and connect with the ground below. Allow your weight to sink into the floor, chair, or cushion.
Notice all the sounds around you, and allow them to just be. Take note of the shade and light, and the air is touching your body.
Sense how the sky is above you, the horizon is stretched out around you, and the earth below you, supporting your weight.
Let your mind release and empty out everything that doesn't need to hold onto. Allow it to leave, flow out, and away. Let your body do the same thing. Let it release everything that it doesn't need to hold onto. Allow it to leave; flow through you, and away.

Take yourself away from the things that you have been through in your day. Bring all your energy to your center and ground yourself in the present moment. Start to notice the area around you. Breathe along with space, and notice the rise and fall of every breath. Notice how it's coming and going, its sensation, temperature, and sound.

Breathe down into the area where your body weight rests, below your spine, into your root Chakra. Breathe into this area. Allow it soften and grow with your breath, bring nourishment and life force energy into it.

Let the root connect into the ground below you, deep within the earth. Bring in the color red, the color of earth. Allow your root to be bathed in red: grounding, embodying, empowering you the present moment. Allow your root to take everything it so desires. Speak these words: "I am here," "I have every right to be at this moment, as I am," "The earth will support me."

Once you are ready, continue up to your belly, just below the belly button, to your Hara, emotional intelligence, pleasure, movement, creativity, and choice chakra.

Move your breath into your Hara. Allow this area to soften gently and expand with your breath, bring in life force energy and nourishment. Invite in the color orange, the setting sun's color. Allow your Hara to be bathed in the color orange: motivating, empowering, and balancing. Allow your Hara to be fed and say: "I honor all my needs," "I will allow myself nourishment."

Once you feel ready, move your focus on the soft area just below the breastbone, your Solar Plexus, your power chakra.

Breathe into this area, letting the solar plexus to expand and soften gently along with your breath. Invite the color yellow in, the color of the sun. Allow your solar plexus to be bathed in the sunshine: nurturing, restoring, and replenishing. Allow the solar plexus to take everything it needs. Say the following: "I am worth my weight in gold," "I am enough," "I am more than enough," "I greatly value myself."

Once you are ready, move up to the center of the chest, the heart, unconditional love and self-development chakra.

Breathe slowly into your heart, allowing it to expand and soften with your breath. Allow in the color green, a spring color, or the color rose pink, whichever speaks to you. Allow your heart to be bathed with healing, renewal, and nourishment. Allow your heart to take in all it desires and speak, "I am nourished with love," "I will give and receive love freely," "I am completely loved."

Once you are comfortable and ready, move onto your neck, the throat, personal will and self-expression chakra.

Let the throat to expand, soften, and breathe. Invite in the color blue, the sky's color. Allow your breath to be the sky into your throat, freeing creativity and self-expression, softening control needs, opening, and clearing. Allow the throat to take in what it needs. Say, "I will go with life's flow" "I express myself" "I speak and hear the truth."

Once you are ready, move your focus up to the forehead, between the eyebrows, the third eye, intuition and wisdom chakra. Allow it to breathe, expand, and soften gently.

Invite in the color indigo, the color of the night sky. Allow your third eye to be bathed in indigo; understanding, insight, clarity, balancing, and soothing. Allow the third eye to take all it desires. Say; "Everything is unfolding as it should."

In your own time, move your focus to the top of the head, your crown, the oneness chakra. Allow your crown chakra to breathe.

Bring in the color violet and softly bathe your crown chakra in the violet; harmonizing, restoring, and balancing. Allow your crown to take everything it needs. Say, "I am one with the whole" "I am one with the universe."

Once you feel ready, bring yourself back to the whole, back into the normal flow of the breath, back into your center. Breathe deeply into the core, and say "I am perfect as I am" "I am whole."

Let the words' energy enter your spirit, emotions, mind, and body. Allow your body to take everything it needs. In your time, allow yourself to become aware of the air touching your body. Then notice all the sounds near you and far away.

Let your chakras close a little, all you need is the intention. Notice the support you have below. Take note of how it feels now and hold you in loving kindness, for the amazing, unique, and beautiful person you are. Once you feel ready, bring you a meditation to a close and slowly open your eyes and notice how you feel and how your surroundings have seemed to change.

This meditation should not be used an everyday practice. Use this only when you feel like you need to improve your breathing technique. You can also set a schedule for when you use this meditation, twice a month, with the change of the seasons, or any other schedule that works best for you.

Part 6

Spiritual Path in Everyday Life

Chapter 18: Organizing Spiritual Work on Daily Life

The phrase positive thinking sounds great on the surface; most people would rather have positive thoughts rather than negative ones. But this phrase is also a fluffy term that is often easily dismissed within the real world. It doesn't carry the same kind of weight as a phrase like "hard working" or "work ethic." But these kinds of views are changing.

People and research are telling us that positive thinking is not only about being happy, or pasting a smile on your face for the world to see. Positive thoughts add some real value to your everyday life and can help you to build skills that will last longer than a pasted on smile.

A positive psychology researcher from the University of North Carolina, Barbara Fredrickson, has helped to prove the power of positive thoughts in our everyday life. Let's look at some of what she has found, and what it means to you.

First, let's look at what negative thoughts will do to your brain. Imagine this for me.

Pretend you are walking along in the woods, and a tiger suddenly walks out on the path in front of you. When you see the tiger your brain will create a negative emotion, in this example, it would be fear.

Researchers, for a long time, have known that negative responses will cause you to perform a specific action. Like if a tiger crosses your path, you will likely run. Nothing else in the world, at that moment, matters. Your complete attention is on that tiger, the fear it has caused, and how you plan on getting away from it.

Basically, this means that a negative emotion will narrow the focus of your mind and thoughts. At the moment, you could have the choice to grab a stick, climb a tree, or pick up a leaf, but your brain will ignore these other options because they don't seem relevant when you have a tiger standing in front of you.

This is a great thing to have if you need to save life and limb, but in the world today, and in modern society, you don't have that fear of walking across a tiger in the woods. The bad thing is, the brain still has that programmed response to negative emotion, and it shuts out the rest of the world and limits what you see.

Another example will be if you are fighting with somebody. The emotions and anger you feel at that moment may completely consume you so much that you are unable to think about anything else. Or if you are stressing about all the things you need to do today, you might end up finding it hard to focus on the things you need to do or even to get started because the length of your to-do list has you paralyzed. Maybe you feel bad because you've not been eating healthy or exercising, and all you can think about is your willpower and thinking that you are lazy causing you not to have any motivation.

In all of these examples, your brain shuts you off to the outside world and focuses on the emotions of stress, fear, and anger, just like with the tiger. The only thing that negative emotions do is preventing your brain from seeing other options that may be around you. It's a survival instinct.

Now, what do positive thoughts do to the brain?

Fredrickson created an experiment to see the impact that positive emotions have on the brain. In the experiment, she split her subject into five separate groups and showed each of them a different movie clip.

Two of the groups were shown clips that cause positive emotions. One group was shown things that caused a sense of joy, and the second group was shown things that caused a sense of contentment.

The third group was the group the control group and they were only shown things that created no significant emotional change.

The other two groups were shown clips that would cause negative emotions. One of the groups saw images that caused fear, and the other was sown things that caused anger.

After they had seen the images, all the participants were asked to picture themselves in a place that would cause that same emotion to come up. They were asked to write down the things that they would do. They were each handed a sheet of paper that had 20 fill-ins the blank lines that began with "I would like to..."

The participants that had been shown images that caused anger and fear weren't able to write down as many responses. While the participants that were shown images that caused contentment and joy were able to write many more actions than even the control group.

This means when you feel positive emotions such as love, joy, or contentment; you can see more things that you can do in life. This is some of the findings that showed that positive emotions could broaden your sense of possibilities and open up the mind.

But more interesting discoveries came later.

Benefits from positive emotions don't end when the emotion ends, in fact, you receive the most benefit from these emotions with an enhanced ability to build greater skills that you can use later in your life.

Look at this example. Children that run outside, swing along tree branches, and play with friends are developing physical, social, and creative skills by moving athletically, playing and communicating with others, and learning how to explore the world around them. This is because the emotions of joy and play are prompting the child to build these skill sets that will be valuable and useful to them later in life.

The skills that they have learned will last them a lot longer than the actual emotions that initiated the learning. Negative emotions have the opposite effect because building skills for the future are irrelevant to the brain at that moment in time when you have an immediate danger or threat.

As you can see these thoughts and emotions greatly impact your everyday life, so it's important that you learn more about positive self-talk and thinking.

Don't misunderstand what I mean by positive thinking either. This doesn't mean you turn a blind eye to the bad things in life. Positive thinking only means that you will approach these unpleasant moments productively and positively. You believe that only the best will happen.

Being able to think positively often starts with self-talk. If you don't know what self-talk is, it's the stream of unspoken communication that runs through your mind. These thoughts have the ability to be negative or positive. Self-talk can sometimes come from reason or logic, and it can sometimes arise from misconceptions because of the lack of information you have about something.

If your self-talk tends to be mainly negative, then your outlook on life is going to be mainly pessimistic. If your self-talk tends to be more positive, then you will be more optimistic.

Researchers, like Fredrickson, continue to explore all of the effects that optimism and positive thinking has on your health. A few of these benefits are:

- Better coping skills when you are facing stress or hardships
- Improved cardiovascular health and a reduced risk of dying from heart disease
- Improved physical and psychological well-being
- More resistance to the common cold
- Lower distress levels
- Lower depression rates
- A longer life

Negative self-talk normally comes in one of these four forms:

Polarizing
You tend to see things as either only good or only bad. You don't have a middle ground. You tend to feel as if you have to be perfect or you are a complete failure.

Catastrophizing
Your thoughts automatically go to the worst outcome possible. You regular coffee shop accidentally gets you order wrong, and you believe that the rest of your day is going to be horrible.

Personalizing
When something goes wrong, or something bad happens, you blame yourself for it. An example would be that you hear your friend's night out was canceled, and you automatically think it's because nobody wanted to be around you, so they canceled.

Filtering
You increase the problems of the negative parts of a situation and completely ignore all of the positive ones. An example would be that you had an amazing day at work. You got everything done before you were supposed to, and you boss complimented you on your speediness and quality of work. The evening, you only think about doing more tasks that next day and completely forget about the compliments you received from your boss.

Don't worry though; it's easy to change out your negative thoughts with positive ones, it will just take some time and effort. It's just like creating a new habit. Here are some ways to get started.

Identify areas where you need to change
If you are looking to become more optimistic and practice more positive thinking, figure out the places and areas in your life where you tend to be more negative. This could be your

commute to work, your relationship, anything. Start small by focusing only on one area at a time.

Check yourself
Occasionally check in with yourself during the day to see what you're thinking. If you notice that your thoughts are mostly negative, try to figure out how you can turn them positive.

Don't be afraid of humor
Allow yourself to laugh or smile, especially when you are going through something rough. Find the humor in everything that happens during the day. When you can laugh at life, then you will feel less stressed.

Take up a healthy lifestyle
Try to exercise at least 30 minutes a few days a week. If you can't do 30 minutes at one time, your break it up into three ten-minute chunks. Exercise causes a positive effect on your mood and will help to reduce stress. Having a healthy diet will help to fuel your body and mind.

Surround yourself with positivity
Make sure that the people you spend your time with and adds positivity to your life. They should be supportive and positive and can provide you with helpful feedback and advice. If you are surrounded by negative people, it will only increase your stress and your negativity.

Practice positive self-talk
Follow this rule: don't say things to yourself that you would never say to your friend. You need to be encouraging and gentle. If negative thoughts come up, evaluate them with rational, and then say some positive affirmations. Think of the things that you are most thankful for.

Summary on How to Engage in Meditation

Reflection offers time for unwinding and uplifted mindfulness in an upsetting existence where our faculties are regularly dulled. Research proposes that reflection has the potential for something other than impermanent pressure help.

Contemplation techniques to try

Figuring out how to ponder can be basic, and it's probably the best thing you can accomplish for your wellbeing and by and large prosperity. Reflection is a particularly powerful method for stress alleviation since it empowers you to mitigate worry at the time and to make changes in yourself that will assist you with being less receptive to the stressors you face later on. Figuring out how to ruminate can be fun as there are such a significant number of reflection methods that can be powerful in the event that one style contemplation doesn't feel right, another style will. Figure out how to think a few distinct ways, and see what approach works best for you.

Care Meditation

Care reflection might be one of the all the more testing types of contemplation for reflection tenderfoots, yet it is a compensating structure that brings numerous advantages, both for the novice and for the individuals who practice consistently. For those simply figuring out how to ponder, care contemplation requires no props or readiness (no candles to light, mantras to pick, or methods to adapt); long haul practice can bring a more settled personality and less reactivity to push. The key component of care reflection is an attention on the present minute. Instead of concentrating on something outside of oneself, care reflection requires an emphasis on "now." Learn increasingly about care contemplation and careful living.

Strolling Meditation

Figuring out how to think with a mobile reflection is basic, and gives a portion of the unwinding advantages of activity just as the standard advantages of contemplation. The way in to a mobile reflection isn't only the strolling itself, obviously, it's the attitude where you walk. Strolling contemplations can be quick or moderate, can be rehearsed with an unmistakable personality or with the guide of music or a mantra. Strolling reflection is particularly valuable for the individuals who like to remain dynamic and may feel worried with the quiet and stillness of a portion of different techniques, similar to care contemplation. Learn contemplation with this straightforward strolling reflection instructional exercise, and adjust your pace or center as you find what feels directly for you.

Mantra Meditation
Mantra reflection is another basic system for the individuals who are new to contemplation. On the off chance that keeping your mind totally calm feels like an over the top test, mantra contemplation may be simpler. It joins a portion of the advantages of positive confirmations with the advantages of reflection with the reiteration of a solitary word or sound. A few people feel somewhat awkward with rehashing "om" or murmuring, yet you can utilize whatever mantra you like. Similarly, as with strolling contemplation, the key fixing with mantra reflection is the thoughtful state you accomplish and not really the mantra you use, however it's a smart thought to pick a mantra you're OK with. This is a simple one to begin with.

Care in Daily Life
While care contemplation normally includes keeping the mind totally clear of considerations and keeping up that state, care can be developed from multiple points of view for the duration of the day. Fundamentally, remaining completely present with

whatever you are doing and keeping up an attention on the physical experience of the present minute can enable you to keep up care as you experience your day. There are approaches to develop care, and as you're figuring out how to think, attempt to develop care too—it can enable you to rehearse contemplation all the more effectively, and can fit into a bustling calendar generally effectively.

Chocolate Meditation
At the point when you're seeing how to contemplate, here's a moderately brisk and exquisite procedure to attempt. The chocolate reflection is a type of care contemplation that is frequently utilized in care based pressure decrease (MBSR) classes, is basic for fledglings, connects with a few detects, and has a worked in remuneration of making the flavor of chocolate feel progressively exceptional. Utilizing dim chocolate for this activity brings its very own advantages. In case you're searching for something straightforward and new, attempt the chocolate contemplation.

Breathing Meditation
Breathing reflection is one of the most prominent types of contemplation as a result of its straightforwardness and effortlessness, just as its accommodation (breathing is continually happening, so it's an advantageous stay for contemplation). The breath gives a characteristic center that is subtle, however consistently there, and makes a characteristic beat to become mixed up in. You can work on breathing reflection for a couple of minutes, or for more, and consistently discover unwinding.

Shower Meditation
One relieving strategy for those seeing how to ponder is the shower reflection. A shower contemplation consolidates the standard advantages of reflection with the advantages of an alleviating, hot shower, which can loosen up tired muscles,

give a loosening up air, and permit an impermanent sentiment of break from stressors. Being in the water can likewise assist you with staying wakeful, something that is significant yet at times testing in case you're figuring out how to think when tired. Attempt a shower reflection, and be spotless, loose, and prepared for bed (or a low-stress day) when you're done.

Smaller than expected Meditations
For the individuals who feel they don't possess energy for full-length reflection sessions (20 minutes is a decent normal measure of time), or for the individuals who might want to encounter a portion of the advantages of contemplation between longer sessions, scaled down (contemplations around 5 minutes long) are an incredible strategy to attempt. Smaller than normal reflections are extremely straightforward and fit in well with even the busiest of timetables. Figure out how to reflect in shorter blasts, and work up to longer sessions, or simply utilize this procedure for fast and helpful pressure alleviation.

Conclusion

Thank you for reaching the end of this book. It is my hope that it was informative and able to provide you with all of the tools you need to achieve your goals whatever they may be.

I sincerely hope that you are able to use the information in this book to better your life.

Awakening the Kundalini is a special opportunity that not everyone can do in his/her lifetime. Although it may be difficult, consider even the hardships as gifts that will make you a better person at many levels. Remember that other people like you have undergone the activation and have managed to overcome it —seek them and ask for help if you need to.

It is said that the Spirit has its reasons for doing things, and we humans are simply complying with its wishes. It communicates with us through synchronicities (meaningful coincidences), events, dreams, sudden insights, and much more. The more aligned we are with the Spirit, the more blessed we become. So, try your best to become more spiritual and listen to what the divine is trying to tell you.

Do not be troubled when you think you have "sinned" or that you are becoming less spiritual. The Spirit may have allowed you to move away from it to teach you valuable lessons. If you find the need to return, just do so without overly chastising yourself. Even if you are an enlightened individual, it never means that you must never commit mistakes.

The activated Kundalini represents our connection with the Divine. We can still be human if we want to, but we also gain the advantage of being Divine while still in our flesh. This is not an obligation but more of an experience for us to learn from and enjoy. So, take it easy, and do more of what you want if you truly desire it. You will be able to do more now.

The next step is to reaffirm every day that you are on your way to becoming a better, fuller you. Believe in yourself and your ability to make the changes necessary to realize your goals.

Once you've removed the clutter from your mind, you will turn to overthink into focused achieving every day. You may have heard many times over, "easier said than done." Well, you should be excited to learn how to do what you set your mind to do. You've wanted to make a change for a long time. Taking steps to make your goals come to fruition is something many people never achieve.

www.ingramcontent.com/pod-product-compliance
Lightning Source LLC
Chambersburg PA
CBHW071804080526
44589CB00012B/682